The Fire and the Fountain

An Essay on Poetry

JOHN PRESS

UNIVERSITY PAPERBACKS

BARNES & NOBLE INC: NEW YORK

Printed in Great Britain

University Paperbacks are published by
METHUEN & CO LTD
11 New Fetter Lane, London, EC4
and BARNES & NOBLE INC
105 Fifth Avenue, New York 3

TO MY MOTHER
AND TO THE MEMORY OF
MY FATHER

Contents

Sweet fire the sire of muse, my soul needs this;
I want the one rapture of an inspiration.
O then if in my lagging lines you miss
The roll, the rise, the carol, the creation,
My winter world, that scarcely breathes that bliss
Now, yields you, with some sighs, our explanation.

GERARD MANLEY HOPKINS

Just in this Moment, when the morning odours rise abroad,
And first from the Wild Thyme, stands a Fountain in a rock
Of crystal flowing into two Streams. . . .

WILLIAM BLAKE

Acknowledgements

IN the preparation of this book I incurred certain debts of gratitude which I now gladiy record.

Mrs. W. B. Yeats has generously allowed me to illustrate my argument and to embellish my pages with numerous quotations from the verse and prose of W. B. Yeats; Miss L. Crompton patiently deciphered and typed the much longer first draft of my manuscript; and although my wife's share in the book is far from easy to define, it is perhaps enough to say that but for her constant advice, criticism, and encouragement I should not have completed the task that I began.

Permission to use quotations from copyright works, as detailed in the relevant footnotes, has also been given by the following in respect of the authors named:

W. H. AUDEN: the Author; Faber & Faber Ltd.; and Random House, Inc., New York.

T. S. ELIOT: the Author; Faber & Faber Ltd.; and Harcourt, Brace & Company, Inc., New York.

DAVID GASCOYNE: the Author, and Mandeville Publications.

ROBERT GRAVES: the Author; Cassell & Co. Ltd. (*Collected Poems, 1914–1947*); Hamish Hamilton Ltd. (*The Common Asphodel*).

THOMAS HARDY: Macmillan & Co. Ltd.; The Macmillan Company, New York; and the Trustees of the Hardy Estate.

W. R. RODGERS: the Author, and Martin Secker & Warburg Ltd.

DYLAN THOMAS: J. M. Dent & Sons Ltd.; and New Directions, Norfolk, Connecticut.

W. B. YEATS: Macmillan & Co. Ltd.; and The Macmillan Company, New York.

J. P.

1955

Preface to the Second Edition

Although I have made no major alterations to the text of the first edition, I have corrected a number of minor inaccuracies, some of which were pointed out to me by reviewers and other readers. I am grateful to Professor Bonamy Dobrée, Miss Nina Epton, Mr. Raymond Le Goy, Mr. David Masson, Mr. Raymond Mortimer, Professor V. de Sola Printo, Mr. Peter Quennell, Sir Herbert Read and Mr. Michael Riviere, who gently reproved me for my errors and added to my store of knowledge.

Some readers, notably Dame Edith Sitwell, have disagreed with my observations on the music of poetry. I retain my former opinions; and if anybody should quote, as an example of a 'musical' line, Poe's

> The viol, the violet, and the vine

I should counter with the song that Chee Wee Gibbon sings in John Phillips's novel, *The Second Happiest Day*:

> Oh violate me in the violet time,
> In the vilest way that you know.

In the ten years which have elapsed since the original publication of *The Fire and the Fountain* I have reflected on various problems discussed there, but have come no nearer to solving them. The best succinct account of the creative process known to me is a remark made by the American song-writer Frank Loesser, who wrote, among other masterpieces of their kind, the lyrics for *Guys and Dolls*:

> Some people's heads are arranged so that they
> keep getting colds. I keep getting songs.

August 1965   J.P.

THE FIRE AND THE FOUNTAIN

In this book Mr. Press sets out to describe and analyse the moment of poetic inspiration, and to trace the growth of a work in the poet's mind. It is a profoundly original study of what makes a poet and what makes a poem, drawing on the work of the great English poets from Chaucer to Eliot.

UNIVERSITY PAPERBACKS

Chapter One

WILLIAM BLAKE has told us how artists, and other men who are blessed with the Divine Vision, experience an Eternal Moment:

> For in this Period the Poet's Work is Done, and all the Great
> Events of Time start forth & are conceiv'd in such a Period,
> Within a Moment, a Pulsation of the Artery. . . .

The purpose of this book is to estimate the significance of this Moment for the poet, and to trace the way that a poem grows in his mind. Blake, with his hatred of logical analysis, might indeed have objected that a poem does not grow by discernible stages, since it is given to the poet in an instantaneous flash by the Angels of God when the doors of our perception have been cleansed:

> Just in this Moment, when the morning odours rise abroad,
> And first from the Wild Thyme, stands a Fountain in a rock
> Of crystal flowing into two Streams. . . .

Yet even if we accept the truth of Blake's doctrine that the poetic process is a mystery which the analytic faculty is powerless to solve, we may still endeavour to learn what distinguishes a poet from his fellow men and how his senses come to be so renovated and cleansed that a poem may rise in him like a fountain. We may discover that a poem presents itself to a poet in a variety of guises and that, even if we can discern the moment when it begins to take shape in the poet's conscious mind, its true origin lies farther back and deeper down, in a childhood experience or in a racial memory. Finally, remembering that even Blake, with his unwavering belief in heavenly guidance, worked incessantly to convey the minute particulars of the Divine Vision with the utmost clarity, we may study the methods by which the poet deliberately shapes what he has been given into the distinct outlines of a perfected work of art.

The belief that the poet is directly inspired by divine agencies has been held at all times and in all places. Isaiah describes how he could proclaim the Word of God only when his unclean lips had been purified by a seraph with a live coal in his hand, and Milton uses just such an image when he dedicates himself to the task of leaving behind 'something so written to after-times, as they should not willingly let it die'. He will create

a work not to be raised from the heat of youth, or the vapours of wine; like that which flows at waste from the pen of some vulgar amourist, or the trencher fury of a rhyming parasite; nor to be obtained from the invocation of dame memory and her siren daughters, but by devout prayer to that eternal Spirit, who can enrich with all utterance and knowledge, and sends out his seraphim with the hallowed fire of his altar to touch and purify the lips of whom he pleases.[1]

Blake asserts even more furiously than Milton his belief in inspiration: 'Reynolds' opinion was, that genius may be taught, and that all pretence to inspiration is a lie or deceit, to say the least of it. If it *is* deceit, the whole Bible is madness. This opinion originated in the Greeks calling the Muses daughters of Memory.'[2]

Blake, like Milton, attacks the theory that Memory is responsible for the shaping of a poem and that from Memory the poet derives his impressions and his distinctive utterance. Such a theory was repugnant to one who detested the philosophy of Bacon, the intellectual revolution of the seventeenth century, the sensationalist philosophies of the eighteenth century, and the materialist doctrines of contemporary science. Blake believed in angels and in the eternal truths of the imagination:

> The atoms of Democritus
> And Newton's particles of light
> Are sands upon the Red Sea shore
> Where Israel's tents do shine so bright.

Thus he could say in a letter to Thomas Butts about one of his Prophetic Books: 'I may praise it, since I dare not pretend to be any other than the Secretary; the Authors are in Eternity.'[3]

It is not surprising that Yeats should have attributed some of his poems to visitations by supernatural agencies, since throughout his life the influence of Blake was powerful and fruitful. His study of Blake reinforced his temperamental belief in the supernatural which had been fostered and strengthened by a childhood passed in the Irish countryside, where the invisible world was still

---

[1] *Reason of Church Government*. Blake noted this passage in the margin of his copy of Reynolds's *Discourses*.
[2] *Notes on Reynolds*. [3] 6 July 1803.

felt as a constant presence, the natural counterpart of the visible world. Deliberate research into the occult, the discovery that he possessed certain psychic gifts, and a longing for spiritual illumination, adulterated with a less creditable wish to make an impression on others by uttering cryptic and oracular pronouncements, drove Yeats to adopt an attitude peculiar to himself and alien to the general current of poetical belief of his time. Because he was a great poet and because he wore whatever mask he chose to adopt with superb grace and dignity, we are impressed by what he tells us. It is not easy to decide in what sense and to what degree Yeats believed in the supernatural visions and experiences that came to him, for although he was too sophisticated to accept any revelation with the same unquestioning spirit that Blake habitually displayed, he genuinely felt that such revelations had a significance for him, and that his whole being was enriched by the communications imparted to him so mysteriously. In a note on his poem 'The Cap and Bells' he describes its genesis and its place in his thought:

> I dreamed this story exactly as I have written it, and dreamed another long dream after it, trying to make out its meaning, and whether I was to write it in prose or verse. . . . The poem has always meant a great deal to me, though, as is the way with symbolic poems, it has not always meant quite the same thing. Blake would have said 'The authors are in eternity', and I am quite sure they can only be questioned in dreams.[1]

We may disregard as unreliable the testimony of a poet who tended to sacrifice strict matter-of-fact truth to the demand of myth and the artistic coherence of an attitude. We may dismiss Yeats's accounts of his experiences as the fables of an Irish Romanticist, whose faith in the unseen is hard to distinguish from credulity and obscurantism. No such charges could be levelled against Valéry, who miraculously combined the calculating precision of the mathematician with the imaginative passion of the poet. He once admitted that sometimes God gave him a line of poetry and that this single line was enough, for, having been granted a nucleus, he could then proceed to construct his flawless architectural patterns. We need not pause to inquire exactly what Valéry meant when he attributed his inspiration to God: it is enough for us to note that he acknowledged the existence of an

[1] W. B. Yeats, *Collected Poems* (1933), p. 440.

external source of power and illumination from which he received a gift that he had not deliberately sought. A detached observer may find it a shade ironical that whereas Valéry chose to describe this phenomenon in religious terms, Hopkins should employ imagery that is almost pagan to convey his want of this same power:

> Sweet fire the sire of muse, my soul needs this;
> I want the one rapture of an inspiration.
> O then if in my lagging lines you miss
> The roll, the rise, the carol, the creation,
> My winter world, that scarcely breathes that bliss
> Now, yields you, with some sighs, our explanation.

Hopkins, in writing these words, gives the lie to his own assertion that he was forsaken by inspiration. 'The roll, the rise, the carol, the creation'. Few lines in the language are so radiant with that pulsing beauty which, defying rational analysis, quickens our responses and convinces us that we are in the presence of a rare quality that can be apprehended but not described.

Belief in the reality of inspiration does not necessarily lead to any one dogmatic assertion about the source of inspiration or about the means by which it manifests itself. It is humbler and wiser to accept certain experiences without formulating elaborate verbal explanations to account for them. Wordsworth, like Traherne, experienced the sense of strange glory, the feeling of oneness with the universe, when body and spirit know themselves to be an organic unity perfectly in harmony with the universe and denizens of eternity as well as of time. When he is content to record the impact of such moments, we are persuaded of the truths that he describes with incomparable force and exactness. Paradoxically, when he generalizes about the nature of his intimations and explains them in the terms of a coherent philosophy his verse loses not only its formal beauty but also the power to convince us intellectually. Not content with showing us what *is*, the poet intervenes with the meddling intellect, which he had once attacked, to demonstrate what it means.

It is possible to maintain that inspiration comes from God, from Heavenly Wisdom, from seraphim, or from any member of the angelic hierarchy who chances to strike a responsive chord in the

[1] 'To R. B.'

4

myth-making faculty of the poet. Possible but not essential. It is equally plausible to hold that inspiration is the product of mental disequilibrium, of dreams, or of the unconscious activity of the mind.

The belief that poetry springs from a state of ecstasy akin to madness is so old and well established that we need take only a brief glance at the evidence in support of the theory. Plato, in a famous passage, seems to make madness a necessary qualification for the successful writing of poetry: 'He who having no touch of the Muses' madness in his soul, comes to the door and thinks he will get into the temple—he, I say, will not be admitted.'[1]

Elizabethan theory on the subject can be seen in Shakespeare's linking of the lunatic, the lover, and the poet, or in Drayton's couplet on Marlowe:

> For that fine madness still he did retain
> Which rightly should possess a poet's brain.[2]

A similar notion is expressed by Schiller who talks of 'the momentary and passing madness that is found in all creators' or, to cite a living critic, by Montgomery Belgion who roundly asserts that 'the excitement in which alone, and independently of the will, literary inspiration is possible must be a form of madness'.[3]

It will be noted that in all these passages the word madness is hedged about with qualifying phrases: 'the Muses' madness', 'fine madness', 'momentary and passing madness', 'a form of madness'. What appears at first sight a bolder statement is to be found in the Leslie Stephen Lecture delivered by A. E. Housman at Cambridge on 9 May 1933. Since Housman's wanderings round Little Bethel have been chronicled and criticized by Ezra Pound in his *Polite Essays* no detailed examination of his thesis is necessary. It will be enough to quote the most startling passage, and one that is particularly relevant to the problem of madness and poetry. After an attack upon the chilliness and the poverty of the poetry written in the eighteenth century, Housman makes the following pronouncement: 'As matters actually stand, who are the English poets of that age in whom pre-eminently one can

---

[1] *Timaeus*.   [2] 'To Henry Reynolds, of Poets and Poesy'.
[3] *The Human Parrot*, p. 33.

hear and recognise the true poetic accent emerging clearly from the contemporary dialect? These four: Collins, Christopher Smart, Cowper and Blake. And what other characteristic had these four in common? They were mad.'[1]

It is true that Housman later modifies this statement by admitting that neither Collins nor Cowper wrote his poetry while he was confined in the madhouse and that Blake was never certified as mad, but the initial force of his dramatic declaration 'they were mad' is scarcely diminished by the saving clause so prudently inserted. Like a skilful advocate, Housman ensures that we shall remember and be convinced by those facts that lend support to his argument. He implies that, in the eighteenth century, the best poetry was the product of madness and that madness was, so to speak, the sign of a poet's authenticity. If this were true it would throw revealing light upon the poetic process in general, since it is unlikely that what occurred in the eighteenth century was unique and unrelated to the poetic activity of other ages.

We know that poetry of a high order can be written by a man who is mad when he writes it. Smart's greatest poem, as Housman is quick to remark, was written when he was suffering from the effects of mental disorder. It was in Northampton Asylum that John Clare wrote some of his finest poems:

> I lost the love of heaven above,
>   I spurned the lust of earth below,
> I felt the sweets of fancied love,
>   And hell itself my only foe.
>
> I lost earth's joys, but felt the glow
>   Of heaven's flame abound in me,
> Till loveliness and I did grow
>   The bard of immortality.
>
> I loved, but woman fell away;
>   I hid me from her faded fame.
> I snatched the sun's eternal ray
>   And wrote till earth was but a name.
>
> In every language upon earth,
>   On every shore, o'er every sea,
> I gave my name immortal birth
>   And kept my spirit with the free.

[1] Housman, *The Name and Nature of Poetry*, p. 38.

In the presence of such lines we recognize that our knowledge both of madness and of poetry is strictly limited. The confident eighteenth century which omitted Smart's masterpiece from his collected poems on the grounds that it bore 'melancholy proofs of the recent estrangement of his mind'[1] seems far away. We at least realize the extent of our ignorance.

Nevertheless, the isolated examples of Smart and of Clare should not lead us to misinterpret the relation between madness and poetry, or to accept Housman's implications about the nature of poetry. Collins and Cowper wrote poetry in spite of their madness, not because of it. If Blake was mad, we must extend our definition of madness to include all those mystics and visionaries who have seen the forms of eternity revealed to them in this transitory world. It is significant also that Housman fails to mention the insanity of Swift and the bouts of mental turmoil to which Johnson was subject. Housman is trying to show that men whose deepest feelings were secretly in rebellion against the tyranny of the intellect were, for that reason, true poets. Swift and Johnson, however, wrote poetry of the kind that Housman was attacking, typical poetry of the Enlightenment. They were not true poets; their madness is therefore irrelevant and can be ignored for purposes of the argument. Burns is not mentioned by Housman, for although, by Housman's own standards, he was a genuine poet, he was, unfortunately, indubitably and boisterously sane.

We can, however, be grateful to Housman for drawing our attention to this question of madness among eighteenth-century poets, even if we find his diagnosis faulty. It is possible to adumbrate an alternative theory that may take into account the available facts and offer some explanation of the links between madness and poetry. It is clear that the best poets of the epoch, Pope, Swift, Johnson, Gray, Collins, Cowper, Smart, and Blake were endowed with an exceptionally powerful nervous sensibility, and that most of them had a temperamental leaning towards the melancholia which is the obverse side of the eighteenth-century medal, whereon brutality, animal vigour, and fierce common sense are so triumphantly engraved. These poets were living at a time when educated society was a strong, closely-knit group.

---

[1] Housman, op. cit., p. 39.

Membership of the Republic of Letters gave a man a sense of security, emotional as well as financial, a feeling that he belonged to a society that needed him and did not look on him as an eccentric outcast crying vainly in the dark. Thus the dangers that might arise from excessive sensibility were mitigated by the stabilizing influence of social intercourse. We see in Pope a great poet in whom the interaction of his private temperament and his public life combined to produce verse of a harmonious perfection and balance unequalled in the language. The ferocity of Swift's imagination, which might have pushed him over the edge long before his final breakdown, was tempered by his absorption in the great world until political bitterness and private grief broke down his resistance and the flood of savage indignation swept him into the gulf of lunacy. We do not know the nature or the extent of the agonies that Johnson fought with in his solitude, but we may safely assume that it was his strong sense of being a member of a great society that helped to keep madness at bay. Even so retiring and shy a poet as Gray felt keenly the approbation or the neglect of the fashionable world and was bitterly hurt when the publication of 'The Bard' and 'The Progress of Poesy' was greeted with mockery and complaints of incomprehensibility. These poets were, at least in part, dependent upon society, sharing its assumptions and using their peculiar gifts so that they might communicate with the ordinary members of that society.

It was otherwise with Collins, Cowper, and Smart. Standing outside the fashionable, intellectual society of their time, indifferent to its demands and unconcerned to submit to its dictates, they were unaided by any outward check upon the abnormal workings of their imagination. Cowper's mental condition was further complicated by the overwhelming impact of Evangelical revelation that came near to shattering him. It seems improbable that his mental breakdown was caused by his conversion to the Evangelical faith, but one effect of his newly-found religion must have been to emphasize the uniqueness of his soul, and to weaken the ties that bound him to the vigorous society, intent upon earthly activities, for which he might have written had revelation not been granted to him. The lonely deer became the stricken deer.

Blake rejected more vehemently than Cowper the standards prevalent in the Republic of Letters, but was saved from the perils of isolation by the accidents of birth and of occupation. Born into the lower-middle class and compelled to labour for his living as a craftsman in the heart of industrial London, Blake the visionary was also Blake the revolutionary, who aided a fellow revolutionary to escape from England and himself stood trial for treason, a member of an earthly society of suffering men as well as an inhabitant of Jerusalem. His visions of Heaven and Hell are all the more convincing because he was at the same time the poet of London, not the bustling, prosperous London of Johnson and of Reynolds, but the pullulating, despairing city made hideous by the harlot and by the afflicted chimney-sweep:

> I wander thro' each charter'd street,
> Near where the charter'd Thames does flow,
> And mark in every face I meet
> Marks of weakness, marks of woe.[1]

In such poems Blake reminds us of the great poet of our day who discovers the horror of emptiness and the foretaste of hell in the tubes and in the crowded streets of the metropolis; although Mr. Eliot derived his imagery of the monstrous city from Dante and from Baudelaire more than from Blake:

> Unreal City,
> Under the brown fog of a winter dawn,
> A crowd flowed over London Bridge, so many,
> I had not thought death had undone so many.[2]

If Blake was rooted firmly in the world because of his hatred for the prosperous and cultivated *bourgeoisie*, Burns was safely anchored by his determination to enjoy the pleasures and the security of that same *bourgeoisie*. He frankly admitted his desire for a collectorship which might bring him, as he said, a thousand a year, literary leisure, and a decent competence.

I have tried to suggest that there is some relation between madness and poetry in the eighteenth century but that the connexion between madness and Housman's 'genuine poetry' is not as simple as he maintained and that his definition of genuine poetry is inadequate. Leaving the eighteenth century, we may now turn to a consideration of the problem in more general

[1] 'London' (*Songs of Experience*).   [2] *The Waste Land*, ll. 60–63.

terms. So far, we have seen that a special kind of madness may lead to the writing of poetry and that common or garden certifiable madness may also inspire poetry. Can we advance beyond these limited discoveries and supplement these meagre observations?

Coleridge drew an analogy between delirium and mania on the one hand and Fancy and Imagination on the other. If we may expand that analogy we can perhaps understand the traditional association of madness with poetic genius. The poet, as we shall discover in a later chapter, is gifted with a more than usually acute nervous sensibility. Roger Fry pointed out in his essay on 'The Artist's Vision' that the tremendous intensity with which an artist contemplates ordinary objects is, biologically speaking, a blasphemy. The poet's concentration on his objects of study, his remarkable powers of coining metaphors, his command of striking imagery, and his transfiguring gift of imagination may also smack of a similar blasphemy. The curve of his imagination rises through sensibility to vision and finally to ecstasy, and all is well if he remains in command of his imagination. The danger is that fancy may turn to delirium, imagination to mania, and that from the heights of ecstasy he may plunge downwards. The nature of this descent has been described by a poet who,

> wandering
> Through unnamed streets of a great nameless town
> As in a syncope, sudden, absolute,
> Was shown the Void that undermines the world:
> For all that eye can claim is impotent—
> Sky, solid brick of buildings, masks of flesh—
> Against the splintering of that screen which shields
> Man's puny consciousness from hell: over the edge
> Of a thin inch's fraction lie in wait for him
>
> Bottomless depths of roaring emptiness.[1]

When Nijinsky aspired to dance the War the imaginative pressure splintered the screen and the soaring mind was brought low. It was a sound impulse that guided Bernard Shaw to proclaim the sanity of art, but in his criticism, as in his plays, he lacks insight into the depths of darkness and despair that can, perhaps, be illuminated only by the poetic imagination. His remark that it

[1] David Gascoyne, 'Inferno'.

is easier to write poetry than prose and his strictures upon Shakespeare both spring from this inability to comprehend the nature of poetry. After paying tribute to Shakespeare's gifts as a poet, he proceeds to chide him for his weakness as a dramatist and thinker, not realizing that the drama and thought are contained within the poetry, that the characters of Macbeth, Hamlet, and Cleopatra are revealed by the tone, texture, and rhythm of the verse, that each play has something of the quality of a symphony in which the conflicting themes are finally resolved by the artist who designed them. The sanity of art is not merely the apotheosis of common sense, but a precarious balance attained only after dangerous explorations through dark places. It is a sanity plucked from insanity as safety is plucked from danger, the calmness at the heart of a whirlwind.

Shaw, like the men of the Enlightenment, regarded madness as a humiliating and terrible reminder of the forces that the advance of human wisdom had, as yet, failed to bring under control. Some artists and philosophers of the nineteenth and twentieth centuries have accepted madness and schizophrenia as states of mind from which certain types of artistic creation may luxuriantly flower. It is worth noting that no form of madness seems capable of turning a man who is not a poet into a poet. Madness may release certain potentialities of the mind, as with Cowper, Smart, Clare, Hoelderlin, and De Nerval, but it is doubtful whether it can create new abilities. Ophelia sings a bawdy song when she goes mad, and it is a mark of Shakespeare's genius that, in rhythm and tone, it is the kind of song that might have come from her lips when she was sane.

Many people are unwilling to accept the theory of Inspiration in the sense of a message or a vision from God, because they doubt whether God exists. Others reject any attempt to discuss poetic inspiration in terms of madness, on the grounds that all art is essentially sane and that preoccupation with mental abnormality is perverse and dangerous. These old speculations have a way of creeping back in new disguises and, in our day, theories of the unconscious activity of the mind appeal to those who want to combine religious scepticism, scientific accuracy, and imaginative perception.

Ancient literature is full of stories about dreams and their interpretations, but no systematic attempt to decipher the meaning of dreams was made until our own time. Those who believed in God humbly accepted their dreams as a message from heavenly powers. Milton explicitly states his belief in their divine origin:

For God is also in sleep and dreams advise.[1]

Those who were uneasy about their dreams had recourse to wise men who possessed, or claimed to possess, the power of divination but, in general, they were content to record their dreams and to recognize that, beyond the little world of reason and order that men precariously build, there stretches a darkness from which an occasional, cryptic message is transmitted. In the age of Shakespeare, the natural and the supernatural were not sharply divided, and part of his incomparable richness comes from the ease with which he was able to tap those sources which dried up after the Scientific Movement of the late seventeenth century: 'It is the infinite depth of the unknown called by religious people God, which gives depth to poetry.'[2]

It was left to the late nineteenth century to rediscover deliberately that infinite depth which had been ignored or despised by the heirs of Descartes. In ages when the sense of wonder was stronger than the desire to analyse, men had accepted that depth as a supernatural reality. Men of the present age, unwilling to employ the concept of the divine, have had recourse to a more elaborate hypothesis.

Plato had noted in *The Republic* the existence of passions which lay concealed within us: 'in dreams . . . the wild beast in us . . . becomes rampant. . . . In phantasy it will not shrink from intercourse with a mother or anyone else, man, god or brute . . . in every one of us . . . there exist desires, terrible in their untamed lawlessness, which reveal themselves in dreams.'[3]

The accuracy of Plato's diagnosis was confirmed more than two thousand years later by Freud who, with scientific thoroughness, investigated the nature of these terrible passions and explored the sources of our buried life. Even before he began his researches, a few nineteenth-century poets and critics had sensed the exis-

[1] Satan is, however, recognized as the inspirer of evil dreams. See *Paradise Lost*, Book V, 799–809.

[2] Capetanakis, *A View of English Poetry*.

[3] Book IX, opening section, F. M. Cornford's translation (1941), p. 290.

tence of powers that work within us while we sleep, powers from
which poetry may draw strength and joy. Wordsworth speaks of

> that blessed mood,
> In which the burthen of the mystery,
> In which the heavy and the weary weight
> Of all this unintelligible world,
> Is lightened:—that serene and blessed mood,
> In which the affections gently lead us on,—
> Until, the breath of this corporeal frame
> And even the motion of our human blood
> Almost suspended, we are laid asleep
> In body and become a living soul;
> While with an eye made quiet by the power
> Of harmony, and the deep power of joy,
> We see into the life of things.[1]

It is not always a blessed mood that is the fount of poetry.
'Kubla Khan' was written when Coleridge's conscious mind had
been laid asleep by the drugs which he had taken in an effort to
gain relief from the intolerable burden of the world. Matthew
Arnold's best poetry takes its origin from the sense of isolation
which, at certain moments, he appears to have experienced with
peculiar force. In such poems as 'Isolation' a cry is torn, not from
his urbane, cultivated mind, but from the depths of his being:

> Who order'd that their longing's fire
> Should be, as soon as kindl'd, cool'd?
> Who renders vain their deep desire?—
> A God, a God their severance ruled;
> And bade betwixt their shores to be
> The unplumb'd, salt, estranging sea.

The image of the sea frequently recurs in Arnold's verse at the
emotional climax of the poem, sometimes as a symbol of completion, of richness and fulfilment, always as a symbol of elemental power. Occasionally, he uses capital letters as if to emphasize
the immensity of that ocean which man, in his loneliness, regards
with fear and wonder:

> And the width of the waters, the hush
> Of the grey expanse where he floats,
> Freshening its current and spotted with foam
> As it draws to the Ocean, may strike

[1] 'Tintern Abbey Revisited', ll. 38–50.

Peace to the soul of the man on its breast:
As the pale Waste widens around him—
As the banks fade dimmer away—
As the stars come out, and the night-wind
Brings up the stream
Murmurs and scents of the infinite Sea.[1]

Again, in one of his finest poems, 'The Buried Life', Arnold employs the same image in order to achieve his effect:

A man becomes aware of his life's flow,
And there arrives a lull in the hot race

.   .   .   .   .

And then he thinks he knows
The Hills where his life rose,
And the Sea where it goes.

The Victorian critic E. S. Dallas drew attention to a world that lies within us beyond the control, or even the comprehension, of the calculating, reasoning intelligence:

In the dark recesses of memory, in unbidden suggestions, in trains of thought unwittingly pursued, in multiplied waves and currents all at once flashing and rushing in dreams that cannot be laid, in the nightly rising of the somnambulist, in the clairvoyance of passion, in the force of instinct, in the obscure but certain intuitions of spiritual life, we have glimpses of a great tide of life, ebbing and flowing, rippling and rolling and beating about where we cannot see it.[2]

Not content with noting the existence of this subterranean world, Dallas points out its relation to the world of the imagination: 'Incidentally . . . the unconscious life of the mind bears a wonderful resemblance to the supposed features of the imagination. . . . To lay bare the automatic or unconscious action of the mind is indeed to unfold a tale which outvies the romances of giants and ginns, wizards in their palaces, and captives in the Domdaniel roots of the sea.'[3]

Dallas was elaborating in picturesque language an observation that Shelley had made in 1821: 'Poetry differs in this respect from logic, that it is not subject to the control of the active powers of the mind, and that its birth and recurrence have no necessary connexion with the consciousness or will.'[4]

---

[1] 'The Future'.
[2] *The Gay Science* (1866).
[3] Ibid.
[4] *A Defence of Poetry*.

Once such an admission has been made, a new importance will be attached to dreams, to dream-like states of mind, and to the images generated therein. Shelley, in one of his fragments, describes sleep in terms that we might employ to depict the place of the unconscious mind in our lives:

> I went into the deserts of dim sleep—
> That world which, like an unknown wilderness,
> Bounds this with its recesses wide and deep.

As the nineteenth century wore on, artists, poets, and philosophers, such as Poe, Beddoes, De Nerval, Kierkegaard, Rimbaud, and Van Gogh, began to explore the realm of night and to recognize that the intimations which we receive from the dark places beyond the borders of our normal waking life are proof that, in civilizations and in men alike, there are irrational powers raging beneath the tranquil surface of our daily existence which lie outside the control or even the comprehension of the calculating, reasoning intelligence. Freud himself recognized that his was a work of consolidation rather than of discovery. Speaking to an assembly, on the celebration of his seventieth birthday, he disclaimed the title of discoverer of the unconscious which was being thrust upon him: 'The poets and philosophers before me discovered the unconscious; what I discovered was the scientific method by which the unconscious can be studied.'[1] Partial confirmation of this disclaimer is to be found in the fact that although *The Waste Land*, with its obsessive recurrence of dream-like motifs, might be taken as a poetic exposition of Freudian analysis, T. S. Eliot's methods were prepared for him not by Freud but by other poets.

Freud's investigations into the nature of man and into the working of his mind supplement the intuitions of the poets and the philosophers with some valuable clues about the relationship between poetry and the unconscious activity of the mind. He has demonstrated that, even in this scientific age, we habitually think and feel in metaphorical, figurative, and imaginative formations. The unconscious mind may even be described as a poetry-making organ: 'For the unconscious mind works without the syntactical

---

[1] Cited by Lionel Trilling in his essay 'Freud and Literature', reprinted in *The Liberal Imagination* (1950). This quotation is to be found on p. 34 of the book. I have drawn heavily upon this essay in the pages that follow.

conjunctions which are logic's essence. It recognizes no *because*, no *therefore*, no *but*; such ideas as similarity, agreement and community, for example, are expressed in dreams imagistically by compressing the elements into a unity.'[1]

The products of the unconscious mind, if this account of the process is accurate, bear a striking resemblance to poetry, especially to contemporary poetry, for simultaneity, condensation, vivid imagery, and the fusion of diverse elements are the characteristic marks of such poetry. A poem may come to the poet in an instantaneous flash, in the same way that a mathematician may suddenly perceive a set of new relationships, or a musician may know how a movement of a quartet will sound before he can distinguish the individual themes.

We must, however, beware of thinking that poetry is merely the product of the unconscious mind. Such a belief ignores the social purpose of the poet, the need to communicate with an audience, and the conscious shaping of his raw material that is one of the poet's chief tasks. Even the unconscious mind, though it may dispense with logic, works with a purposive intent. The poet cannot even throw logic overboard, for, as Coleridge has insisted, poetry has 'a logic of its own, as severe as that of science, and more difficult, because more subtle, more complex, and dependent on more and more fugitive causes'.[2]

It is precisely the need for conscious and strict control that distinguishes the making of a poem from the activity of the unconscious mind. Hazlitt, in one of his essays, likens the control exercised by the poet to the despotic rule of a tyrant. Part of the fascination afforded by poetry springs from the dialectical process that informs it, the conflict of themes, the tension arising from the interplay of normal speech rhythm counterpointed against the formal pattern of the metre, the interaction of the poet's conscious mind and his unconscious mind, the conflict between the poet's desire to satisfy himself, and his need to satisfy his audience. Freud has aided us to understand how complex the human mind is, and we are misusing his researches if we apply them crudely and mechanically to the study of poetry, in order to demonstrate that poetry is nothing but an overflow of the

---

[1] Trilling, op. cit., p. 53.
[2] *Biographia Literaria.*

unconscious mind. It is the poet's sovereign mind that enforces harmony upon the turbid flux of existence.

There is another idea of Freud's which some poets and critics have found suggestive—the notion of the death-wish that Schopenhauer had adumbrated. The followers of W. H. Auden were, at times, a little too slick in their use of this concept, which they employed in order to give a spurious impersonality and depth to their self-pitying uneasiness and discontent. It was part of the fashionable stock-in-trade of those who wanted to display their grasp of contemporary thought and their awareness of the human situation, and who found in Freudian jargon a substitute for patient meditation and hard thinking. Yet this concept, if its implications are fully understood, throws light upon those apparent contradictions and paradoxes that seem to underlie the nature of each one of us and to infect the most prosperous and highly-organized society. It gives a clue to the infinite complexity of those tangled impulses that fight for mastery within us, and hints at man's essentially tragic nature. It is, in fact, an idea likely to be congenial to the poet, even if, philosophically, the evidence for its truth is thin and dubious. The poet, in search of a myth that will fructify his imagination, finds, in the notion of the death-wish, an element of the irrational mystery from which so much poetry takes its origin. The finest expression of this myth is to be found in the words which Capetanakis put into the mouth of Abel when he speaks of 'My brother Cain, the wounded':

> And then he chose the final pain for me.
> I do not blame his nature: he's my brother;
> Nor what you call the times: our love was free,
> Would be the same at any time; but rather
>
> The ageless ambiguity of things
> Which makes our life mean death, our love be hate.
> My blood that streams across the bedroom sings:
> 'I am my brother opening the gate'.[1]

The postulate of the unconscious mind, like the theory of inspiration, draws our attention to the existence of forces that are not subject to the control of the ratiocinative faculties, and reminds us that there are regions where 'all the answers break or

[1] 'Abel'.

sound impure'.[1] The exact nature and significance of these forces
is a matter for legitimate dispute, and may always continue to be
so, but any doctrine of poetry that fails to take them into account
is likely to be trivial and parochial. We are beginning to recognize that even those myths that appear to be grossly unscientific
may contain elements of truth which, at one time, could be
expressed only by symbols and by legends. In fact, such myths,
however crude, may be more scientific than the vulgar desire to
explain away whatever does not conform to a schematic philosophy in which all component parts are neatly tabulated and
docketed. Theories of inspiration which assume that the Muse
endows her votaries with the gift of song have one great merit,
however rudimentary and clumsy they seem to a sophisticated
audience. They recognize that, in the poetic process, there is a
mystery which cannot be airily dismissed and which must be
humbly accepted before any theorizing can be attempted. To
ignore the depth and magnitude of the enigma is to stultify all
one's thinking about poetry, however ingenious and logical it
may appear. The ancient belief in some form of inspiration and
the persistence of this doctrine throughout the centuries are the
tribute of rational man to the imaginative truths that are the
ground of all his speculative inquiries.

It is true that, from time to time, robust and sceptical voices
have been raised against this belief in inspiration. William Morris
assures us that 'there is no such thing. It is a mere matter of craftsmanship.' Morris showed in his life and in his poetry what honest,
joyous craftsmanship could do. Endowed with an unquestioning,
healthy joy in the natural world, superbly equipped to take
pleasure in making things with skill and perseverance, Morris
was too happy and vigorous a man to experience the sense of
inadequacy and of bewilderment from which a profound search
for truth may spring. If Tennyson deliberately averted his eyes
from the depths of emptiness before him, Morris was so keenly
absorbed in his craftsmanship that he was unaware that there were
such depths to avoid. His legendary figures remain creatures of
a fairy-land enclosed within the pages of a hand-illuminated
book, whereas the figure of Tithonus is a living, suffering human
being, a projection of the uncertainty and of the uneasiness that

---

[1] Capetanakis, 'The Prophets'.

Tennyson was never able to subdue completely, a symbol of the divided longings of us all. In his denial of the reality of inspiration Morris gives us an insight into his strength, and a deadly proof of his limitations.

Reynolds had expressed a similar distrust in talk about genius, imagination, and inspiration. In poetry, a little sublime obscurity is permissible (it was such jovial condescension that infuriated Blake), for poetry belongs to the injudicious region of the mind:

> But when, in plain prose, we gravely talk of courting the Muse in shady bowers; awaiting the call and inspiration of Genius, finding out where he inhabits, and where he is to be invoked with the greatest success; of attending to times and seasons when the imagination shoots with the greatest vigour, whether at the summer solstice or the vernal equinox; ... when we talk such language or entertain such sentiments as these, we generally rest contented with mere words, or at best entertain notions not only groundless but pernicious.[1]

Hobbes put a similar objection even more forcibly and with a sardonic humour that he often employed in order to destroy what he regarded as a superstitious convention. His dig at Christian poets must have been particularly infuriating to those who believed simultaneously in Jehovah and in the Muses, in the majesty of Sinai and in the beauty of Parnassus. Heathen poets, runs his argument, might well claim to be the mouthpieces of a divine spirit,

> But why a Christian should think it an ornament to his poem, either to profane the true God or invoke a false one, I can imagine no cause but a reasonless imitation of custom, of a foolish custom, by which a man, enabled to speak wisely from the principles of nature and his own meditation, loves rather to be thought to speak by inspiration, like a bagpipe.[2]

Such objections to the theory of inspiration spring from a laudable desire to show good sense, even in the presence of poetry, and to resist all tendencies to lapse into mumbo-jumbo. The employment of esoteric jargon and the attendant perils of mystery-mongering are ever-present temptations that beset all who lay emphasis upon the mystery of poetry. Such a belief should be a stimulus to hard thought, not a substitute for it. Even

---

[1] *Discourses*. Cf. Bacon's remark at the close of his discussion of poetry: 'Let us now pass on to the judicial place or palace of the mind.

[2] *Answer to Davenant*.

the ponderous, avuncular homily of Reynolds and the crude Philistinism of Hobbes may have the salutary effect of forcing us to re-examine our beliefs about the nature of poetry. Morris, Reynolds, and Hobbes are saying, in effect, that talk about inspiration is much ado about nothing, a foolish, ridiculous superstition quite unworthy of the attention of sensible men. The introduction of the word 'bagpipe' is an obvious device by which serious consideration of the problem is evaded. Any religious or philosophical doctrine can be brought into ridicule by such tricks. Any great poem can be distorted, if only the denigrator ignores the spirit in which it is conceived, the tone in which it is written, and the convention which the poet employs. Rymer on *Othello*, Voltaire on *Hamlet*, and Tolstoy on any masterpiece of western culture exhibit that remarkable combination of intellectual acuteness and imaginative blindness which is so depressing to contemplate. All that they say is logically impeccable and totally irrelevant.

There are two possible answers to Morris, Hobbes, and Reynolds. One is to point out that their failure to recognize the existence of inspiration is their misfortune and that no satisfactory theory of poetry can be constructed on the basis of their imaginative deficiencies. A second answer, closely allied to the first, is that a sense of humility, of dependence upon some power outside oneself, has been felt as a reality by many of those best qualified to judge: 'I always feel as though I stood naked for the fire of Almighty God to go through me. . . . One has to be so terribly religious to be an artist.'[1]

Such testimony is worth at least as much as the assertions of men who pride themselves on their obtuseness, disguised as common sense. Plato, Isaiah, Shakespeare, Milton, Shelley, and Yeats, to name only a few poets, have recorded their convictions and experiences in such a way as to make it clear that inspiration plays a part in the creation of poetry, and that no theory of poetry or of prophecy is valid if it ignores this basic truth.

Belief in this theory does not imply any renunciation of the critical intelligence, nor is it an excuse for a slack and imprecise use of language. We may be unable to trace the origin or the nature of inspiration, but we can follow the way in which it

[1] D. H. Lawrence, *Letters*.

operates and observe some of its more obvious characteristics
We can even distinguish the working of inspiration in poetry
from its working in the other arts, which suggests that the use of
the word may be no more than a convenient way of describing a
number of complex and varied forces which we group under one
heading for the sake of having a neat terminology at our disposal.
The name that we give these forces is immaterial, provided that
we accept their existence and remember that vain disputation
about nomenclature is one of the prime sources of confusion.

It is clear that inspiration comes fitfully and that it makes its
presence felt in a variety of guises. Sometimes it will dictate a
whole poem or a long passage; sometimes it will offer the tantalizing gift of a single line. It may even visit a poet with nothing
but the raw material of his verse. Yeats, on his death-bed, awoke
from a dream and dictated the prose draft of a poem at 3 a.m.
on 7 January 1939, but the poem was not completed until 13
January.[1] The spirits who communicated 'A Vision' to Yeats,
through the automatic writing of his wife, announced explicitly:
'We have come to give you metaphors for poetry.' He believed
that the new richness and power that characterized his later verse
came as a result of his visionary experiences, but he does not
suggest that he, like Blake, is the mere secretary of angelic poets.

The fleeting character of inspiration was well known to Pope
who, on waking from sleep, even in the middle of a freezing
night, would arouse his amanuensis to record the ideas that had
disturbed his slumbers.[2] Balzac referred to the will-o'-the-wisp
element in the working of inspiration, the unpredictable course
that it followed and the impossibility of recapturing the fugitive
gleam once it had vanished. Yeats found in the 'sudden thunder
of the mounting swan' a symbol of inspiration.[3] A metaphor is
neither an argument nor an explanation and the use of such a
symbol will not satisfy those who are sceptical about the reality
of inspiration. Those, however, who admit the fact of inspiration
will recognize that the symbol directs the mind to the contemplation of what must necessarily remain a mystery. In its brilliance
and its mystery the swan, rising into the heavens, breaking the

---

[1] The poem in question was 'Cuchulain Comforted'. Henn, *The Lonely Tower*, p. 321.
[2] The Duchess of Newcastle also awoke her servants for this purpose.
[3] Jeffares, *W. B. Yeats: Man and Poet*, pp. 223 and 327.

tranquillity of the air, stands for that unique complex of emotions which shake the poet's mind and spur him into song.

A second noteworthy characteristic of poetic inspiration is that it confines its visitations to those who are already poets. There are examples of young children producing musical compositions, mathematical discoveries, and works of art under the influence of what one can only describe as inspiration. I do not know of any child who has written poetry of any value before his fifteenth or sixteenth year. Similarly, uneducated men are, occasionally, capable of working out the most intricate mathematical problems and of painting or drawing pictures of remarkable merit. Such men are never inspired to write first-rate poetry. We may reasonably ask ourselves what it is that distinguishes poetry from the other arts and sciences, and why it is that inspiration never turns a man into a poet but refuses to visit him until he has become a poet by other means. If we can answer that question, we may learn something about inspiration as well as about poetry.

I suggest that the fundamental distinction between poetry and the other arts is the part played in the former by memory. The prime requisite of the musician and of the painter is an ability to arrange patterns of sounds or of shapes in a way that is emotionally and intellectually satisfying. The mathematician is a man especially gifted in the perception of formal relationships (which helps to explain the ancient links between music and mathematics). It is, therefore, possible for a child or an illiterate man to be endowed with an unusual ability to discern formal patterns and to relate them to one another. If he is fascinated by symbols and by the process of abstract thought, he will be inspired to become a mathematician; if his aural senses are highly developed, he will turn to music. Should he be gifted with an unusual degree of manual skill he may, at an early age, produce remarkably able drawings.[1] There is no guarantee that these prodigies will become great painters, musicians, or mathematicians in adult life, since the ability to perceive formal relationships is not the sole requisite in any art or science, and their subsequent failure or success in no way affects the validity of the argument. The vital fact is that

---

[1] Leonardo wrote on the back of a drawing: 'Let no man who is no mathematician read the elements of my work.'

lack of education and of experience will not prevent a child or an illiterate man from producing certain types of art, which spring from the ability to recognize and to communicate formal qualities.

Poetry differs from music and from painting in that it is made with meaningful words and not with visual or with aural patterns. Even the musical quality of words in poetry must be intimately related to the meaning, unless by the music of poetry we mean the crude rhythmic and emotional effects produced by the employment of 'romantic' words in a monotonous and heavily-marked metrical pattern. Before we can write poetry we must have a firm grasp of both the formal and the emotional meaning of words. This grasp cannot be achieved until education and experience have developed whatever faculties may be latent within us. Words are the instruments of poetry and words have no power to move us unless they are charged with the intellectual and the emotional associations that arise out of experience.

Blake was right in affirming his belief in inspiration, but wrong in denying the importance of memory. Hobbes was wrong in believing that the power of writing poetry is given to every sensible man who cares to use his judgement, but right in asserting the role of memory in poetic composition: 'Time and Education begets experience; Experience begets memory; Memory begets judgment and fancy: Judgment begets the strength and structure, and Fancy begets the ornaments of a poem. The ancients therefore fabled not absurdly in making memory the mother of the Muses.'[1]

The emotional prejudices of Hobbes led him to deny the existence of inspiration, although there is nothing in his theory of memory that makes such a denial logically inevitable. To lay emphasis on the working of the memory in the poetic act is not to diminish the mystery of the act, for in the writing of a poem the memory is functioning in a special way. It is this unusual, profound, and exciting stirring of the memory that constitutes the gift of poetic inspiration, which is not the infusion of knowledge into a virgin mind, but the setting in motion of the intricate process by which experience is transmuted into poetry. Unless experience is present there is nothing on which inspiration can

[1] *Answer to Davenant.*

work. Unless the gift of handling words is present the product of inspiration will be shapeless and worthless.

If these twin premises are accepted, much that at first sight is paradoxical falls into place. We can begin to understand why it is that poetic inspiration visits those who are accomplished poets and, conversely, why poets who believe in the reality of inspiration are also masters of their craft. One day, as he was waiting for the Irish mail at Euston, certain lines came into Yeats's head. He retired to the waiting-room and reappeared within half an hour, bearing a sheet of Euston hotel notepaper on which he had written the complete poem:

> Through winter-time we call on spring,
> And through the spring on summer call,
> And when abounding hedges ring
> Declare that winter's best of all;
> And after that there's nothing good
> Because the spring-time has not come—
> Nor know that what disturbs our blood
> Is but its longing for the tomb.[1]

We must accept the fact that inspiration suddenly came to the poet, provided that we do not forget that the poet's mind was already prepared to receive what was given to it so unexpectedly. From 1910 onwards, Yeats began to construct a religious system that was to incorporate in its structure magical experience, doctrines of spiritualism, and cyclical determinism. The idea of recurring cycles was ever-present in the poet's mind at this period:

> Another Troy must rise and set,
> Another lineage feed the crow,
> Another Argo's painted prow
> Dive to a flashier bauble yet.[2]

> So the Platonic Year
> Whirls out new right and wrong,
> Whirls in the old instead;
> All men are dancers and their tread
> Goes to the barbarous clangour of a gong.[3]

[1] 'The Wheel'. See J. B. Hone, *W. B. Yeats*, p. 360.
[2] 'Two Songs From A Play, I.'
[3] 'Nineteen Hundred And Nineteen II'.

Speculation about death was another preoccupation troubling the poet. In 'The Wheel', the revolution of the seasons and the movement of the blood, related to each other and to the great wheel of being that is the rhythm of all thought, all action, are shown to be linked emotionally with the longing for the tomb. Yeats could be inspired to write this poem only because the elements of the poem were already present in his mind, ready to be blown into incandescence by that fortuitous wind of inspiration, whose power and mode of operation were first described by Shelley: 'The mind in creation is as a fading coal, which some invisible influence, like an inconstant wind, awakens to transitory brightness.'[1]

Nor is it merely the subject-matter of the poem that lies dormant in the poet's mind awaiting the summons of inspiration to emerge into the light of day. The technical devices, the rhythm and the metre of a poem that may seem to rise on the poet's lips as spontaneously as the song of a bird have, in fact, a long history behind them, a history of conscious work, of deliberate effort, of unremitting experiment. The poet may toil for long periods and his work will perhaps lack all trace of inspiration, yet his craftsmanship and the skill that grows with the practice of his trade are not wasted. When inspiration finally comes he is ready to take advantage of the unexpected gift. The poem falls suddenly, with the tremendous power of an avalanche, impelled by the cumulative weight of experience and of technical mastery so painfully acquired in the barren, dispiriting months. Part of the effect produced by 'The Wheel' can be traced to the contrast between the first four lines of the poem and the last four. The full rhymes in the first half of the poem reinforce the confidence and the certainty of our expectations. The eagerness of our hunger for new experience is conveyed by the resonant quality of the verse. The mood of the last four lines is subtly different. A note of anxiety, of impatience replaces the challenging, imperious ring which characterizes the opening of the poem. This uncertainty is reflected by the shift to another type of rhyme, imperfect and muted, synchronizing with the altered mood of the poem. Such technical mastery did not come suddenly by accident. We know that Yeats deliberately fashioned and re-fashioned his style,

[1] *A Defence of Poetry.*

subduing his undisciplined fancies and his wavering rhythms to a new synthesis in which richness harmonized with austerity. He cut out the abstractions which had cluttered his verse, made his rhythms more taut and muscular, transformed his rhymes from decorative embroidery into an integral, functional part of the whole poem. Thus, when 'The Wheel' came to him in a flash of inspiration, it came perfectly formed, emotionally and technically, with the inevitability of genius.

The analysis of 'Kubla Khan' by Professor Livingstone Lowes in *The Road to Xanadu* reinforces the conclusions drawn from our examination of 'The Wheel'. It is now generally recognized that the fragments of knowledge consciously acquired by Coleridge and the memories of actual experiences, which were apparently buried and forgotten, rose to the surface and coalesced into a poem composed in a state of trance. Less well known is the fact that, in the months preceding the writing of 'Kubla Khan', Coleridge had indefatigably practised a series of technical exercises in an effort to find new metrical forms. Apparently the labour was wasted, the results were nil, and one might dismiss the whole episode as an arid pursuit of a sterile prize. Professor Lowes, however, suggests that these experiments ultimately bore fruit in the complete mastery of rhythm to be found in 'Kubla Khan', a mastery that was entirely new and, at first glance, inexplicable.

One occasionally reads a report of a game of Rugby in which a player, suffering from concussion, remains on the field and gives a brilliant performance, playing 'like a man inspired'. The cliché is more accurate than the newspaper reporter may know. The effect of the concussion has been to induce a trance-like condition wherein the inhibitions and hesitancies of the waking state are temporarily obliterated. Unsuspected powers are revealed and the player raises his game, or has it raised, to a higher pitch of intensity than he has ever previously attained. Nevertheless, he can take advantage of the potencies released by the concussion only because his skill as a Rugby player has been consciously developed by years of training.

In the same way, the poet must patiently train his own particular faculties so that he may be ready when inspiration descends upon him like a thief in the night. Those who find the analogy

between poetry and Rugby too crude or incongruous may prefer
an explanation couched in more orthodox terminology:

> I do not assume, in this or any other poetic experience, that the elements
> are casual, or the occasion arbitrary. Automatism is not the same thing as
> *chance*: inspiration is not a *blind* impulse. As in a chemical experiment, for
> success the instruments must be clean, the quantities precise, and the tem-
> perature even. Analogous conditions in the poet are probably only secured
> by mental habits of a similar exactitude. It may be for this reason that good
> poets are usually writers of exceptionally clear prose.[1]

Any theory of poetic composition which ignores the reality of
inspiration is likely to be both shallow and provincial. It is noteworthy that denial of this reality should come mainly from
inferior poets or from those who are not poets at all, and that
many great poets have testified to inspiration's sovereign power.
Although there is no general agreement about the precise way
in which inspiration descends upon the poet, there is virtual
unanimity about its salient characteristics—its tantalizing, evanescent quality, its independence of human volition, and the
remarkable, paradoxical manner in which it combines an apparently capricious mode of operation with a logical inevitability.

The concept of poetry and the problems confronting the poet
vary from age to age, yet it is no rhetorical falsification to speak
of the European poetic tradition and of the great line of poets
from Homer to Yeats. For the poets of every age are united in a
common devotion and in a common dedication—a devotion to
their native tongue and a dedication to the Muse, a Goddess who,
luminous and serene, remains the primal source of that light
which irradiates the poet.

[1] Herbert Read, *Collected Essays in Literary Criticism* (2nd ed.), p. 115, footnote.

Chapter Two

WE have seen, in the last chapter, that the Muse habitually descends only upon those who are worthy to receive her. In this chapter we must seek to discover whether there are any distinguishing characteristics which mark a man as a true poet. We may begin by considering two answers to this problem which are commonly given. The first assumes that the poet is a Bard and that poetry is primarily the noble utterance of a noble soul. It is an assumption found in Shelley, who declared that 'Poetry is the record of the best and happiest moments of the happiest and best minds';[1] and it is a doctrine put forward even more emphatically by Augustine Birrell: 'A poet's soul must contain the perfect shape of all things good, wise and just. His body must be spotless and without blemish, his life pure, his thoughts high, his studies intense.'[2]

These two sentences admirably summarize Milton's opinion of the matter and of his own character (as a young man, he seems to have regarded his poetic powers as a kind of magical endowment which would flow away from him, like Samson's physical strength, if he divested himself of his chastity), but they are so clearly inapplicable to the majority of poets that they scarcely need refuting. Unfortunately, the concept of the poet as a high-minded Bard was largely responsible for the faults that disfigure the two most influential anthologies of the past hundred years, *The Golden Treasury* and *The Oxford Book of English Verse*. Chief among these defects is a curious inability to recognize, or reluctance to admit, that certain fundamental qualities of human beings have been depicted by most of the finest English poets. Hatred, obscenity, lust, ferocity, and bitterness are notably absent from these anthologies, although they are abundantly present in life and in the corpus of English poetry.

By an unhappy chance, the third most influential anthology of recent times, *The Spirit of Man*, reinforces the particular view

---

[1] *A Defence of Poetry.*
[2] *Obiter Dicta: Second Series, Milton.*

28

of poetry implicit in the pages of its two predecessors. Robert Bridges was, of course, deliberately trying to elevate the minds of his countrymen in the middle of a war, and therefore chose such passages of verse as served to emphasize the glorious and heroic qualities of men. In his pages, we find man the Platonist, the Christian, the Mystic, the Pilgrim, the lover of Beauty. We find little mention of certain other activities of man that, on any just view of humanity, deserve our attention. There is scarcely a hint that man eats, drinks, commits fornication, dances, plays games, makes jokes, gossips, and runs away in the hour of battle. If it is argued that such activities belong to the body rather than to the spirit of man, we can only reply that if poetry is concerned solely with a bloodless abstraction, a mere etiolated spectre, it can never retain its hold upon our hearts.

Those who stress the nobility of the poet are often the most purblind opponents of all that is most vital in contemporary poetry. The young Tennyson, lonely and self-tormented, was dismissed as effeminate and obscure until he became the leonine Bard whose views on the French were so healthy and manly. It may be merely a legend that Queen Victoria wanted to make Swinburne her Laureate on the death of Tennyson; it is certain that she would never have contemplated the appointment in the eighteen-sixties when he had nothing to commend him but his genius and had not lavished his gifts upon the production of what Hopkins called 'long waterlogged lines' about the Armada and 'blethery bathos' about babies.[1] The abuse hurled at T. S. Eliot for the first twenty years of his poetic life is a melancholy reminder that each generation gives birth to its full quota of dunces.

W. B. Yeats once said of a young poet: 'No, he's too serious, too honest: the Muse prefers the gay, the warty lads.' I think that Ernest Hemingway was making the same point when he remarked that 'a serious writer may be a hawk or a buzzard or even a popinjay, but a solemn writer is always a bloody owl'. Both are claiming that a certain gaiety and vigour are the hallmarks of a genuine writer. The assumption that poetry is concerned with the beautiful things of the spirit, and with nothing else, has done more to degrade the idea of poetry than any other

[1] *Letters*, I, p. 304.

single belief. Large numbers of people do not read poetry, since they believe that its very nature excludes all passion, wit, intellect, and masculinity. A glance at the flabby, trivial poems in the latter portion of *The Oxford Book* is enough to show that the popular view of poetry is not without some foundation.

The lingering preconception that poetry must elevate the mind, that the poet is, like Moses, a law-giver, has led to some remarkable pronouncements and judgements on individual poets and poems. Southey was horrified at Herrick's exquisitely written lyrics because of their pagan levity. Kingsley dismissed the work of Keats as if it were a regrettable display of enervating sensuality unworthy to be compared with the serious poetry that ennobles all who read it:

Let the poets of the new school consider carefully Wolfe's *Sir John Moore*, Campbell's *Hohenlinden, Mariners of England* and *Rule Britannia*,[1] Hood's *Song of the Shirt* and *Bridge of Sighs* and then ask themselves as men who would be poets, was it not better to have written any one of those glorious lyrics than all which John Keats has left behind him; and let them be sure that, howsoever they may answer the question to themselves, the sound heart of the English people has already made its choice.[2]

The omission from *The Golden Treasury* of Spenser's *Epithalamium* and Marvell's 'To His Coy Mistress' has a direct bearing on the present topic. Palgrave advanced the excuse that Spenser's masterpiece was not acceptable to the taste of Victorian England, and it may be that the glowing beauty of the poem would have offended the sly prurience of Palgrave's readers. It is more difficult to account for the absence of 'To His Coy Mistress', which is less overtly sensual than one or two of the songs printed in the first portion of the book devoted to the Elizabethans. I suspect that Palgrave did not relish the tone of this magnificent poem, combining, as it does, wit, passion, irony, and an unfailing urbanity. A simple expression of love, a fervent description of a mistress, even the voluptuous regret that we find in Keats, might pass uncensored by the austere critic, but this complex, sophisticated rendering of sensual experience was pro-

[1] James Thomson was, of course, the author of this poem. It is in the final scene of his masque, *Alfred* (1740).
[2] Cited by Raymond Mortimer, *Channel Packet* (1942), p. 166.

foundly disturbing. The songs of Lodge or of Constable could have been written by a Bard in a carefree moment of relaxation from his arduous poetic duties; it was unthinkable that a Bard could ever have composed 'To His Coy Mistress', still less the dark songs and elegies of John Donne. It is noteworthy that Donne finds no place in Palgrave as either a sacred or a profane writer, nor can we suppose that a man of Palgrave's wide reading was ignorant of Donne's work. Admission of Donne into the canon would have proved fatal to the theory of poetry which Palgrave held with lofty conviction.

I believe that a similar emotional fastidiousness, a high-minded shrinking from uninhibited passion, accounts for Robert Bridges's failure to sympathize fully with the poems of Gerard Manley Hopkins. The charges of Marianism, perversity, and an unhealthy blending of asceticism and sensuality indicate that the sense of literary decorum which Bridges so assiduously cultivated was outraged by the raw, unmitigated violence, by the naked intensity of sensation that informed almost every poem written by Hopkins. Canon Dixon understood that the terrible crystal of Hopkins's poetry was a sign of the authentic fire of genius. Bridges must have sensed that a full acceptance of this poetry would have shattered the philosophical calmness and assurance that could find satisfaction in symmetrical Platonism, and contemplate the harmonious working of the spirit of man with a serenity undisturbed by the agony of mind which so tormented Hopkins.

The ideas about the nature of poetry engendered by these three famous anthologies need to be supplemented by wider reading, that shall take into account those aspects of poetry neglected or concealed by the three anthologists, either from deliberate intention, or, more probably, because a self-protective mechanism guided their choice. A careful study of Aldous Huxley's *Texts and Pretexts* is a valuable corrective to a narrow critical sensibility, for this anthology is a proof that poetry is concerned with the full man, body, mind, and spirit, with man in his splendours and miseries, his greatness and his ridiculous, odious pettiness. Those whose minds have been thus awakened to a sense of the full range of English poetry will discover for themselves the variety of great poetry, the naked thew and sinew of the poet's language, the untrammelled force of the poetic mind. They will learn to value the intellectual power and the muscular beauty of Dryden's translation of Juvenal's *Sixth Satire*; to pay homage to the greatness of *Don Juan*; to admire the brilliance and the vitality of Pope. They will realize that Wordsworth's record of uttering nothing base has little bearing on his stature as a poet and that most English poets of the front rank, from Chaucer onwards, have uttered a great many lines that an over-delicate stomach would find extremely base.

Those who belong to the Bardic school are usually, though not inevitably, conservative by temperament. A man who believes that the task of the poet is to give enduring expression to the noblest values of society implicitly accepts the general framework of society as just and well ordered. His conservatism may even extend beyond the bounds of his own society to include the universe at large, and take on the quality of a cosmic toryism that sees the wisdom of God revealed in the arrangement of society no less than in the pattern of created things. Such a belief insensibly grows as material prosperity and literary reputation increase, until it hardens into an unshakeable conviction. Literary taste is reinforced by doctrinal orthodoxy, and the blunting of the senses leads the judgement to value the enunciation of general truths rather than the precise description of sensuous experience. An academic conservatism, with a strong grip upon the world of letters, seeks to impose its formal decorum upon the passionate life of poetry.

Inevitably there arises a fierce reaction against this religious, political, and literary conservatism. Those whose sense of pity and of justice is outraged by the cruelties inflicted upon men in the name of society denounce society as a gigantic sham. The revolutionary theory of poetry, which appears, at first sight, to be diametrically opposed to the conservative theory of the Bard, casts the poet in a new role. He is no longer the mouthpiece of the ruling classes but, to his glory and his shame, the revolutionary outcast, the idealist, despising the corruptness of society, the prophetic voice heralding a new era.

The revolutionary theory of poetry is largely derived from a study of a few nineteenth-century poets. Any attempt to apply it to poets as diverse as Ben Jonson, Marvell, Dryden, Pope, Keats,

Clare, and W. B. Yeats, would quickly reveal its limitations. There are, besides, two fundamental objections to the theory that have now to be considered.

The first is that the distinction between literature and life has not been observed. It is generally recognized that the lives and the works of poets may present a marked contrast to each other and that the chastest and tenderest of poets on paper may, in daily life, be cantankerous and lecherous. In much the same way, the description of a poet as a revolutionary is misleading unless we define more closely wherein his revolutionary qualities manifest themselves. In one sense, a poet ought to be a revolutionary. He must break through the deadening acceptance of stale ways of perceiving and feeling the visible and invisible worlds about him. For him everything should appear unique and fresh, the familiar being transfigured as it was for Traherne and for Blake. Again, he should reject the flabby, ready-made verbal counters which the common run of humanity wearily adopts to communicate its jaded, mechanical perceptions of the environment. Poetry is not always called upon to be the advance-guard of language, to use T. E. Hulme's striking phrase, but unless it is constantly prepared to assume that role it is in danger of dying of inanition. Hobbes was making the same point when he wrote: 'As the sense we have of bodies consisteth in change and variety of impression, so also does the sense of language in the variety and changeable use of words. I mean not in the affectation of words newly brought home from travel, but in new and with all significant translation to our purposes of those that be already received.'[1]

The purposes to which a poet may turn his revolutionary faculties may vary widely. He may use his gifts to further a politically conservative philosophy, a philosophy of rebellion, or a philosophy of complete indifference to the contending factions that dominate society. We should reserve the name of revolutionary poet for a man who employs the resources of language in a new way to convey his vision of the world in which he lives, experiences, and suffers. We need some other term for the poet who expresses, in the language of yesterday, his contempt for the society of today and his aspirations for the society of tomorrow. W. B. Yeats, who rejected almost all the doctrines of the progressive,

[1] *Answer to Davenant.*

humanitarian school, and who longed for the concentration of power and wealth in a few hands, is a far more revolutionary poet than Ernest Jones who, a hundred years ago, denounced the iniquities and prophesied the overthrow of the ruling classes in Victorian England. The essence of a poet is to be found less in his opinions than in his idiom.

The second objection to the theory is even graver than the first. Although this revolutionary doctrine may, as I said, appear to be diametrically opposed to the tenets of the Bardic school it is, in reality, complementary to them, the obverse side of the medal. Just as Fascism and Communism, though superficially hostile to each other, unite in their detestation of liberal humanism, even so these two poetic theories are agreed on one basic dogma. Both assume that the poet employs his gifts in order to affirm certain values; both judge him by the contents of his spiritual manifesto. It matters little whether one believes that a poet should justify the social order of today or celebrate the social order of tomorrow. The root error springs from the judgement that the poet exists in order to subserve any political, religious, or ethical code. Such a presupposition breeds the false approach to poetry by which we appraise a poet in the light of what he states, instead of experiencing the total poem that he has written. This distinction may appear to be splitting hairs; it is, in fact, fundamental to any true understanding of poetry.

The point may be raised that, unless we judge a poet by what he says, we are evacuating poetry of all moral content and reducing it to a sequence of patterned sounds, thereby reverting to the triviality of the aestheticism fashionable in the nineties. If the concept of great poetry is a valid one, we must admit a scale of values by which we can distinguish the elegant minor poem from the superb major poem, and we cannot afford to ignore the content of the poem, the moral element that gives depth to the poet's vision. We can agree unreservedly with this argument, provided we recognize that the values inherent in great poetry arise from the poetry and are not imposed upon it by the didacticism of the poet. We consider one poem greater than another because it seems to us more universal in its scope and more true in its philosophy. I believe that no poem can win that recognition from us unless it expresses with complete fidelity the personal vision of the poet. The more piercing, exact, coherent, and complex the vision, the greater the poem, but the essence of the vision is its individuality, its undistorted reflection of the total experience of one man. The presentation of a set of dogmas, held even with complete sincerity, can never be a substitute for this personal experience in which belief and doubt, passion and thought, memory and desire are so closely blended that nobody can distinguish the one from the other. The poem is a whole world of order and beauty, instinct with the morality that grows from the acceptance and the understanding of experience. It is not the expression in rhyme and metre of political and religious formulae.

This distinction helps to explain why *Samson Agonistes* is a greater poem than *An Essay on Man*. In the same way that *Paradise Lost* flares up into a glowing magnificence when Milton forgets his ostensible purpose of justifying the ways of God to man, *Samson Agonistes* has the power to move us because it is not merely a story from the Old Testament that serves to illustrate the miraculous working of Providence. The poem's unique splendour arises from its mingling of the divine legend with the remembered experiences of the poet's life. The myth comes alive because it is an ever-present reality for Milton or, if we prefer to put the matter in another form, because his own life is presented within the framework of the Biblical story, thereby becoming endowed with the universality, the impersonal truth, of great poetry. In reading the poem we are not giving intellectual assent to a theological proposition, but sharing in the revelation of God's power and mercy that came to a poet in the course of a lifetime's action and suffering. When we read *An Essay on Man* we miss the authentic note of personal conviction that we find in the poetry of the highest order. Pope writes a set of brilliant variations on a theme provided by his friend Bolingbroke, a Catholic commentary on a Deistical text. Despite some individual passages of remarkable merit, the *Essay* fails to attain the perfect fusion of diverse elements that marks the completely satisfying poem. Paradoxically, the *Moral Essays*, and, in particular, the essay 'Of the Characters of Women', though slighter in form and less ambitious in purpose, have a greater artistic and moral unity than *An Essay on Man*. The contemplation of women's frailty (their moral weakness and their delicate, evanescent beauty), aroused in Pope all the scorn, the tenderness, and the stoical acceptance of sadness that lay so deep in his nature. The ingenious philòsopher and famous man of letters gives place to the great poet contemplating the pattern of human existence with the smile that both mocks and pities and with the heart that understands.

No theory about the poet's nature is valid unless it recognizes that what a poet *is* must always be of more significance than what he avowedly *believes*, just as the poem must be judged for what it *is* and not for what it overtly *states*. The black Tennysonian melancholy reveals more of the essential quality of his poetry than his commonplace reflections on democracy and the French. Swinburne's peculiar response to pleasure and to pain determined his whole development as a poet, whereas his shrill revolutionary sentiments were so much froth upon the deep current of his emotional life. It is certainly true that he wrote better verse while under the spell of Mazzini than while under the tutelage of Watts-Dunton, but it is equally true that he wrote his finest verse while he was under the influence of nobody and of nothing except his acutely morbid sensitivity, the nature of which has been admirably defined in a recent study of the poet.[1] Swinburne was a man whose deepest concern was with the turmoil of his own passions. His political and social beliefs were, even at their most profound, a projection outwards of the inner strife and anarchy by which he was perpetually racked until he retreated to the haven of suburban versifying and scholarship.

The past thirty or forty years have witnessed a growing recognition that the official biographies of nineteenth-century poets are both inadequate and misleading. Little by little, new evidence has appeared that has thrown light upon the obscure recesses of the Victorian mind, despite the deliberate obstructive tactics of surviving Victorians who, like Peter Bell, reluctant to lift the all-concealing tunic or frock-coat,[2] have attempted to resist the new movement, withholding documents and doing what they could to

---

[1] Humphrey Hare, *Swinburne.*
[2] Shelley, 'Peter Bell The Third':

> But from the first 'twas Peter's drift
> To be a kind of moral eunuch;
> He touched the hem of Nature's shift,
> Felt faint—and never dared uplift
> The closest, all-concealing tunic.

discredit the researchers. The justification for the most thorough probing into the intimate life of a poet is that we may thereby discover the mainspring of his poetic activity.

Furthermore, such a critical approach emphasizes the truth that poetry is written by man in all his complexity of thought and passion. It concentrates on the naked reality of the poet, passing beyond his mere opinions to scrutinize the intricate web of desires and fears which lies quivering beneath the surface of rational behaviour that we present to the world. Above all, the analysis of the psyche reveals that the mystery at the heart of poetry mirrors the strange contradictions of the human spirit. It teaches us that human weakness may go hand in hand with spiritual discernment, that pain and degradation may break down the barriers of the mind and release the poetry that lay imprisoned there, that our conventional valuations of conduct must be revised in the light of humility, and of our growing knowledge that the poet is a creature at once more interesting and more tragic than the Revolutionary or the Bard.

A recognition of these truths is to be found in a passage by De Quincey where, in the course of speculations about the poetry of Wordsworth, he attempts to explain the nature of its origins:

Wordsworth's intellectual passions were fervent and strong: but they rested upon a basis of preternatural animal sensibility diffused through all the animal passions (or appetites), and something of that will be found to hold of all poets who have been great by original force and power, not (as Virgil) by means of fine management and exquisite artifice of composition applied to their conceptions.[1]

The essential character of a poet resides in his temperamental constitution, in the basic impulses that flow through him and provide the store of energy that animates his being. We have had numerous studies of the poet's mind, soul, imagination, opinions, and beliefs, but few people have seriously considered what one may call the physiology of poetry. A poet's political or religious philosophy, though of biographical interest, is of secondary importance for readers of his poetry, and for the poet himself. Despite all fluctuations of belief and shifts of opinion one thing is sure: the poet, if his poetry is to have lasting richness and vitality, must be able to draw upon those deep sources of animal

[1] *Literary Reminiscences.*

passion that lie coiled within us. A man can suffer from almost any disease of mind or of body and still be a poet, provided that he is not afflicted with emotional anaemia. Coleridge knew that opinions and beliefs, however metaphysically ingenious and elaborate, were but superstructures and that a poet could find no lasting strength except from

> The passion and the life, whose fountains are within.

Once this is realized, we shall understand why the Bardic school and the Revolutionary school fail to grasp the vital facts about the poet's nature. They are focusing attention upon the secondary attributes of the poet and neglecting the primary source of power which alone can set in motion the dynamic process that culminates in a poem. It is as though we were to examine the machinery that stands in a generator hut and ignore the waterfall that lies beyond the obscuring trees.

Wordsworth himself used a phrase almost identical with that of De Quincey's when he remarked that a poet must be possessed of 'more than usual organic sensibility'. He must, in fact, respond to the visible world more intensely or more profoundly than the average man whose perceptions have been blunted by the familiar routine imposed upon him by the mechanics of living. He may employ his vivid sensibility in whatever way he chooses, placing it at the service of any party or creed, but unless he possesses this gift of sensuous vitality his poetry will infallibly sink beneath the weight of that dullness which Pope intuitively recognized as the besetting weakness of well-meaning hacks who decide to express their opinions in verse.

It is too much to expect that all five senses of a poet will be equally acute and voracious. Shakespeare was exceptionally well endowed with sensual perception, and it may be hazarded that part of his superiority to all other English poets springs from the fact that all his senses were abnormally powerful and exact, whereas in most poets one or two senses predominate over the rest.[1] We commonly think of Shakespeare as the fullest and richest of poets and I believe that we are thereby unconsciously paying tribute to the perfect balance and to the flowering abun-

---

[1] When Buchanan said that Rossetti's poetry exuded 'one profuse sweat of animalism' he was paying an unwitting tribute to the opulent splendour of Rossetti's sensuality which has helped to preserve his finest verse from oblivion.

dance of his sensual faculties. His verse has more *body* than the verse of any other poet, and it is significant that this word has two connotations, for it can mean flavour, as when we say that a wine is full-bodied, and it can also convey the notion of flesh as opposed to mind. Shakespeare's verse is pre-eminent in precisely these two particulars, for it celebrates with peculiar strength and sweetness every conceivable activity of the human animal. Shaw, who may be ranked with Tolstoy as the greatest moralist of the late nineteenth century, was genuinely horrified by the writings of a man whose plays were so unmistakably not for Puritans. Shakespeare depicts with unrivalled accuracy and sympathy the Old Adam in us who, redeemed by Imagination and royally endowed, enjoys the kingdom of the senses. Coleridge said of Shakespeare that he 'darts himself forth and passes into all the forms of human character and passion'.[1] He was able to do this only because his intellectual apprehension of human character was reinforced and invigorated by an inexhaustible flow of animal vitality that suffused his whole being. It is notoriously difficult to decipher Shakespeare's philosophy, because in him thought was not an intellectual activity dissociated from living. Shakespeare's philosophy resides in his total response to experience, incorporated in the rhythms of his verse, and drawing sustenance from the depths and range of his sensuality.

Claudio's speech in *Measure for Measure* illustrates my contention that Shakespeare's verse is distinguished above all by the amount of body in it. In reply to Isabella's comfortable philosophizing about death and dishonour, Claudio, brushing aside all abstractions, faces the brute facts:

> Ay, but to die, and go we know not where;
> To lie in cold obstruction and to rot;
> This sensible warm motion to become
> A kneaded clod; and the delighted spirit
> To bathe in fiery floods, or to reside
> In thrilling region of thick-ribbed ice;
> To be imprisoned in the viewless winds,
> And blown with restless violence round about
> The pendent world; or to be worse than worst
> Of those that lawless and incertain thoughts
> Imagine howling.

[1] Cf. Arnold's remark that Pope had a 'quick and darting spirit'.

Almost every word falls with the impact of a blow, placed with the utmost precision. The weight of phrases such as 'cold ob-struction' and 'kneaded clod' is a proof that language in the hands of a supreme master takes on an immediate, physical quality that reflects the intensity of the writer's response to experience. The word 'thrilling' is here employed in such a way that we are reminded of its root meaning and made conscious of the terrible coldness of the thick-ribbed ice pressing down upon the flesh and infusing its freezing current into every particle of the body. Shakespeare invests the civilized man's apprehension of the spiri-tual agony of death with the immediacy of physical fear that belongs to primitive man. The last triumph of the poet is to express in highly subtle and articulate language the primal instincts that lie submerged within us all. It is, paradoxically, the abundance of animal sensibility that may open the doors of spiritual perception, just as it is the concrete particularities of flowers, trees, and stones that are more truly supernatural than the abstract world of ideas and concepts which we construct for our mental convenience in our daily lives.

Lesser poets than Shakespeare may count themselves fortunate if more than one of their five senses should prove to be unusually vivid. Comparatively little attention has been devoted to what I have called the physiology of poetry, and it would greatly con-tribute to our understanding of poetry if the organic sensibility of all poets were to be studied with the same intelligent care that has been lavished upon Wordsworth by Professor J. C. Smith.[1] We commonly expect a poet's gift of observation to be keen and demand that he should have great descriptive powers. This demand is reasonable only if we remember that we have no business to limit a poet's powers of description and of observa-tion to things *seen*. Over-emphasis on the visual capacity of the poet is a legacy of the belief that poets ought to peer lovingly at flowers, like Lord Tennyson, and to report upon their structure and colouring as minutely as a botanist. Such a doctrine is com-forting to the poet who likes to walk in the country, particularly if he is short-sighted, but it has no binding force upon those whose tastes and visual peculiarities are of another pattern. Even

[1] J. C. Smith, *Wordsworth*. I wish to acknowledge my debt to this short but invaluable study upon which I have freely drawn for illustrations to my argument.

if a poet's visual faculty is the strongest of his five senses his impressions of the world will be influenced by the mechanical structure of his eyes. Robert Graves has examined the verse of a number of our major poets to demonstrate the variety of the ways in which a poet may see.[1] Before we can appreciate the quality of a poet's verse to the full we need to know a great deal about the way that the world appears to him: whether, for example, he is long-sighted or short-sighted; whether he sees a landscape as a unified design or as a series of individual shapes; whether he is attracted by the pattern of still objects or by the disturbing effect of moving objects; whether his eyes are too weak to endure bright sunlight, but extremely sensitive to the quality of different shades of colour. The list could be extended, and I cite these examples only to show that even the visual faculty in poets considered in isolation is by no means straight-forward and uncomplicated.

It is instructive to compare the attitudes of Wordsworth and of Yeats to the natural objects around them. Wordsworth, it is clear, nourished his genius by a long and loving scrutiny of the phenomena that he chanced to see. His absorbed contemplation of flowers and of birds is well known, but, in addition to these conventionally poetic subjects, he derived satisfaction from a study of things that are less obviously beautiful. For example, his admiration for cabbages in all stages of growth and of decay, and for the iridescent scales of a dead trout (much to Shelley's horror) suggests that he possessed an interest in visual shapes and plastic values that is found more often in painters than in poets. He was seemingly gifted with the patience of the naturalist that enabled him to observe a butterfly or a bee for half an hour.

Yeats, on the other hand, showed almost complete indifference to the minutiæ of nature although he was an entomologist in his youth and although his father urged him to cultivate his gift of precise observation. We learn from his letters to Lady Gerald Wellesley that he never bothered to look at external nature, perhaps because, like Baudelaire, he was incapable of becoming sentimental over vegetables. Even the landscapes he loved best seldom moved him to describe them exactly. All that we know about Coole is that there are wild swans drifting on the darkening

[1] Robert Graves, *The Common Asphodel*, pp. 295–306.

flood, great trees, pure clouds, and woods where one can wander at peace. Yeats was more concerned with the total sense of richness and beauty arising from a scene than with constituent parts. Nature existed as the harmonious background for the leisurely flowering of the personality, the function of the landscape being to evoke memories or to provide symbols for an esoteric philosophy:

> Under my window-ledge the waters race,
> Otters below and moor-hens on the top,
> Run for a while undimmed in Heaven's face
> Then darkening through 'dark' Raftery's 'cellar' drop,
> Run underground, rise in a rocky place
> In Coole demesne, and there to finish up
> Spread to a lake and drop into a hole.
> What's water but the generated soul?
>
> Upon the border of that lake's a wood
> Now all dry sticks under a wintry sun,
> And in a copse of beeches there I stood,
> For Nature'd pulled her tragic buskin on
> And all the rant a mirror of my mood.[1]

Few poets have been more sensual than Yeats, but he found no stimulus in the careful observation of nature and was therefore content to ignore those significant details that had been as food and drink to Wordsworth. His genius being essentially dramatic, Yeats needs an appropriate stage-setting, much as the playwright welcomes a magnificent *décor*. The beauty of his meditations is heightened by the stage properties that he handles with consummate art, evoking an atmosphere of superb tranquillity with the utmost economy of description. The following poem contains the minimum of detailed observation, yet the emotional effect produced by the mention of the trees and of the garden gravel is considerable. It is these natural forms that give depth to his reveries, much as moonlight may bind a landscape into a melodious unity:

> If you that have grown old were the first dead
> Neither catalpa tree nor scented lime
> Shall hear my living feet, nor would I tread
> Where we wrought that shall break the teeth of time.

[1] 'Coole and Ballylee', 1931.

Let the new faces play what tricks they will
In the old rooms; night can outbalance day.
Our shadows rove the garden gravel still,
The living seem more shadowy than they.[1]

Take from this poem the catalpa tree, the scented lime, or even the garden gravel, and what remains is far less vivid. Their appearance, which Wordsworth might have described in detail, is irrelevant to Yeats; their function is to induce in us the appropriate mood so that the poem may slowly work its spell upon us.

A study of Yeats's poetry should dispel the notion that a poet is an inspired bird-watcher who celebrates in ecstatic language the rural beauties of innocent nature. The importance attached to the poet's eye and the belief in the moral superiority of the country to the town spring from the prejudices of earnest Wordsworthians who, having lost their faith in traditional religion and having made town-life unbearably hideous, found in a worship of the countryside a substitute for faith and an anodyne for nerves that had been shattered by relentless industrialism. It is important to remember that the sensuous equipment of the poet is not confined to the sight alone, and that dull or defective vision is not a fundamental defect in a poet, provided that his total response to the world is passionate.

This is not to deny that precise observation can give rise to magnificent lines. One of the characteristic marks of a poet is to see the world sparkling with freshness and to present that vision so accurately that we are aware of a new revelation. Some lines of poetry become so much a part of us that we can never look at what they describe without a quickening of the pulse, and a sense of gratitude for their share in opening our eyes to the perennial fascination of the commonest sights. Sometimes the poet directs our attention to a hitherto unnoticed beauty of birds, flowers, fruit, or trees:

Each tree heart-deep the wrangling rout receives—
    Save for the whir within,
You could not tell the starlings from the leaves;
Then one great puff of wings and the swarm heaves
    Away with all its din.

                                        Rossetti

[1] 'The New Faces.'

The hedgerow hips to glossy scarlet turn,
Haws swarm so thick till bushes seem to burn.
And blackthorn sloes, some hung in misty dew,
True to the season, darken into blue.

Clare

The wrinkled sea beneath him crawls.

Tennyson

When drop-of-blood-and-foam-dapple
Bloom lights the orchard-apple,
And thicket and thorp are merry
With silver-surfèd cherry.

Hopkins

And in the autumn Procne came again
And leapt upon the crooked sloe-bough singing
And the dark berries winked like earth-dimmed beads
As the branch swung beneath her dancing feet.

Peter Quennell

The poet's eye may, on the contrary, light upon objects and scenes that most people would find ugly or disturbing or commonplace until they are transformed by the poet's vision which can reveal the unsuspected qualities possessed by simple things. Every action and every object, however coarse or trivial, can be redeemed by the zest and the intensity with which it is contemplated. Just as Van Gogh discovered that an old chair could be as exciting as a handsome girl or as a landscape, so the poet may find the base and the sordid transfigured in the light of his long, patient, unflinching scrutiny. There is a line of Browning's that bears witness to the sensitivity of his eye, his ability to determine exactly the quality of the objects presented to it:

Those morbid, olive, faultless shoulder-blades.

The poet's eye is indeed terrifyingly acute because it is not blurred by the conventional acceptance of surface appearances with which most of us are content. A poet looks at the world as if for the first time and brings back his report upon what he has seen. Occasionally, we are shocked by the violence of the description. Dryden's translation from the Sixth Satire of Juvenal is a terrible document because it is an eye-witness account that depicts the actions of human beings in the fashionable world,

44

stripped of the pretences which we normally agree to take as the truth about one another:

> The Secrets of the Goddess named the Good,
> Are even by Boys and Barbers understood:
> Where the Rank Matrons, Dancing to the pipe,
> Gig with their Bums, and are for Action ripe;
> With Musick rais'd they spread abroad their Hair;
> And toss their Heads like an enamour'd Mare.

Like the child in Hans Andersen, the poet, ignoring the make-believe of polite society, pierces through to the naked reality, however disquieting the result may be. One task of the poet is to jolt us out of our familiar acceptance of what we observe in our daily lives, by showing us hitherto unsuspected facets of common objects, or by presenting an ordinary scene in a fresh guise, pointing out queer relationships between objects, revealing the poetry that lies beneath the stale routine of living. The innocent eye of the child and the experienced heart of the man combine in the poet to communicate both the freshness and the significance of what is seen.

Precision, zest, unsentimentality—these are the qualities that we may legitimately demand in the poet's account of the world around him, whether he is describing human beings, the countryside, or an urban scene:

> Here, at the fountain's sliding foot,
> Or at some fruit-tree's mossy root,
> Casting the body's vest aside,
> My soul into the boughs does glide;
> There, like a bird, it sits and sings,
> There whets and claps its silver wings,
> And, till prepared for longer flight,
> Waves in its plumes the various light.
>
> Marvell

> In the worst inn's worst room, with mat half-hung,
> The floors of plaister and the walls of dung,
> On once a flock-bed, but repair'd with straw,
> With tape-ty'd curtains, never meant to draw,
> The George and Garter dangling from that bed
> Where tawdry yellow strove with dirty red,
> Great Villiers lies. . . .
>
> Pope

C*

What care our Drunken Dames to whom they spread?
Wine no distinction makes of Tail or Head.
Who lewdly Dancing at a Midnight-Ball,
For hot Eringoes and Fat Oysters call:
Full Brimmers to their Fuddled Noses thrust,
Brimmers the last Provocatives of Lust,
When vapours to their swimming brains advance,
And double Tapers on the Tables dance.

Dryden

Look steadily—how the wind feasts and spins
The brain's disc shivered against lust. Then watch
While darkness, like an ape's face, falls away,
And gradually white buildings answer day.

Hart Crane

A twitch, a twitter, an elastic shudder in flight
And serrated wings against the sky,
Like a glove, a black glove thrown up at the light
And falling back.

D. H. Lawrence

It is clear from these quotations that a poet is able to give considerable pleasure to his readers if he is lucky enough to possess a sharp eye. It is equally true, though less generally realized, that a poet's verse is enormously enriched if he is liberally endowed with the other four senses. One reason for this failure to appreciate the importance of this endowment is that it is far harder to convey sound, smell, taste, and touch in verse than it is to evoke an image. There is, however, little doubt that these other senses play a considerable part in the making of a poem's sound, shape, and texture. They are so closely allied that in any consideration of them we shall slide imperceptibly from one to the other in order to discover what contribution they can offer to the poem's total effect.

Wordsworth's poetry has incontestable grandeur, akin to that of the mountains which he celebrated with such reverential insight, yet only the most ardent Wordsworthians would deny that there is in his verse a certain bleak austerity which is a sign of a sensual deficiency in the man.[1] One remembers Haydon's anecdote about Wordsworth: 'In the corner stood the group of

[1] Wordsworth condemned Goethe for his 'inhuman sensuality', spoke disapprovingly of 'poetical sensualists', and called Byron 'reprehensible, perverted and vicious'.

Cupid and Psyche kissing. After looking some time, he turned round to me with an expression I shall never forget and said "The Dev-ils".' Equally significant is Wordsworth's cold dismissal of Keats's attempt in *Endymion* to recapture the spirit of the ancient world as 'a pretty piece of paganism'. Shelley, who possessed a shrewd wit that he all too rarely used, diagnosed in Wordsworth a 'low-tide in soul, like a stagnant laguna'. He represents Nature as a woman speaking to Peter Bell—Wordsworth:

> She laughed the while, with an arch smile,
>   And kissed him with a sister's kiss,
> And said—'My best Diogenes,
> I love you well—but if you please,
>   Tempt not again my deepest bliss.
>
> 'Tis you are cold—for I, not coy,
>   Yield love for love, frank, warm and true;
> And Burns, a Scottish peasant boy—
> His errors prove it—knew my joy
>   More, learned friend, than you. . . .'

It is, therefore, with no sense of surprise that we read of Wordsworth's comparative insensibility to music and to perfumes. Coleridge's affirmation that Wordsworth had no ear for music is borne out by Quillinan's more specific judgement that he lacked an ear for instrumental music. 'The Solitary Reaper' is based upon an experience of Wordsworth's friend Wilkinson and tells us nothing about Wordsworth's response to music, although it serves as a reminder that he was extremely adept at juggling with the emotions that he recollected or invented in tranquillity. It seems likely that the senses of sound and of smell are closely linked, if we may rely upon the evidence of poetry. For it will often be found that poets deficient in the one sense are similarly obtuse in the other and, furthermore, that a sensitivity to music often goes with an exquisite response to different scents. Scott, who, like Wordsworth, was indifferent to music, resembled him also in his blunt sense of smell. James Payn goes so far as to say that Wordsworth could not distinguish the scent of a bean-field in bloom, thereby reinforcing Southey's contention that Wordsworth had no sense of smell. Southey also tells us of the one occasion that a scent appears to have moved Wordsworth deeply: 'Once and once only in his life, the dormant power was

awakened; it was by a bed of stocks in full bloom, at a house
which he inhabited in Dorsetshire, some five and twenty years
ago, and he says it was like a vision of Paradise to him; but it
lasted only a few minutes, and the faculty has continued torpid
from that time.'[1] Even when describing a smell, Wordsworth
reverts to visual imagery, just as Victor Hugo, who was notoriously indifferent to music, instinctively turns to a visual image
to save him from floundering in unfamiliar waters:

> Comme sur la colonne un frêle chapiteau
> La flûte épanouie a monté sur l'alto.

It is only fair to add that, although Wordsworth may have
been deaf to instrumental music and deficient in a sense of pitch,
he possessed considerable powers of judgement when it was a
matter of assessing volume or timbre. Yet, compared with Shakespeare, Milton, or Shelley, it is clear that his perceptions of sound
and of smell were rudimentary. It is noteworthy that all these
poets express one of these senses in terms of the other:

> O! it came o'er my ear like the sweet sound
> That breathes upon a bank of violets,
> Stealing and giving odour.
>
> Shakespeare

> . . . a soft and solemn-breathing sound
> Rose like a steam of rich-distilled perfumes,
> And stole upon the air.
>
> Milton

Even more remarkable is Shelley's mode of comparison:

> And as a vale is watered by a flood,
>
> Or as the moonlight fills the open sky
> Struggling with darkness—as a tuberose
> Peoples some Indian dell with scents which lie,
>
> Like clouds above the flower from which they rose,
> The singing of that happy nightingale
> In this sweet forest, from the golden close
>
> Of evening till the star of dawn may fail,
> Was interfused upon the silentness.

[1] Cited by J. C. Smith, *Wordsworth*, p. 12.

One may hazard the generalization that while a keen visual faculty in a poet does not necessarily imply that his other sensual faculties are remarkably acute, those poets noticeably rich in any one of the other four sensual perceptions are likely to be unusually well endowed with the remaining three. Herrick's verse, for example, survives largely because it is interfused with a palpitating awareness of texture, smell, taste, and sound:

> So smooth, so sweet, so silvery is thy voice,
> As, could they hear, the damned would make no noise,
> But listen to thee (walking in thy chamber)
> Melting melodious words to lutes of amber.

Two further examples drawn from seventeenth-century poets will show the way in which the sharpness of the impression that we receive is conveyed by an appeal to more than one of our five senses:

> The dew no more will weep
> The primrose's pale cheek to deck;
> The dew no more will sleep
> Nuzzled in the lily's neck.
>
> Crashaw

> I saw fair Chloris walk alone
> When feather'd rain came softly down,
> Like Jove descending from his tower
> To court her in a silver shower.
>
> Strode

In our own day, the austerity of T. S. Eliot's thought is made acceptable as poetry because, from time to time, it takes on the sensuous beauty of a temple-flower tree on whose black, leafless boughs the delicate blossom rises.

A comparison between the sensual endowments of Wordsworth and of Keats may help us to understand how a poet's organic sensibility is directly reflected in the texture of his verse. Wordsworth, whom Carlyle described as having 'great jaws like a crocodile's', was as indifferent to the taste of the food that he masticated as to the smell of the bean-field in bloom. Nor does he seem to have been acutely sensitive to the feel of objects, to the subtle gradations of texture. It is true that the sense of touch helped him to escape from the imprisoning trances that held him in a state of suspended animation, all normal bodily faculties in abeyance. 'Many times when going to school', he told Miss Fenwick, 'have I grasped at a wall or a tree to recall myself from this abyss of idealism to the reality.' In other words, he used the sense of touch as a means of reassuring himself that the external world had an objective existence, rather as Doctor Johnson attempted to refute the philosophy of Idealism by kicking a stone. There is nothing to indicate that Wordsworth derived sensuous pleasure from touch, or that he found it a means of giving depth and delicacy to his verse. The matchless range of Keats's animal sensibility was beyond his reach, his comprehension, and his sympathy.

The poetry of Keats, like that of Shakespeare, is deeply rooted in sensual reality, and on these grounds alone one can justify the comparison that has often been drawn between them. The importance of the senses in poetry has been noted by Robert Graves, who very justly remarks: 'In my experience, poetic imagery concerned only with the visual senses is far less cogent than that concerned with the so-called "grosser" senses of hearing, touch, taste and smell.'[1] He goes on to contrast Shelley's imagery, which is 'remote and almost wholly visual', with the 'sensuous, intimate' imagery of Keats. Some of the most characteristically beautiful lines of Shelley convey his response to light or to fire:

> Men scarcely know how beautiful fire is—
> Each flame of it is as a precious stone
> Dissolved in ever-moving light, and this
> Belongs to each and all who gaze upon.
>
> As the dissolving warmth of dawn may fold
> A half-unfrozen dew-globe green and gold
> And crystalline till it becomes a wingèd mist,
> And wanders up the vault of the blue day,
> Outlives the noon, and on the sun's last ray
> Hangs o'er the sea, a fleece of fire and amethyst.
>
> Or as on Vesta's sceptre a swift flame
> Or on blind Homer's heart a wingèd thought.
>
> Bright as that wandering Eden Lucifer.

How different are the lines of Keats that seem to contain the essence of his genius. Robert Graves explains their dissimilarity by a reference to the contrast in the two poets' animal natures:

[1] *The Common Asphodel*, p. 19, in the section entitled 'The Grosser Senses'.

'Shelley was a volatile creature of air and fire: he seems never to have noticed what he ate or drank, except sometimes as a matter of vegetarian principle. Keats was earthy, with a sweet tooth and a relish for spices, cream and snuff, and in a letter mentions peppering his own tongue to bring out the delicious coolness of claret.'[1]

The last two stanzas of the 'Ode on Melancholy' reveal Keats's extraordinary responsiveness to sensuous experience:

> But when the melancholy fit shall fall
>   Sudden from heaven like a weeping cloud,
> That fosters the droop-headed flowers all,
>   And hides the green hill in an April shroud,
> Then glut thy sorrow on a morning rose,
>   Or on the rainbow of the salt-sand wave,
>   Or on the wealth of globèd peonies;
> Or if thy mistress some rich anger shows,
>   Emprison her soft hand, and let her rave,
>   And feed deep, deep upon her peerless eyes.
>
> She dwells with Beauty—Beauty that must die;
>   And Joy, whose hand is ever at his lips
> Bidding adieu; and aching Pleasure nigh,
>   Turning to poison while the bee-mouth sips:
> Ay, in the very temple of Delight
>   Veil'd Melancholy has her sovran shrine,
>   Though seen of none save him whose strenuous tongue
> Can burst Joy's grape against his palate fine;
>   His soul shall taste the sadness of her might,
>   And be among her cloudy trophies hung.

The visual images are reinforced by an appeal to the other senses. We are meant to feel the softness of the April shroud and the roundness of the peonies, to experience the full force of the word 'shroud' which suggests the sadness of death implicit in the mingled sun and showers of April. The peonies and the salt-sand wave are akin in texture and in depth to the skin and to the eyes of the rich, angry mistress. There is the further suggestion that the sensuous elements of Nature are to be found richly concentrated in a woman's flesh, or, if one reverses the metaphor, that

[1] Graves is mistaken about the pepper and the claret. Keats makes no mention of the incident: the assertion that he peppered his tongue with Cayenne was made by Haydon. Charles Cowden Clarke dismissed Haydon's story as odious twaddle. I think that Haydon was telling the truth.

Nature is impregnated with an almost sexual warmth and sweetness. In the last stanza three images of taste occur as symbols of the power of Melancholy, a sign that Keats turned to the grosser senses for illumination as naturally as Wordsworth relied upon his visual faculties to express his most intense spiritual perceptions.

The Odes are the most harmonious expression of Keats's maturing sensibility, but all his verse is suffused with this voluptuous response to experience. Smell, taste, and touch have rarely been more explicitly conveyed than in two famous stanzas from 'The Eve of St. Agnes':

> A casement high and triple-arch'd there was,
> All garlanded with carven imageries,
> Of fruits and flowers, and bunches of knot-grass,
> And diamonded with panes of quaint device,
> Innumerable of stains and splendid dyes,
> As are the tiger-moth's deep-damask'd wings;
> And in the midst, 'mong thousand heraldries,
> And twilight saints, and dim emblazonings,
> A shielded scutcheon blush'd with blood of queens and kings.

> . . . And still she slept an azure-lidded sleep,
> In blanchèd linen, smooth, and lavender'd,
> While he from forth the closet brought a heap
> Of candied apple, quince, and plum, and gourd;
> With jellies smoother than the creamy curd,
> And lucent syrops, tinct with cinnamon;
> Manna and dates, in argosy transferr'd
> From Fez; and spicèd dainties, every one,
> From silken Samarcand to cedar'd Lebanon.

Keats, like Shakespeare, was able to communicate the thrill of extreme terror. In lines that recall the tremendous agony of Claudio in *Measure for Measure* Keats brings home to us the full meaning of the medieval commonplace *Timor mortis conturbat me*. The dry bones of an abstract reflexion are clothed with tormented flesh:

> The sculptur'd dead, on each side, seem to freeze,
> Emprison'd in black, purgatorial rails:
> Knights, ladies, praying in dumb orat'ries,
> He passeth by, and his weak spirit fails
> To think how they may ache in icy hoods and mails.

It was precisely this intense response to sensation, this avid desire for passionate experience, that enraged those readers of Keats who lacked his temperamental voluptuousness. Kingsley, as we have seen, asserted that the sound heart of the English people had rejected the productions of John Keats. His robust and somewhat shaggy masculinity, combined with his solicitude for health and cleanliness, took alarm at the distressing acuteness of sense that was so offensively visible in the poems of the tuberculous apothecary. Byron's obscene comments upon Keats, which may in part have sprung from his aristocratic prejudice against a young Cockney, are understandable if we allow for his contemptuous attitude towards all that smacked of the boudoir. Lacking Shelley's generosity and delicacy of understanding, he impatiently dismissed Keats as unpleasantly effeminate, failing to recognize the leonine strength that controlled the sweetness.

Although few poets begin to rival Keats in his continuous awareness of smell, taste, and touch, English poetry is wonderfully rich in lines that remind us of the sensual flame that burns in the quivering nervous system of the poet. Darley's Phoenix makes her nest in a tree that shines in our memory as vividly as any tree in poetry, although its appearance is nowhere minutely described in visual terms. We know only that it is bright and burning, yet how unforgettably precise and moving is the description of the whole landscape:

> O blest unfabled Incense tree,
> That burns in glorious Araby,
> With red scent chalicing the air,
> Till earth-life grow Elysian there!

The whole scene is mysteriously unified by the red scent that steals into every recess and corner, melting all things into a sensuous harmony. D. H. Lawrence uses a similar technique:

> When shall I see the half-moon sink again
> Behind the black sycamore at the end of the garden?
> When will the scent of the dim white phlox
> Creep up the wall to me, and in at my open window?

The faint subtlety of the phlox's perfume is suggested by the adjective 'dim' which reinforces, in its turn, the slow, insidious connotations of the word 'creep'. This intercommunication between the senses is, for many poets, as stimulating and as significant as the visionary faculty so highly prized by Wordsworth. Tennyson employs a similar device, in conjuring up the impressions made upon him by the gardens and by the countryside of Lincolnshire where he had passed his childhood:

> Unwatch'd, the garden bough shall sway,
>   The tender blossom flutter down,
>   Unloved, that beech will gather brown,
> This maple burn itself away;
>
> Unloved, the sunflower, shining fair,
>   Ray round with flames her disk of seed,
>   And many a rose-carnation feed
> With summer spice the humming air.

The second stanza, in its rich concentration of imagery, gives proof not only of Tennyson's remarkable command of language but also of the fineness of his sense-perceptions. The botanical exactitude of the second line serves only to accentuate the overpowering profusion evoked by the two final lines. We no longer observe the appearance of the sunflower; instead, we experience its very essence with all our being. It is relevant, as well as amusing, to recall that in vulgar speech the word 'hum' is used to describe a powerful and offensive smell, a sign that the untutored vigour of the common man recognizes the affinities between the different grosser senses. Tennyson, with his unerring feeling for language, chose the word 'humming' in order that its sensuous reverberations might blend the divergent sensual responses into one intricate melody.

Even comparatively minor poems retain their power to please us because of their vivid sensuousness that lives on unquenchably bright. We can still savour the combination of wit, desire, and keen sensitivity to touch that informs Randolph's description of 'A Pastoral Courtship':

> There is no Frog to leap and fright
> Thee from my Arms, and break delight;
> Nor Snail that o'er thy Coat shall trace,
> And leave behind a slimy Lace.
> This is the hallowed shrine of Love,
> No Wasp nor Hornet haunts this Grove,
> Nor Pismire to make Pimples rise
> Upon thy smooth and Ivory Thighs.

The power to communicate atmosphere and to reproduce men's animal delight in the multifarious pleasures of the world is one of the supreme marks of the poet. Equally characteristic of the poet is the ability to convey loathing and disgust, to present whatever is foul in its physical actuality, to evoke the sense of oppressive gloom as well as the feeling of extreme bodily joy. It is the zest, the inexhaustible vitality that matters:

> Whenas the rye reach to the chin,
> And chopcherry, chopcherry, ripe within,
> Strawberries swimming in the cream,
> And schoolboys playing in the stream;
> Then, O, then, O, then, O, my true love said,
> Till that time come again,
> She could not live a maid.
>
> > Peele

> The drunkard now supinely snores,
> The load of ale sweats through his pores.
> Yet when he wakes the swine shall find
> A crapula remains behind.
>
> > Cotton

> Purged by the sword and purified by fire,
> Then had we seen proud London's hated walls;
> Owls would have hooted in St. Peter's choir,
> And foxes stunk and littered in St. Paul's.
>
> > Gray

> Far out in the grey silence of the flood
> They watch the dawn in smouldering gyres expand
> Beyond them: and the day burns through their blood
> Like a white candle through a shuttered hand.
>
> > Roy Campbell

It is only to be expected that the emotions aroused by sexual desire should have been experienced by poets with the utmost intensity. There is little doubt that Browning and Tennyson were endowed with strong animal sensibility, Tennyson in particular displaying an almost morbidly sensitive responsiveness to external stimuli. Unfortunately, Browning was anxious to preserve his reputation as a wrestler with metaphysical difficulties and Tennyson too often remembered the lofty mission to which a Bard was dedicated. It was all too rarely that their naked sensuality was allowed free play unimpeded by their propensity to pronounce moralizing judgements. Both poets speak most passionately through the lips of a woman, as if this device liberated them from the necessity of making an ethical assertion. J. B. Yeats spoke of 'the *anger subtly present* in ethical thought— as it is also in most kinds of argument; how many poems has it laid low?'[1] The girl in Browning's 'The Confessional' is prompted by her agony to utter a cry of the purest and most poignant grief, made more terrible by her memory of utter sensual bliss, and undimmed by any philosophical reflection:

> I had a lover—shame avaunt.
> This poor wrenched body, grim and gaunt,
> Was kissed all over till it burned,
> By lips the truest, love e'er turned
> His heart's own tint: one night they kissed
> My soul out in a burning mist.

Tennyson achieves a similar intensity of utterance when, in 'Fatima', he presents the meditation of a woman thirsting for her lover:

> Last night, when some one spoke his name,
> From my swift blood that went and came
> A thousand little shafts of flame
> Were shiver'd in my narrow frame.
>   O Love, O fire! once he drew
>   With one long kiss my whole soul thro'
> My lips as sunlight drinketh dew.
>
> The wind sounds like a silver wire,
> And from beyond the moon a fire
> Is poured upon the hills, and nigher
> The skies stoop down in their desire;
>   And isled in sudden seas of light,
>   My heart, pierced through with fierce delight,
> Bursts into blossom in his sight.
>
> My whole soul waiting silently,
> All naked in a sultry sky,
> Droops blinded with his shining eye:
> I will possess him or will die.

Tennyson's miraculous perceptiveness is revealed in a few stanzas from *In Memoriam*:

[1] *Letters to his Son*, p. 198 (his italics).

Till now the doubtful dusk reveal'd
    The knolls once more where, couch'd at ease,
    The white kine glimmer'd and the trees
Laid their dark arms about the field;

And suck'd from out the distant gloom
    A breeze began to tremble o'er
    The large leaves of the sycamore,
And fluctuate all the still perfume;

And, gathering freshlier overhead,
    Rock'd the full-foliaged elms and swung
    The heavy-folded rose and flung
The lilies to and fro, and said

'The dawn, the dawn', and died away,
    And East and West without a breath
    Mixt their dim lights, like life and death,
To broaden into boundless day.

Tennyson was always particularly sensitive to atmosphere, to the damp richness of decay no less than to the luminous serenity of the summer landscape. In one of his early poems we catch a glimpse of the dark sensuality that proved so fertile a soil for the flowering of his genius, a sensuality that was only partially concealed by the noble decorum thought proper for a Victorian laureate:

The air is damp and hushed and close
As a sick man's room, when he taketh repose
    An hour before death;
My very heart faints and my whole soul grieves
At the moist rich smell of the rotting leaves
    And the breath
Of the fading edges of box beneath
And the year's last rose.
Heavily hangs the broad sunflower
    Over its grave i' the earth so chilly;
Heavily hangs the hollyhock,
    Heavily hangs the tiger-lily.

Since Tennyson's day such exquisite writing has been suspect, partly because any attempt to reproduce his brilliant delicacy of observation and of feeling inevitably suggests that the poet is striving to imitate an obsolete mode of apprehension. It is always difficult to write in a style that an earlier poet has brought to perfection, especially as one can never be sure that one's emotional reactions will not be faked in order that they may conform to the expected pattern. A poet may even feel that he ought to suppress certain genuine impulses, lest he may be accused of writing pastiche. Some puritanical critics might consider that Laurie Lee's poems exhibit a highly self-conscious and sophisticated rehashing of Tennysonian formulæ. The metre of one of his most beautiful lyrics certainly recalls the stanzaic form of *In Memoriam* but the poem seems to me completely fresh and original. The first eight lines suffice to prove that Laurie Lee is a man whose senses respond to the challenge of the metropolis with the leaping vitality that we have the right to expect in a poet:

> The green light floods the city square—
>   A sea of fowl and feathered fish
>   Where squalls of rainbirds dive and flash
> And gusty sparrows chop the air.
>
> Submerged, the prawn-blue pigeons feed
>   In sandy grottoes round the Mall
>   And crusted lobster-buses crawl
> Among the fountains' silver weed.

If we demand that poets shall experience keenly all that is beautiful in the world, we need not be surprised that their expressions of disgust have a terrible physical immediacy. Once we accept this we shall understand why it is that Shakespeare has recorded in horrifying language some of the baser aspects of human thought and behaviour, and why it is that even his most obscene passages bear the stamp of his genius. We shall learn to admit that the revulsion and the disgust that lacerated Swift are fit subjects for poetry. The difference between Swift and Shakespeare is that while Swift is habitually overwhelmed by nausea, like a sick man laid prostrate, Shakespeare almost always commands his disgust and can, thereby, communicate to us the physical sense of contamination that he suffered in his contact with vileness. Hamlet's onslaught upon his mother reveals Shakespeare's bodily revulsion at the mere thought of sensual grossness, his tormented awareness of the moral vileness that contaminates the individual or the realm like an ulcerous sore:

> Let the bloat king tempt you again to bed;
> Play wanton on your cheek, call you his mouse;

And let him, for a pair of reechy kisses,
Or paddling in your neck with his damn'd fingers. . . .

The one word 'paddling' conveys precisely the sense of greedy, furtive lust that characterizes the bloat king.

Dryden's tremendous exuberance enables him to portray coarseness and lust so vigorously that they become monumental, thereby losing something of their base, disgusting quality. Yet how admirably does Dryden paint for us the cruder manifestations of human desires:

She duely, once a Month, renews her Face;
Mean time it lies in Dawb, and hid in Grease;
These are the Husband's Nights; she craves her due,
He takes fat kisses, and is stuck in Glue.
But, to the Lov'd Adult'rer when she steers,
Fresh from the Bath, in brightness she appears.

And with what conviction does he reconstruct the conditions of life and the social habits of the noble savage:

Those first unpolisht Matrons, Big and Bold,
Gave Suck to Infants of Gygantick Mold;
Rough as their Savage Lords who Rang'd the Wood,
And fat with Akorns Belcht their windy Food.

Some poets whose sensuous faculties have been unusually keen have explored the subtle inter-relationships of the five senses. This kind of investigation may be variously estimated and I do not propose to discuss it at any great length, if only because any adequate treatment of the subject would lead us far astray from our main theme. It is enough to note that, in the mid-nineteenth century, what had hitherto been an occasional hint scattered here and there in English poetry became part of a systematic technique. We have seen how Shakespeare, Herrick, Milton, and Shelley represent music in terms of the other senses. William Strode compares the softness of music with the falling of snow upon wool, and Crashaw employs one sensuous image after another to convey the effect of the nightingale's song as she vies with the lutanist. Milton's famous description of the divine harmonies of music contains a striking anticipation of modern practice:

How sweetly did they float upon the wings
Of silence, through the empty-vaulted night,
At every fall smoothing the raven down
Of darkness till it smiled!

Despite such examples, general critical opinion in the eighteenth century remained stolidly impervious to any suggestions
that the compartments between the five senses were not so water-
tight as was generally supposed. Fielding refers to the absurdity
of the opinion which a 'blind man entertained of the colour
scarlet; that colour seemed to him to be very much like the sound
of a trumpet'. Dr. Johnson also mentions this comparison, equating
it with the dictum of Dionysius who 'tells us, that the sound of
Homer's verse sometimes exhibits the idea of corporal bulk'.

In the mid-nineteenth century, poets began to search for a unity
that was believed to lie beneath the different manifestations of
the senses. Baudelaire's sonnet 'Correspondances' and Rimbaud's
attempt to affix colour-values to the vowel-sounds mark the
beginning of the new desire to probe more deeply into the
ramifications of the senses. Such minute analysis may be wel-
comed as a sign of an increased subtlety and accuracy, of a desire
to record the slightest quiver of the nerves, the most impercep-
tible stirrings of the sensual organs. Or it may be less favourably
regarded as the morbid propensity of minds unhealthily stimulated by the inhuman glare and noise of the metropolis to crave
for a thrill, the literary equivalent of drug-taking. Indeed, the
drug-addict is said to enjoy a heightening of the senses akin to the
perception of sense-relationships that we find in Baudelaire,
Rimbaud, and their successors. Finally, we may look upon the
whole process as a logical extension of the early Romantics' use
of language, as an attempt to find a verbal freshness that should
correspond with the emotional fervour which they sought to
reproduce in their verse. Originality of feeling, unless it is to
grow stale almost at once, must be buttressed by originality of
language.

Thus we find in the late nineteenth century and in the twentieth century a use of epithets that Fielding would have dismissed
as absurd. Swinburne excited the nerves of his generation by the
virtuosity with which he handled the sensuous properties of
language:

Ah yet would God this flesh of mine might be
Where air might wash and long leaves cover me,
Where tides of grass break into foams of flowers
Or where the wind's feet shine along the sea.[1]

Hopkins compares a mountain bathed in evening light with

a stallion stalwart very-violet-sweet

and makes us feel the oppression of darkness that weighs down upon the tortured soul when he uses this superb image:

I wake to feel the fell of dark not day.

Dame Edith Sitwell has practised this technique with a virtuosity unparalleled since the days of Swinburne and of Hopkins. When we read such phrases as 'the hairy sky' and 'The morning light creaks', we should remember that she has frequently acknowledged her debt to Hopkins and that she has admired Swinburne ever since the days of her girlhood when she stole away to pour a libation upon his grave.

A poet who distorts the normal use of language in order to convey with the utmost fidelity and immediacy of sensation the sensuous quality of the object or the emotion which he is describing, and who endeavours to shock his readers into awareness of the exact physical properties of the world about them, is running a considerable risk. It is all too easy to manufacture a series of perverse images with a frigid calculation that is the antithesis of the impassioned response to life which distinguishes a poet. The charlatan's impudent manipulation of epithets is a modish trick as far removed from genuinely sensuous observation as was the pompous formality of minor eighteenth-century verse from the Miltonic grandeur or from the Augustan perfection.

It may indeed be thought that my emphasis on the poet's animal sensibility may lead to a serious misconception of poetry, and of the poet's character, to an over-rating of the poet's ability to convey sensuous impressions and to a corresponding undervaluing of his intellectual, moral, and spiritual resources. A critic of my general argument might choose to attack it on the grounds that animal sensibility alone can never make a man a poet, and

[1] *Laus Veneris*. Cf. his reference to 'sounds that shine'.

that the cult of sensibility has had deplorable results in life and in literature. He might point out that, although Dorothy Wordsworth's sensibility was as great as, possibly even greater than her brother's, she was unable to write poetry whereas he left behind some of the most superb verse in the language. Furthermore, the poets of the nineties prided themselves on the refinement of their sensibility, the acuteness of their perceptions, and attempted to build the art of poetry upon the sensual foundation that we are asked to admire. Such a doctrine produced a crop of untidy, self-indulgent lives, but comparatively little poetry of any merit. It is, doubtless, very pleasant for a poet to excuse his sexual misdemeanours by pleading that his animal passions are bound to be preternaturally strong, and even more comforting for the incipient Don Juan to derive from his amorous impulses the certainty that he is a poet. Nevertheless, it is doubtful whether the cause of poetry or of morality is thereby advanced. And if this animal sensibility is as important as has been claimed, we ought to rank Keats above all other poets, certainly far above Wordsworth. Is it not truer to say that the faults which vitiate Keats, his over-luscious imagery, his mawkish self-indulgence, his cloying sweetness, spring precisely from that sensibility to which we are required to pay such unqualified homage? That hectic sensuousness, so characteristic of tuberculosis, may endow poetry with an unearthly richness, but it can never be the inevitable basis of all poetry. Chopin realized that his temperament contained within itself the seeds of disintegration and always, before giving a recital, would play Bach, so that his nerves might be calmed by the music of one whose genius was built upon more enduring foundations than the sensual appetites.

Such arguments, however cogent they may be in themselves, do not affect my main contention, for although I have insisted that the first prerequisite of a poet is a powerful organic sensibility, I have never maintained that it is the sole prerequisite. The possession of a delicate sensibility without the power to transmute its promptings into poetry is responsible for the proliferation of a class of people whom we may describe as half-artists, men and women who are acutely conscious of the world's beauty and forever tantalized by their creative impotence. The poets of the nineties, though genuinely responsive to colours, perfumes,

and shapes, lacked the intellectual and moral drive that might
have controlled their undirected sensibility. What vitiated them
was not the possession of sensibility but the lack of a central,
unifying passion. As for the accusation that poets and would-be
poets often lead sexually irregular lives, it may be conjectured
that this particular form of sensuality is inseparable from the
temperamental endowment that makes it possible for them to be
poets:

> You think it horrible that lust and rage
> Should dance attendance upon my old age;
> They were not such a plague when I was young;
> What else have I to spur me into song?

Whether we regard these lines of Yeats as rhetorical defiance or
as disturbing truth, we can at least agree in holding that the poet's
sensual appetites form an integral part of his personality and that
they must be carefully studied if we are to evaluate his poetry.
Hopkins wrote a remarkable letter about Keats, in which he
attempts to trace the relationship between his sensuality and his
poetic achievement. We may discern in his judgement the
severity of the priest rather than the sympathy of the poet, but at
least he has not shirked the problem that is raised by the peculiar
quality of Keats's genius. I have suggested that Kingsley's whole-
some manliness and Byron's buck masculinity were affronted by
the embarrassingly warm profusion of feeling that suffuses the
poetry of Keats. The Christian asceticism of the Jesuit priest was
equally perturbed by the tone of Keats's verse: 'It is impossible
not to feel with weariness how his verse is at every turn abandon-
ing itself to unmanly and enervating luxury. It appears too that
he said something like "O for a life of impressions instead of
thoughts".'[1] Hopkins goes on to lament the moral perils to which
Keats thus exposed himself, and also suggests that his intellectual
growth was hampered by his self-indulgent habits: 'His mind had,
as it seems to me, the distinctly masculine powers in abundance;
but while he gave himself up to dreaming and self-indulgence, of
course they were in abeyance.' The most interesting part of the
criticism follows, and I quote it because it shows that, despite

---

[1] 'The kind of man Keats was gets ever more horrible to me. Force of hunger for
pleasure of every kind, and want of all other force—that is a combination.' Carlyle, in
his Journal for Dec. 1848.

his moral condemnation of Keats's animal sensibility, Hopkins realized that the potential superiority of Keats to all his contemporaries lay in precisely that sensuality which was so offensive to the moral earnestness of the Catholic priest. Keats would, says Hopkins, have moved beyond an adolescent brooding upon his own sensations into more profound modes of experience. Only God knows how his life would have altered, but we men can prophesy with some confidence that 'his genius would have taken to an austerer utterance in art. Reason, thought, what he did not want to live by, would have asserted itself presently, and perhaps have been as much more powerful than that of his contemporaries as his sensibility or impressionableness, by which he did want to live, were keener and richer than theirs.'[1]

This seems to me a very just statement of the relationship between the sensual endowment of a poet and his poetic achievement. A rich animal sensibility may be frittered away or left undeveloped, either through laziness or though sheer inability to harness its power to any form of artistic expression. A man may thus have all the qualities usually found in a poet, except the power of turning them into poetry. Animal sensibility is not enough: but, without it, moral fervour, a devotion to the public good, a meditative spirit, and an accurate knowledge of prosody are all in vain. A man cannot become a poet simply by taking thought, and the old saying that a poet is born, not made, is a recognition of the truth that the deep resources on which a poet draws spring from the temperament with which he is endowed at birth and from the emotional experiences of his childhood.

In his essay on Hopkins, Sir Herbert Read draws attention to the quality by which we can always recognize a poet. It is interesting to note that the thought in this passage re-echoes almost exactly the thesis advanced by De Quincey:

He [Hopkins] had that acute and sharp sensuous awareness essential to all great poets. He was physically aware of textures, surfaces, colours, patterns of every kind; aware acutely of earth's diurnal course, of growth and decay, of animality in man and of vitality in all things. Everywhere there is passionate apprehension, passionate expression, and equally that passion for

---

[1] *Further Letters*, pp. 233–9. Hopkins says also that 'in this fault he resembles, not differs from Shakespeare'. He is replying to Coventry Patmore's contention that Keats was a feminine genius among men and the 'unlikest' of our poets to Shakespeare.

form without which these other apprehensions are spendthrift. But the form is inherent in the passion.[1]

How fruitful the marriage between form and passion can be a brief examination of the poetry of Pope will show. I choose Pope in preference to any other great poet because, despite the advocacy of a handful of critics in the past twenty years, the nature of his genius is still misconceived. We are still told that he was a brilliant but cold writer of polished verse, that, at best, he was only a master of wit-writing, and that it is vain to attempt to elevate him to the rank of poet. It is understandable that those who repeat the judgements of the textbooks should persist in this attitude, but it is not easy to see why those who actually read Pope should be so blind to his quality. For the most obvious fact about Pope is the intensity of his feelings, the painful acuteness of his sensibility. The famous lines from *An Essay on Man* hint at the disadvantages of a morbid sensitivity, and it may be conjectured that Pope is referring to his own experience, his own suffering:

> Say what the use, were finer optics giv'n,
> T' inspect a mite, not comprehend the heav'n?
> Or touch, if tremblingly alive all o'er,
> To smart and agonize at every pore?
> Or quick effluvia darting through the brain,
> Die of a rose in aromatic pain?

It was his exquisite feeling that enabled him to describe the most delicate shades and textures, the most subtle variations of colour and the most aetherial qualities of light. He normally preferred the minute to the conventionally sublime because his sensibility was stirred by tiny particulars rather than by vague immensities:

> The spider's touch, how exquisitely fine!
> Feels at each thread, and lives along the line.

His imagination, like the spider's touch, rejoiced in the exploration of sensual experience, the observation of barely perceptible differences in surfaces and in hues, the ever-shifting play of light upon a changing scene. The blurred, the formless, and the coarse were alien to his perception and to his moral discrimination. His genius could depict the flight of the Sylphs, invisible to mortal

[1] Herbert Read, *Collected Essays in Literary Criticism*, pp. 47-48.

eyes, because he experienced the lightest movement and the most evanescent sound:

> Some to the sun their insect-wings unfold,
> Waft on the breeze, or sink in clouds of gold;
> Transparent forms, too fine for mortal sight,
> Their fluid bodies half dissolv'd in light.
> Loose to the wind their airy garments flew,
> Thin glitt'ring textures of the filmy dew,
> Dipt in the richest tincture of the skies,
> Where light disports in ever-mingling dyes,
> While ev'ry beam new transient colours flings,
> Colours that change whene'er they wave their wings.

The keenness of Pope's eye was matched by the acuteness of his other senses. Consider the mastery which he displays in his portrayal of the sufferings inflicted upon the neglectful Sylphs. The passage is, of course, a polished piece of mock-heroic writing, almost a parody of Claudio's agonized fears in *Measure for Measure*, but it would fail in its purpose were it not for Pope's ability to convey with complete fidelity the actual quality of the pain that the Sylphs would feel, the response of their nerves to a thrilling sensation:

> Whatever spirit, careless of his charge,
> His post neglects, or leaves the fair at large,
> Shall feel sharp vengeance soon o'ertake his sins,
> Be stopp'd in vials, or transfix'd with pins;
> Or plung'd in lakes of bitter washes lie,
> Or wedg'd whole ages in a bodkin's eye:
> Gums and Pomatums shall his flight restrain,
> While clogg'd he beats his silken wings in vain;
> Or Alum styptics with contracting pow'r
> Shrink his thin essence like a rivel'd flower:
> Or, as Ixion fix'd, the wretch shall feel
> The giddy motion of the whirling Mill,
> In fumes of burning Chocolate shall glow,
> And tremble at the sea that froths below!

Pope's nerves, always sensitive, were frequently exacerbated by the cruel insults heaped upon him, especially by those which dwelt upon his deformed body. It may even be that his excessive and vulnerable sensibility dates from his first experience of being ridiculed as a contemptible dwarf, either by a woman, or by the companions who watched him expose his miserable carcass at a brothel. He seems to have regarded his enemies in the light of noxious insects, and his nerves, sharpened by hatred, responded to the odious characteristics of his foes as if they were disgusting smells and sights. Pope's satire is great poetry because his hatred glows with an animal ferocity that sniffs the air like a tiger, and because his emotions are invariably regulated by an iron intelligence:

> Rufa, whose eye quick-glancing o'er the Park,
> Attracts each light gay meteor of a Spark,
> Agrees as ill with Rufa studying Locke,
> As Sappho's di'monds with her dirty smock.
> Or Sappho at her toilet's greasy task,
> With Sappho fragrant at an ev'ning Masque:
> So morning Insects that in muck begun,
> Shine, buzz, and fly-blow in the setting sun.

The sense of physical revulsion is triumphantly conveyed both in that passage and in the incomparable portrait of Sporus. Byron pointed out how one image follows another in this devastating onslaught, and how the whole passage glitters with sensuous intensity. We may note how all the senses are brought to bear upon the detested object in the first four lines:

> Yet let me flap this bug with gilded wings,
> This painted child of dirt, that stinks and stings;
> Whose buzz the witty and the fair annoys,
> Yet wit ne'er tastes, and beauty ne'er enjoys.

Sporus is compared with an insect, a timid spaniel, a shallow, a puppet, and then, most loathsomely, with a toad:

> Whether in florid impotence he speaks,
> And, as the prompter breathes, the puppet squeaks;
> Or at the ear of Eve, familiar Toad,
> Half-froth, half venom, spits himself abroad,
> In puns, or politics, or tales, or lies,
> Or spite, or smut, or rhymes, or blasphemies.

We are driven to moral condemnation by the evidence of the senses; and it is characteristic of his genius that moral infirmity, as well as intellectual meanness, affects Pope like a filthy smell or a repulsive insect. Even Hervey's literary affectation is presented in terms of his sexual ambiguity and his sexual ambiguity in terms of an evil spirit incarnate in a reptile:

His wit all see-saw, between *that* and *this*,
Now high, now low, now master up, now miss,
And he himself, one vile Antithesis.
Amphibious thing! that acting either part,
The trifling head or the corrupted heart,
Fop at the toilet, flatt'rer at the board,
Now trips a Lady and now struts a Lord.
Eve's tempter thus the Rabbins have exprest,
A cherub's face, a reptile all the rest;
Beauty that shocks you, parts that none will trust;
Wit that can creep, and pride that licks the dust.

Pope responded to the beauties of nature as keenly, and to human passions as tenderly, as any Romantic poet, but chose to exercise his gifts on formal landscapes rather than on wild prospects, and on men in society rather than on those who lived in the solitary retreats far away from cities. He loved working in miniature but was equally capable of working on a gigantic scale. Few poets in our language would have been capable of writing either *The Rape of the Lock* or *The Dunciad*: it is difficult to think of any other poet, except Keats or Shakespeare, who could have written them both. It is the power to combine diverse excellencies that is Pope's unique contribution to our poetry. His tenderness was always controlled by his intelligence, his sense of pity by the courage and serenity that protected the Augustans from despair; his sense of beauty was directed by a perceptive irony, an unsleeping wit, that preserved his emotional sensitivity from degenerating into an embarrassing and deliquescent sentimentality; and, underlying the wit, the tenderness, the courage, and the sense of beauty, we can trace the workings of what Matthew Arnold called his quick and darting spirit, and recognize that in him, as in the great Romantic poets, there dwelled what De Quincey described as 'a preternatural animal sensibility diffused through all the animal passions (or appetites)'. This animal sensibility, whether it was concentrated on the delicate Sylphs or upon the noisome insects of the world, whether it was directed upon the follies of society or ranged unimpeded over a wider scene, unfailingly illuminates and vivifies all that it touches. Those who prefer beauty to be untinged with wit, and feeling to be unrestrained by sense, may fail to recognize the vitality with which Pope's verse habitually vibrates. Yet only the most prejudiced can fail to respond to Pope's description of the Grand Tour in Book IV of *The Dunciad*. These lines reveal, as Geoffrey Tillotson has reminded us, a sensibility as immediate and as voracious as that of Keats, a sensibility, moreover, that works in perfect harmony with a luminous intelligence to produce a miraculous piece of art in which the structure, the meaning, and the music are indissolubly wedded:

> To where the Seine, obsequious as she runs,
> Pours at great Bourbon's feet her silken sons;
> Or Tiber, now no longer Roman, rolls,
> Vain of Italian arts, Italian souls;
> To happy convents, bosom'd deep in vines,
> Where slumber abbots, purple as their wines:
> To isles of fragrance, lily-silver'd vales,
> Diffusing langour in the panting gales:
> To lands of singing, or of dancing slaves,
> Love-whisp'ring woods, and lute-resounding waves.
> But chief her shrine where naked Venus keeps,
> And Cupids ride the lion of the deeps;
> Where, eas'd of fleets, the Adriatic main
> Wafts the smooth eunuch and enamour'd swain.
> Led by my hand, he saunter'd Europe round,
> And gather'd every vice on Christian ground.

Had Pope been a less perfectly disciplined artist popular recognition of his genius might have been far more widespread and ungrudging. Ever since the Romantic Movement there has been a tendency on the part of the common reader to believe that the classical spirit is essentially cold and artificial. The correctness that his contemporaries so much admired in Pope has been a stumbling-block to readers of the nineteenth and twentieth centuries. The suspicion lingers on that Pope's correctness is a sign of deficient emotional vitality, a confession of imaginative poverty. Nothing could be farther from the truth. Pope was concerned with perfection of form in order that his passionate imagination might blaze out unimpeded by any flaws in his chosen medium. It was because he so highly valued the language of the heart that he wished to make its message unmistakably clear. Pope's skill and intelligence are such that even his worst detractors have never ventured to deny their power. Yet to admire him solely for these qualities is to misread the meaning of his life and of his work. Like all great poets, he should be read with love and with sympathy as well as with judgement. Those who learn to do so will come to recognize and to salute the fiery spirit and the tender heart that animated the broken body.

I have tried to show that the animal sensibility of which De Quincey spoke is something other than a mere acuteness of the five senses. The possession of such organic sensibility implies the ability to respond to atmosphere and the power to apprehend more deeply than most men the abundant richness of life. Most Englishmen who have given any thought to the matter would say that there is more philosophic wisdom in our poets than in our philosophers. They would maintain that Shakespeare and Keats have a keener perception of truth than, say, Bacon, Berkeley, Bentham, Mill, or Bradley, despite the fact that in their poetry it is difficult to find any precise formulation of philosophical dogmas. Linked with this conviction is the widespread dislike of didactic poetry, the feeling that the poetic faculty is being impeded and even distorted by the imperious demands of an alien theory. These two notions are, I believe, related to each other and to the whole question of animal sensibility.

When we judge that one poem is greater than another we are not usually concerned with the technical skill of the poet as displayed in the versification. A lyric by Campion is no less skilful than a poem such as 'To His Coy Mistress' or 'The Wreck of the Deutschland'. Nor do we judge a poem's greatness by the moral lesson that it attempts to inculcate. It is, for example, difficult to deduce from *Hamlet* or from *Othello* or from the 'Ode on Melancholy' either a moral code or a philosophical meaning, yet few people would deny that these works have a profound significance that touches us more deeply and acutely than any formal philosophical treatise. Such a feeling may be an illusion, but it is one that grows more convincing as time goes on and as our experience grows wider.

The truth seems to be that poetry enlarges and purifies the imaginative vision that lies dormant within us. It does not attempt to solve the riddles of the universe, but it demonstrates, more clearly than any other form of communication, that these riddles exist. We do not learn the meaning of life from *Hamlet* but we come away convinced that life is more abundant and meaningful than we have realized hitherto. The poet reveals something of the power and the vitality that streams through the universe and animates all creation. He awakens our sensual perception and cleanses the imagination that is clogged by the accumulated grit of mechanical routine. It is by virtue of his animal sensibility that the poet can respond to the richness of the world, proving axioms upon his pulses and incorporating into his verse the report of what he has experienced. A poem's imagery, rhythm, tone, texture, and shape all bear witness to the nature of the poet's experience. A poem can never be satisfactorily paraphrased, because the message that is thereby extracted is merely a report about the poem and not even an accurate report. The question: what is the poem's message? is radically misconceived, for the message does not exist except in the imagery, rhythm, tone, texture, and shape which the paraphrase deliberately ignores. The poem, then, has no plain message but it has a meaning that speaks to the reader who will try to understand it. 'By logic and reason we die hourly; by imagination we live.'[1]

Traherne, in his poems and in his *Centuries of Meditations*, celebrated the glory of the world so miraculously revealed to him:

The corn was orient and immortal wheat, which never should be reaped, nor was ever sown. I thought it had stood from everlasting to everlasting. The dust and stones of the street were as precious as gold: the gates were at first the end of the world. . . . And young men glittering and sparkling Angels, and maids strange seraphic pieces of life and beauty! Boys and girls tumbling in the street, and playing, were moving jewels.

You never enjoy the world aright, till the Sea itself floweth in your veins, till you are clothed with the heavens, and crowned with the stars: and perceive yourself to be the sole heir of the whole world . . . till your spirit filleth the whole world, and the stars are your jewels.

It would be sophistry to pretend that the animal existence of the average man is tinged with this cosmic grandeur, yet our wandering in the maze of sensual error is a sign of our common humanity no less than of our mortal frailty. Those who have most lyrically extolled the turbulent life of the flesh are among the most profound and convincing of moralists, as even the sternest teachers have recognized. Newman dwells upon the folly of limiting a young man's reading to what his instructors deem to be morally elevating:

[1] J. B. Yeats, op. cit., p. 231.

You have refused him the masters of human thought, who would in some sense have educated him because of their incidental corruption: you have shut up from him those whose thoughts strike home to our hearts, whose words are proverbs, whose names are indigenous to all the world, the standard of their mother tongue, and the pride and boast of their countrymen, Homer, Ariosto, Cervantes, Shakespeare, because the old Adam smelt rank in them.[1]

Hopkins noted that Tennyson never achieved 'that sort of ascendancy Goethe had or even Burns, scoundrel as the first was, not to say the second; but then they spoke out the real human rakishness of their hearts and everybody recognised the really beating, though rascal, vein'.[2]

A poet may, as he grows older, disavow his youthful allegiances and turn his back upon them, but he can never wholly cast aside his birthright of sensual endowment. Milton's exuberant delight in the world's richness and fulness, nurtured by his Mediterranean travels, burned in his veins long after the Puritan ethos had come to dominate his mind. Donne renounced his pagan sensualities for the service of God, but the ardour, the leaping paradoxes, and the emotional complexities of his profane verse could not but inform the divine poems of his later years, and Hopkins, who curbed the flesh for Christ's sake, displays a naked, agonizing sensuality in the stabbing images of his religious poetry.

It may seem paradoxical that a poet should attain imaginative wisdom by the exercise of his animal passions, especially to an age such as our own that combines a dreary materialism with the worship of windy abstractions like the State, thereby degrading both the life of the body and the truths of the spirit. The poet continually reminds us that man is created to enjoy the glorious abundance of the world and that acceptance of its complexity is the prelude to philosophic wisdom. By his active imagination, that feeds on his sensual perceptions, the poet affirms the beauty and the value of the world, and reminds us that the Negative Way is not the only way to spiritual discernment:

Henry More . . . says that those who would 'make their whole nature desolate of all animal figurations whatever' find only 'a waste, silent solitude, and one uniform parchedness and vacuity. And yet, while a man fancies

[1] *The Scope and Nature of University Education* (Everyman ed.), pp. 228–9.
[2] *Letters*, ii, p. 25.

himself thus wholly Divine, he is not aware how he is even then held down by his animal nature; and that it is nothing but the stillness and fixedness of melancholy that thus abuses him, instead of the true Divine principle.'[1]

In the light of this passage we may understand why it is that the stature of a poet, his intellectual, moral, and spiritual greatness, is so intimately bound up with the force and the quality of his animal sensibility. Unlike those philosophers who attempt to impose an ideal and supposedly higher mental world upon the visible world perceived by the senses, the poet, believing that good and evil, like joy and sorrow, are inextricably linked, accepts the tensions, the paradoxes, and the contradictions that make up the pattern of existence. The transience of beauty, the deceitfulness of the passions, and the broken imperfections of human life that drive the philosopher into the refuge of an unchangeable world of pure abstractions, are, for the poet, the fascinating themes upon which he can build his symphonic variations. His art would be immeasurably poorer were it not for the conflicting elements in human life and the intricacies of the human heart. He remembers also that the lilies of the field, doomed to the briefest of lives before being cast into the oven, are yet clothed in glory, and such knowledge strengthens his belief that the evanescence of the sensual world does not affect its value or its beauty.[2] Keats was expressing some such conviction when he spoke of 'Negative Capability, that is, when a man is capable of being in uncertainties, mysteries, doubts, without any irritable reaching after fact and reason'.[3] Blake's assertion that 'Everything that lives is holy' and his declaration that 'Eternity is in love with the productions of time' supplement Keats's intense feeling for the sensual qualities of created things and call our attention to the richness of the Affirmative Way. They remind us that Christianity has always valued the body, that, with its symbols of bread, wine, fire, and water, it has glorified the basic elements of earthly life and that it preaches a world redeemed by an Incarnation in history. Even the body,

---

[1] W. R. Inge, *Christian Mysticism*, p. 18 (footnote).

[2] Carlyle speaks of 'the Concrete in which lies always the Perennial', and Hardy says of Angel Clare: 'Some might risk the odd paradox that with more animalism he might have been the nobler man.'

[3] *Letters* (To G. and F. Keats, 21 Dec. 1817).

tortured and vilified as it may be in the course of a lifetime, 'is the temple of the Holy Ghost, not the prison-house of a soul which will one day escape out of its cage and fly away'.[1]

Shakespeare is perhaps the supreme example of a poet who accepts unhesitatingly the animal figurations of our nature. He never imposes a moral code upon his experience, but allows it to grow out of his passionate response to every facet of human life. His understanding is always grounded in his sensual perceptions and therefore is never distorted by the impatient desire of the logical mind to invent a neatly-rounded system. Shakespeare, being richer in fruitful sensuality than any other poet in the language, is able to convey to us more fully than anyone else the potentialities of man and the truth about the human situation.

In our own day, we have seen, in W. B. Yeats, how a maturing wisdom can accompany a deepening sensuality. The poet who declared that 'Hamlet and Lear are gay' had reached a point at which he could discern a spiritual meaning in the maze of error into which the body is driven. Indeed, so firmly was he wedded to sensual existence, that even the supernatural world was for him the gateway to a more heightened and intense sensual activity than is possible in the natural world. In one of his 'Supernatural Songs' he describes how 'a monk read his breviary at midnight on the tomb of long-dead lovers on the anniversary of their death, for on that night they are united above the tomb, their embrace being not partial but a conflagration of the entire body and so shedding the light he reads by'.[2] Yeats, like the Christian, believes in resurrection, but it is a resurrection, almost a resurgence, not of the body so much as of the senses:

> The miracle that gave them such a death
> Transfigured to pure substance what had once
> Been bone and sinew; when such bodies join
> There is no touching here, nor touching there,
> Nor straining joy, but whole is joined to whole;
> For the intercourse of angels is a light
> Where for its moment both seem lost, consumed.

Long before those lines were written, J. B. Yeats had said that 'the literature of the senses and the literature of despair go hand

[1] W. R. Inge, op. cit., p. 67.
[2] Letter to Mrs. Shakespear, 24 July 1934. Quoted by Jeffares, op. cit., p. 283.

in hand'.[1] W. B. Yeats is one of the few poets who always kept
the courage of his own sensuality, remembering the joy rather
than the folly and the deceitfulness of phenomenal experience:

> I am content to live it all again
> And yet again, if it be life to pitch
> Into the frog-spawn of a blind man's ditch,
> A blind man battering blind men;
> Or into that most fecund ditch of all,
> The folly that man does
> Or must suffer, if he woos
> A proud woman not kindred of his soul.
>
> I am content to follow to its source,
> Every event in action or in thought;
> Measure the lot; forgive myself the lot!
> When such as I cast out remorse
> So great a sweetness flows into the breast
> We must laugh and we must sing,
> We are blest by everything,
> Everything we look upon is blest.

In this chapter I have laid stress upon that animal sensibility
which I take to be the prime requisite and the distinguishing mark
of a poet. It is by virtue of his abundant sensuality that a poet's
total response to phenomenal experience acquires that power and
that intensity from which poetry is likely to spring. We cannot
hope to find any intellectual beliefs or moral convictions that are
common to all poets, because the essence of poetry lies elsewhere.
What we are likely to discover in all poets is the ability to explore
the life of the senses more passionately and more discriminatingly
than the majority of men, and to make clear to us, not the unchanging pattern that the philosopher abstracts from the flow of
events, but the imaginative reality that is implicit in the network
of sensuous relationships in which we are involved.

There remains one other quality common to all poets, at which
so far I have barely hinted—a passionate concern for form. In
subsequent chapters I hope to indicate how the poet's sensibility
is controlled by his shaping spirit of imagination, and how, by his
mastery of language, the conflicting emotions, ideas, memories,
and sense impressions that are the elements of poetry are finally
resolved and reconciled in the imaginative order of the completed poem.

[1] J. B. Yeats, op. cit., p. 85.

Chapter Three

EVERYONE who has tried to write poetry or who has investigated the ways in which poetry comes to be written knows that it is usually a slow, painful, and uncertain process. Even those poets who, like Virgil and Milton, have devoted themselves entirely to their art, have limited their output to so many lines a day and have been able to achieve their stipulated portion only because of their unremitting toil over a long period of years. We have seen that inspiration is, notoriously, so elusive and intermittent that nobody can rely upon being visited by it, or upon the length of time that it will remain when it has chanced to descend upon the lucky poet. Furthermore, we have seen that the writing of poetry is intimately connected with the sensual endowment of the poet, and that inspiration is most likely to visit those whose animal sensibilities are unusually powerful and acute. It is, therefore, not surprising that the composition of a poem should be so uncertain and tantalizing a process, dependent as it is upon such factors as the mysterious working of inspiration and the variable configurations of the animal sensibilities.

Having said this, we can proceed to ask ourselves whether there are any circumstances peculiarly favourable to the composition of a poem and, if so, whether they throw any light upon the way in which a poem grows. Nor should we be surprised to discover that apparently trivial causes may play their part in the making of a poem, for if, as I have maintained, the poet's senses are the source from which a poem springs, the whole development of a poem may well depend upon tiny and unpredictable disturbances of the poet's organic sensibility. We need not expect that all poets should respond to the same stimuli, because the physiology of each poet is unique and reacts in its own individual way to the promptings of sensual experience.[1]

Some poets find an aid to composition in the contemplation of

---

[1] Rosamond E. Harding's *An Anatomy of Inspiration* gives dozens of examples of aids to composition. I have not drawn on her researches without specifically indicating my borrowings.

nature. Those who have been brought up on Romantic poetry tend to think that all poets ought to find inspiration in the beauties of the countryside, and are inclined to dismiss as unhealthy or as morally suspect those who look elsewhere for the experiences that set in motion the poetic faculty. It is not surprising that natural objects and the ever-changing moods of the English land-scape should have profoundly stirred the Romantics and their forerunners. They were acutely conscious of man's relationship with Nature and more deeply aware than their predecessors of the ways in which human beings, physically and emotionally, are wedded to the universe around them, and of the links which bind man to the diurnal process that governs all living things. They were responsive to the underlying rhythm of existence and attempted to incorporate into their verse something of the harmony that they had discovered in the elements of nature. By philosophical conviction, as well as by temperament, they were attuned to the beneficent intimations of woods, mountains, and streams, finding in them not only the subject-matter but also the source of poetry.

James Thomson appears to have been sensitive to atmosphere and to the changing seasons of the year, for we are told that 'The autumn was his favourite season for poetical composition, and the deep silence of the night the time he commonly chose for such studies.'[1] Milton, Crabbe, and Burns showed a similar pre-ference for autumn,[2] and although Wordsworth does not seem to have had any favourite time of day or season of the year for the writing of poetry, he was commonly moved to verse by cer-tain sights and sounds that were an integral part of the country scene in which he passed his life. He tells us that clouds set his thoughts in motion and we know also that the rocking of leafy trees in a high wind and the noise of rain beating on the roof produced in him an agitation of spirit that was the prelude to the composition of poetry. The presence of running water aided him to write, for he states that he composed thousands of lines by the brook that runs through Easedale. Burns was similarly moved by the sound of running water when he took his lonely walks in

[1] Patrick Murdoch, *An Account of the Life and Writings of Mr. James Thomson*, 1762, cited by Grigson, *Before The Romantics*, No. 324.
[2] Cf. Harding, op. cit., p. 66.

search of the Muse, and by the sound of stormy wind in the trees. Keats had his poetic faculties aroused by wind billowing through the trees or across a field of barley.[1]

Hazlitt draws attention to the difference in Wordsworth's and Coleridge's methods of composition. Hazlitt's criticism anticipates our twentieth-century modes of thought by its recognition of the fact that seemingly trivial actions may be an indication of a man's character and that minor idiosyncrasies of behaviour may provide us with a clue to a man's innermost nature: 'Coleridge has told me that he himself liked to compose in walking over uneven ground, . . . whereas Wordsworth always wrote (if he could) walking up and down a straight gravel walk or in some spot where the continuity of his verse met with no collateral interruption.'[2]

Certain odours appear to stimulate the imagination of poets. It is well known that Schiller kept rotten apples in his desk as an aid to composition, but a remarkable passage from W. B. Yeats may be less familiar: 'I elaborated a symbolism of natural objects that I might give myself dreams during sleep, or rather visions, for they had none of the confusion of dreams, by laying upon my pillow certain flowers or leaves. Even to-day, after twenty years, the exaltations and the messages that came to me from bits of hawthorn or some other plant, seem of all moments of my life the happiest and the wisest.'[3]

It may be that we shall never know why he found a source of inspiration in these natural objects, or why the sound of wind released the creative faculties of three poets so diverse as Burns, Keats, and Wordsworth. We should need to know a great deal more than we do about the close and subtle relationship between body and mind and to explore more thoroughly the network of thoughts, desires, and nervous tensions that so tenuously and miraculously link us to one another and to the universe. We know that the output of factory workers is affected by the interior decoration of the places where they work. As far back as Old Testament days, the power of music to cure certain diseases was commonly recognized, and, in our time, the thera-

---

[1] Cf. J. C. Smith, op. cit., p. 7
[2] 'My First Acquaintance with Poets'.
[3] *Essays*, p. 609, cited by Jeffares, op. cit., p. 205.

peutic value of art is becoming increasingly obvious. The ability of certain drugs, foods, and odours to excite sexual desire has for centuries been a commonplace. Such facts make it probable that the mind and the senses influence each other more profoundly and intimately than we often realize. They suggest that the poet, by his sensuous apprehension of experience, gives us a glimpse of a mode of existence in which mind is not separated from body, because the one is impregnated with the other. They hint at an underlying physiology of poetry that is scarcely suspected by those who concentrate solely upon the thought of a poem, regarding its imagery and its music simply as decorations of the main design and argument. Whatever the truth may be, there can be no doubt that the poet is likely to be more than usually responsive to the mysterious influence that radiates from the organic world.

Some poets are stimulated by rhythmical movement rather than by looking at natural objects or by listening to certain sounds. We have seen that both Coleridge and Wordsworth were fond of walking about while they were in the throes of composition; Tennyson wrote 'Break, break, break' as he strode at night through the lanes near Somersby during the winter months that followed Hallam's death. Other poets find the rhythm of machines more potent than the rhythms of the organic world. The monotonous, hypnotic swaying and clattering of railway trains seem to have exerted their influence upon more than one poet, and to have induced in their whole beings a state in which the rhythmical periods of verse were able to formulate themselves.[1] Stephen Spender has recorded two occasions upon which lines of poetry suddenly came into his mind during a railway journey, once in Spain during the Civil War and once in the corridor of a train as it flashed through the Black Country. The lines that glided into his mind in Spain were incorporated into a poem which I propose to discuss in a later chapter; the single line that was granted to him in the Black Country—'A language of flesh and roses'—was never used by him, but remained an isolated fragment, the mere nucleus of a poem that was never written.[2] T. H. Huxley, after attending Tennyson's funeral, returned home by

[1] Victor Hugo called the knife-board of an omnibus his Pegasus: Harding, op. cit., p. 40.　　　　　　　　　　[2] *The Saturday Book*, Fifth Year, p. 65.

train, and, as he thought about the dead poet, the rocking of the train induced a kind of coma that gave rise to an elegiac poem.[1]

The rhythmic movement of a ship may well provide a stimulus akin to that of the rolling train, especially as the sea itself possesses the power to evoke a whole series of numinous emotions. Swinburne, Victor Hugo, Arnold, and Byron all felt the pull of the sea and responded to its pulsating tides, to the rhythmic flow of its massive energy. The intelligent errors of perceptive critics are sometimes more revealing than the accuracies of mediocre commentators, and there is a fruitful mistake in a speculation by a Marxist scholar that shows considerable insight on his part: 'G. Thomson in *Marxism and Poetry* thought that Keats wrote "Bright star . . ." in response to the hypnotic swaying of the ship which was to take Keats to Italy as it rode at anchor in Lulworth Cove. But the sonnet was written in 1819 and not, as Lord Houghton thought, in 1820 when it was copied by Keats into the blank leaf of his copy of Shakespeare's Poems.'[2] The phrase 'hypnotic swaying' is particularly worthy of attention, for it suggests the reason why rhythmic movement has the power of stirring the poetic impulse. One of the functions of rhythm in poetry is to lull asleep those obstinate mental habits in a reader which prevent him from accepting what the poem is trying to convey, and to awaken that imaginative sympathy without which a poem is bound to receive a stony reception from its readers. The poem can perform its work only when the minds of its readers are attuned to its mood. It is possible that a similar process takes place in the mind of the poet before the poem can begin to ripen. The fret and fever of the alert, questioning intellect need to be lulled and the clairvoyant faculty must, at the same time, be awakened. This double result may best be achieved by the poet's surrender to repetitive movement, whether it be the motion of the body as the poet walks along, the tranquil flowing of a stream, the deeper ground-swell of the sea, or the insistent rhythm of the railway train, particularly if these rhythms are experienced in surroundings that minister to the poet's senses.[3]

---

[1] Tillotson, *Criticism and the Nineteenth Century*, p. 228.

[2] Cited by F. W. Bateson, *English Poetry*, p. 11, footnote.

[3] It is reported of Goethe that, on one occasion, he tapped out the rhythms of a poem on the back of a woman to whom he was making love.

The power of music to evoke moods and memories is so well known as to need no demonstration. The highly-trained musician is able to enjoy a piece of music solely as a pattern of meaningful sounds into which no visual images or verbal associations are permitted to intrude. Those who have never been disciplined to such exhilarating austerity find it harder to preserve inviolate the integrity of music. Memories and images flow into their minds, called into existence by the sounds that have such power to influence those who listen to them, however imperfectly and inattentively. Programme music lends itself most readily to this kind of day-dreaming, but those whose literary imaginations are sufficiently active can always contrive to invent their own programmes. A poet may well find in music a stimulus to composition, by reason of its power to awaken in him a mood of heightened awareness. The musician who objects to the impurity of such a procedure forgets that the poet is driven by an imperative desire to make use of all his experiences and to turn them to good account. Like the bee in Swift's *Battle of the Books*, the poet is concerned less with the quality of the objects that he samples than with the substance that he is able to extract from them. He uses the music as a means of quickening his poetic faculties, of sharpening his perceptions, of inducing a mood in which a poem can begin to germinate.

Two beautiful poems about music may serve to illustrate the truth of this generalization—D. H. Lawrence's 'Piano' and Browning's 'A Toccata of Galuppi's'. Both have as their ostensible subject a piece of music. Lawrence makes no pretence of describing the sound of what he hears; it is enough that the music has borne him back through space and time to the days of his childhood:

Softly in the dusk, a woman is singing to me;
Taking me back down the vista of years, till I see
A child sitting under the piano in the boom of the tingling strings
And pressing the small poised feet of a mother who smiles as she sings....

Browning, despite his employment of technical terms, is less interested in the toccata than in its power to conjure up the picture of the past, to set his imagination roving over the lives of the dead who loved and intrigued in Venice long ago:

Here you come with your old music, and here's all the good it brings,
What, they lived once thus at Venice, where the merchants were the Kings,
Where St. Mark's is, where the Doges used to wed the sea with rings? ...

What? Those lesser thirds so plaintive, sixths diminished, sigh on sigh,
Told them something? Those suspensions, those solutions—'Must we die?'
Those commiserating sevenths—'Life might last! we can but try!'

A striking example of the way in which music may sink deep into the whole being of a poet to re-emerge, transfigured, in the rhythms of a poem, is provided by the experience of Swinburne in the eighteen-sixties, during his composition of *Atalanta*. A large portion of this poem was written in the library at Northcourt while Swinburne's cousin, Mary Gordon, played Handel on the organ. Swinburne himself was conscious of the part played by the music in moulding the shape of his first masterpiece:

> I care hardly more than I ever did for any minor music; but *that* is an enjoyment which wants special language to describe it, being so unlike all others. It crams and crowds me with old and new verses, half-remembered and half-made, which new ones will hardly come straight afterwards; but under their influence I have done some more of my *Atalanta* which will be among my great doings if it keeps up with its own last scenes throughout.[1]

Swinburne's imagination had been inflamed by books at a precociously early age, and it was appropriate that the earliest work of his full maturity should have been composed in a library. It is not easy to disentangle the various influences that went to the making of *Atalanta*, and to attribute the growth of its complex pattern to any one cause would be a crude over-simplification. The origins of *Atalanta* must be sought in the emotional disturbances that lay deeply embedded in the poet's buried emotional life. Handel's music, played in the congenial surroundings of Northcourt, evoked a response from Swinburne's whole being, releasing the conflicting elements that lay imprisoned there and helping to shape them into poetry.

The twentieth-century American poet, Hart Crane, found that his best poetry was written to the accompaniment of music. Believing that the guiding principle, or lack of principle, in the contemporary world was distraction, he habitually wrote in a room through whose open window drifted the noise of the traffic, and the strains of jazz proceeding from the radio or from the

---

[1] Cited by Humphrey Hare, *Swinburne*, p. 92.

victrola. The contrast between the nineteenth-century Englishman and the twentieth-century American is piquant, the one sitting in a great country-house listening to the mounting rhythms of Handel, the other half-attentive to the confused sounds of a metropolis, punctuated by the syncopated rhythms of a cosmopolitan musical idiom that seems to reflect the rootless uncertainty of our age. Yet, despite the differing backgrounds against which they worked, both poets were engaged in the common pursuit of turning the raw material of living into poetry and of calling for aid upon any stimulant that might help them to perform their task.

Some of the stimulants to which poets have recourse may seem strange and even undesirable to the world at large. Horace's dictum that no poems can please long, nor live, which are written by water-drinkers, although not to be taken too seriously, nevertheless reminds us that strong liquor has aided a great many poets to produce their poetry. We know that Aeschylus found refreshment in copious draughts of wine while writing his tragedies. Before working on *Catiline*, Ben Jonson, on his own admission, drank well and 'had brave notions'. Addison, according to a Holland House tradition, composed his verse while walking up and down a long gallery with a bottle of wine placed at each end. He continued to walk to and fro until he had finished the composition and the bottles.[1] Fielding refers to 'the opinion of Butler, who attributes inspiration to ale', but does not go on to discuss the matter. A. E. Housman, who found that a glass of beer helped him to compose a poem, suggested that the effect of beer was to deaden the brain and to release the poetry that lay buried deep in the nervous system. It may be that there is a close analogy between the action of hypnotic rhythm and the effect of alcohol upon the organism of the poet. Both deaden the repressive intellect and, at the same time, liberate those modes of apprehension favourable to the growth of a poem that normally lie quiescent in the shadow of the dominating conscious mind. We may, in fact, use the words 'stimulant' and 'stimulus' too loosely and inaccurately, for we often fail to remember that the stimulation of one part of our nature may involve the suppression or the retardation of another. It is, for example, generally agreed that

[1] Cf. F. L. Lucas, *Literature and Psychology*, pp. 170-1.

indulgence in alcohol does not directly excite sexual desire. Its effect is rather to obliterate those feelings of modesty or of anxiety that usually keep the sexual impulses within the limits decreed by the conventions of any given society. In the same way, in talking about stimulants to poetic composition, we should try to distinguish between the faculties that are damped down by so-called stimulants and those that are truly heightened and quickened.

The effects of drug-taking upon poetry may be variously estimated. While it is true that Coleridge, Crabbe, and Francis Thompson were drug-addicts, it is by no means clear that their best poetry originated in the stupor induced by drugs, although it is undeniable that their sense perceptions must have been profoundly affected by the habit to which they had succumbed. Even a comparatively minor form of drug-taking, such as an excessive indulgence in nicotine, may, indirectly, leave its mark upon the character of a poet's work, although he may not deliberately have recourse to it in order to aid him in his composition. It has, for example, been conjectured that Tennyson's heavy smoking may have stimulated his visual imagination to an almost morbid degree of sensitivity. It is probable also that, in his younger days, his port-drinking may have deepened the hypochondriac's melancholy which was part of his genetical heritage.

Reflection upon the trivial external circumstances that help a poet to compose may induce in us a consciousness of our inability to explain the process by which a poem grows. We cannot tell why Keats courted inspiration by dressing up in the traditional poetic robes and laurel crown, as if in anticipation of Yeats's theory that the poet must don a mask in order to discover the truth within himself. Nor can we be certain of the significance that lies behind W. H. Auden's habit of drawing the curtains to blot out the daylight, in order that he may work by the light of a green-shaded lamp. He has said that his visual imagination is poor; it may be that the world illuminated by the sun is, for him, a distraction rather than a source of poetry. Unlike Shakespeare, who permits the pattern of experience to emerge after he has immersed himself in the sensuous world, Auden prefers to abstract his patterns from experience and to meditate upon their inter-relationships. It is typical of his genius that he recurs to the view of the landscape as seen by the hawk or by the airman, creatures who, soaring above the flux of the world, glimpse men and things as moving patterns, whose minute idiosyncrasies, visible in the sunlight to a student of feature and of texture, are ironed out by the immense distance between earth and sky. Perhaps Auden resembles the character described by James Joyce who, 'being as weak of sight as he was shy of mind, . . . drew less pleasure from the reflection of the glowing sensible world through the prism of a language many coloured and richly storied than from the contemplation of an inner world of individual emotions. . . .'[1]

Whatever we may think of Auden's preference for artificial light, we should beware of styling it unnatural or decadent. Most of us have a Wordsworthian tinge in our make-up, which is an excellent thing in so far as our feeling for the natural world is thereby strengthened and enlarged, but which may so colour our judgement that we fail to appreciate the validity of other poetic experiences and modes of expression. The prime concern of a poet is to write a poem, and to accomplish his design he will adopt the methods which he knows to be efficacious. If we must use the word 'natural' in this context, we can only say that the natural stimulus to the writing of a poem is the one that each individual poet finds most potent. As Robert Graves once remarked, the word of command is irrelevant so long as the mountain moves. Addison's wine, Housman's beer, and Byron's hock, soda-water, and dry biscuits were no more and no less natural as stimuli to poetic composition than the brook which flowed through Easedale or the opium which directed the course of Alph, the sacred river.

Stephen Spender, in the article to which I have already referred,[2] tells us that, when writing poetry, Walter de la Mare smokes incessantly, W. H. Auden drinks endless cups of tea, and he himself relies upon smoking and upon coffee. Such aids, he suggests, are not stimuli, but means by which a concentration that has already been attained is preserved. He then offers an alternative hypothesis that the effort of writing poetry so disturbs the normal balance of mind and body that one needs an anchor of sensation for the physical world. May we go a stage farther

---

[1] *Portrait of the Artist as a Young Man.*   [2] 'Poet'.

and say that this particular disturbance is not simply the effect of writing poetry, but rather the cause, and that an abnormal bodily and mental condition may be the necessary prelude to poetry?

This theory, in its extreme form, maintains that the poet, like all men of genius, is the product of genetical abnormality, or even of biological degeneration. We are reminded that many artists have been tubercular, and are asked to believe that their genius is a by-product of, or a compensation for, the ravages of the disease. Over-indulgence in drink, drugs, and venery frequently aggravates the artist's temperamental and physiological deficiencies. Finally, after tracing the artist's heredity, bodily make-up, dissipated behaviour, and physical disintegration, our remorseless investigator pursues his victim beyond the tomb and solemnly declares that he tends to be sterile or to produce children of mediocre ability. Such eugenic speculations are too vague and inexact to form the basis of any fruitful theory about the arts in general, still less about poetry in particular. A list of names as miscellaneous as Byron, Pope, Shelley, Keats, Poe, Hood, Milton, Francis Thompson, Swinburne, Stevenson, Matthew Arnold, Beddoes, and Swift, coupled with the portentous assertion that these poets were either tubercular, alcoholic, lascivious, or sterile, tells us nothing about *The Triumph of Life*, *Don Juan*, or *The Rape of the Lock*. Biological materialism, however valid it may be in its own field, has no claim to be regarded as scientific when applied to poetry. The genes of the biologist are, in this sphere, as irrelevant as the atoms of Democritus and Newton's particles of light.

More convincing, because less extreme, are the suggestions advanced by psycho-analysts that poetry springs from a neurotic and divided temperament. The poet, in their view, is neither a Bard nor a Revolutionary but a man sharply differentiated from the majority of people who make up the society into which he happens to be born. Blake posed the problem in its simplest form when he asked

O why was I born with a different face?

and his question remains strictly relevant whether or not we think that we know the answer. It may be that the poet is born with certain hereditary predispositions of mind and of body that lead him to think and to behave in a way that the majority of his fellow men stigmatize as abnormal. Or it may be that his nature is determined by some deep psychological shock, the origins of which may remain for ever obscure, even to himself. Many psycho-analysts would maintain that a shock of this nature is likely to have been sustained in childhood and that it is almost certain to have been sexual in character. It is probable, for example, that Baudelaire's love for his mother and hysterical dislike of his stepfather provide the key to his whole subsequent emotional development. The evidence in his case is sufficient for us to formulate a plausible theory, but often, it must be confessed, we have no direct evidence about the nature of the wound that leaves its permanent mark upon its victim. We are forced back upon conjecture and, in an age that assigns to sex the pre-eminence formerly accorded to religion, we shall interpret the facts that we know in terms most congenial to our prejudices.

Whatever the true explanation may be, the fact remains that a great many poets have been noted for an eccentricity of behaviour and a deviation from the normal pattern of thought and feeling that seem to spring from the very depths of their nature. Poe, Beddoes, De Nerval, Rimbaud, and Swinburne, to name only the most striking examples, were, at the best, maladjusted and, at the worst, fundamentally and incurably neurotic. The Philistine conviction that the poet is an unhealthy creature, barely to be tolerated, and the counter-assertion that the poet, in his isolation, is persecuted by an insane and corrupt society, both bear witness to the extent to which this theory has gained currency. The belief that some men are the saints of art despite the notorious grubbiness of their lives; the feeling that Hamlet is the perfect type of the poet; that suffering, degradation, and worldly failure are the lot of the true poet—all testify to the prevalence of the doctrine that poetry springs from the deep wounding of the psyche.

This concept of the poet as a man who has inherited certain abnormal proclivities or who has suffered a psychological shock can be remarkably fruitful, especially if we also accept Freud's theory that we embrace pain for some vital purpose, transforming it that we may the better endure further pain. It helps us to see what Yeats meant when he asserted that 'Hamlet and Lear are gay' and to understand the meaning of Rilke's exhortation: 'Love your loneliness and endure the pain it causes you with harmonious lamentation.'[1] It enables us to perceive why Baudelaire was impelled to transmute his tormenting desires and his consciousness of evil into the harmonious splendour of his verse, and confirms our intuitive conviction that Swinburne was not simply an eccentric Old Etonian, nor Tennyson a purveyor of Victorian commonplaces. Indeed, Tennyson was the one English poet of his time who might have followed the way trodden by Baudelaire and by Rimbaud, for he alone was endowed with that morbid sensibility and that sense of the terror underlying all existence which drove the French poets over the border. As he grew older and more prosperous, the sensibility was used to describe, in exquisitely modulated phrases, the landscape of the English countryside. The terror was stifled, or lulled asleep, by the calm routine of a happy marriage. Baudelaire's Paris is an evil, pulsating organism, but Tennyson's London is the jovial city of clubs and eating-houses reminiscent of Dickens at his happiest. It is hard to say whether Tennyson deliberately turned away from the spectacle of evil and laid the ghosts of terror that had haunted his childhood, or whether he outgrew the pain of his early days and forgot the daimons. Had he cultivated his agony he might have been an even greater poet, but he might have destroyed himself in the process.

Illuminating as this theory is, it does not appear to be of universal validity. It helps us to understand much that might otherwise remain obscure in the work of poets such as Poe, Baudelaire, De Nerval, Beddoes, Tennyson, Swinburne, and Rossetti. It suggests fruitful speculation about the emotional development of Pope, Gray, Byron, and Matthew Arnold, although the evidence may be too scanty for us to pronounce a verdict with any confidence. The loneliness, the unhappiness, and the strangeness of so many poets fall into place and are seen as part of the morphology of poetry. The danger is that we may be tempted to regard the sickness of the poet and the corruption of society as the normal conditions in which the art of poetry best flourishes. The poet may come to be proud of his maladjustment, secretly admiring and cultivating his morbidity, persuading the critic to

[1] *Letters To A Young Poet.*

regard poetry as an interesting record of neurosis, and to reject, as crude and obvious, the body of verse that is instinct with animal vitality and robust affirmation of the beauty and happiness of created things. We have only to think of Ben Jonson, Herrick, and Barnes to realize that gaiety and serenity are as much a part of poetry as anguish and despair. Or, if we require further proof of this contention, we can turn to the pages of Marvell whose verse combines so many of those diverse qualities that we have come to regard as characteristic of English poetry, a warm enjoyment of life's pleasures, a vigour that seldom degenerates into brutality, a sense both of the sadness and of the dignity of human life, a love of the English landscape, and a passionate awareness of the joy of being a man. In Dryden also, we find masculinity, sanity, and intellectual force informing poem after poem, the life of reason exalted by a poet who bears witness to the exhilarating powers of the radiant human animal. Even the famous and magnificent lines that begin

> When I consider life, 'tis all a cheat;
> Yet, fooled with hope, men favour the deceit;

are so exuberant in tone that their movement contradicts their message. Nor can we fit Chaucer into any theory that lays stress upon the wounded psyche, and few of us would value a theory that completely fails to account for *The Canterbury Tales*.

It is, indeed, a weakness of this whole conception of poetry that it lays too heavy a stress upon the formative power of discord, isolation, and anguish. It is true that, at one particular stage of cultural development in Western Europe, the psychological disorder of certain poets was transmuted into poetry that enriched our heritage by extending our understanding of the strange, dark places of the human spirit. It is, nevertheless, a mistake to believe that poetry invariably is or ought to be a compensation for the neurotic disabilities of the poet. There are grounds for believing that great poetry springs from joy and from vigour, that both its origin and its end are delight. Professor Livingston Lowes has maintained that Coleridge was aroused to write his finest verse less by the influence of opium than by the deep sense of joy that flooded his being as a result of his friendship with the Wordsworths, from whom he learned to value the glories of creation, the power and the beauty revealed in every aspect of the life that we are privileged to enjoy.

Lionel Trilling has shown that the particular mental illness which we call neurosis cannot be the mainspring of poetry.[1] This is not to deny that some poets, like some scientists and men of action, have been neurotic, and it is true that suffering may help a poet to attain insights beyond the range of the normal, healthy man. Yet neurosis implies mediocrity and failure and, at its worst, the tragic disintegration of the schizophrene. The distinguishing mark of the artist is his power to make something durable and perfect, so that, in a sense, he is the exact antithesis of the neurotic, who is, at best, a half-artist. The artist, who has the power to make his neurosis valuable and objective, by this act transforms his neurosis so completely that we can scarcely recognize it. A poem is never the direct product of neurosis, though it may be the record of a poet's conquest of neurosis, especially in epochs when sickness and malaise seem to infect the common air. We must beware of thinking that the maladies incidental to our day have always been prevalent, or that all poetry takes its origin from the struggle with neurosis. As Trilling reminds us, the early legends of Apollo and of Hercules clearly point to other sources of poetry, to the sense of power and of joy that is diametrically opposed to the anxiety which assails less fortunate ages. Philoctetes may be able to wield his bow only because he suffers from a nauseating wound: Apollo, the god of poetry, is radiant and undisfigured.

Even if we do not believe the theory that poetry springs from a diseased body or mind, we may readily accept the fact that certain poets find it easier to write poetry when in poor health. It is arguable that ill health may weaken those restraints that keep the poetic faculty under control, and strengthen those perceptions that nourish the imagination, and this will appear the less strange if we recall the double effect of certain aids to poetic composition, such as rhythmical movement and drugs, whereby one part of the mind is lulled and another part stimulated. The genesis of the hymn 'Just as I am' is worth considering for the light that it throws upon the mental disturbances which may be induced by sickness. The hymn was written over a hundred

[1] 'Art and Neurosis', reprinted in *The Liberal Imagination*.

years ago by Charlotte Elliott, sister of the Rev. H. V. Elliott:
'All the members of the household were busily engaged with a
bazaar. . . . His sister, Charlotte, who was weak and ill, was at
home alone, much troubled by thoughts of her own uselessness;
then came to her a sudden feeling of peace and contentment, and
she wrote without any apparent effort these verses.'[1]

A pious anecdote of this nature may not be particularly convincing, and I quote it partly because it anticipates, in simple,
almost naïve language, one of the most interesting speculations
of T. S. Eliot:

> I know, for instance, that some forms of ill-health, debility or anaemia,
> may (if other circumstances are propitious) produce an efflux of poetry....
> To me it seems that at these moments, which are characterised by the
> sudden lifting of the burden of anxiety and fear which presses upon our
> daily life so steadily that we are unaware of it, what happens is something
> *negative*: that is to say, not 'inspiration' as we commonly think of it, but
> the breaking down of strong habitual barriers—which tend to re-form very
> quickly.[2]

We know that *The Waste Land* was written in Switzerland
during convalescence after a breakdown and that A. E. Housman
seldom wrote poetry unless he was rather out of health. Plato's
Timaeus held that no man attains to poetic divination except
when asleep or ill, and Charles Baudelaire called the artist a
'perpetual convalescent'. It is true that T. S. Eliot has warned us
against believing that his personal experience is of universal
validity, reminding us that it is doubtful whether a poet of
Dante's stature had to depend on such capricious releases of
poetic energy, but there are grounds for believing that the comparative passivity and quiescence which are induced by illness
may be states of mind favourable to poetic composition.

Blake has left it on record that he was often commanded by his
Spirits to write against his will, and it is clear that a poet must
often surrender to a power outside himself, renouncing all
impatience and striving. Virgil's description of the Sybil and
Charlotte Brontë's preface to *Wuthering Heights* bear witness to
the truth that the artist has to be possessed and mastered by the
creative spirit before he can utter what he desires to say. Robert
Graves believes that Keats regarded the act of poetic creation as

[1] Cited by Thomas Driberg, 'A Purge of Old Favourites', in *The Cornhill*, No. 984.
p. 493 (footnote).   [2] *The Use of Poetry*, p. 144.

the rape of the poet by the Muse, and suggests that Byron's obscenely contemptuous references to him may have had their origin in a masculine distaste for this apparent perversity.[1] Many poets have said that lines of poetry suddenly flow into their minds uninvited and unsought for, when they are completely relaxed; some have warned us that the over-eager wish to write a poem may effectually hamper its composition or produce a poem whose design is flawed by its having been churned out in obedience to the tyrannical will.[2]

We must, however, beware of thinking that a poet need do nothing but wait for the poem to write itself, or that illness will inevitably produce an efflux of poetry. Coleridge remarked that, before a poem could be written, there must be an interaction of the active and the passive powers of the mind; the mathematician Poincaré's account of how latent ideas combined in his unconscious mind, like hooked atoms, reads like a vindication of Coleridge's insight into a profound truth about the creative spirit of man. The poet must learn how to wait and also how to forage, how to yield and also how to possess. He must be able to spring from the deepest passivity into the most furious activity, and he must be fully equipped to take advantage of whatever gift fortune may bring him. Wordsworth was right when he counselled trust in and submission to the beauteous forms of things:

> Come forth and bring with you a heart
> That watches and receives

but wrong in his belief that science and art were inimical to the imagination. For, ultimately, the poet must dominate his medium, even if, for the sake of final conquest, he makes a feigned withdrawal, relaxing the pressure and consenting to a temporary surrender. He learns to take advantage of any help that he can secure from outside agencies, or from any physical abnormality which may aid him in his task. He uses what happens to him in order to further his own ends, his very passivity serving only as the gateway to an increased activity, his patient waiting a time of renewal, his illness the prelude to a more radiant health.

[1] *The Common Asphodel*, pp. 245–7.
[2] Cf. A. E. Housman, *The Name and Nature of Poetry*, pp. 46–50; W. B. Yeats, *Autobiographies*, p. 337; Norman Nicolson, 'The Image in my Poetry', in *Orpheus*, ii, p. 121.

It is obvious that Keats was profoundly influenced by the morbid symptoms of tuberculosis and it may be true, as William Empson asserted in a notorious passage, that 'his desire for death and his mother has become a byword among the learned'.[1] We need not seek to deny those elements in his poetry which come from his toying with the thought of death as a luxuriant, sensual experience, but to explain Keats's poetry in clinical terms, or as a direct result of his desire for death and his mother is to abandon criticism for fantasy. Any just estimate of Keats must take into account the aberrations of his sensibility and the sexual disequilibrium that may have been responsible for the irritation which Byron felt when confronted with his work. The task of criticism is to show to what extent these peculiarities weaken his verse and to what degree they are transmuted into poetry by the poet's ever-maturing power of selection and mastery of his emotional impulses.

The poet makes use not only of his illnesses but also of all those other stimuli which we have been considering in this chapter. They may aid him to compose, but it is misleading to think of him as a dreamy automaton dependent upon chance stimuli, or as a system of reflexes conditioned by external trivialities, like Pavlov's dog. Charles Lamb's description of the poet has not been invalidated by the discoveries of the past hundred and fifty years: 'The ground of the mistake is that men, finding in the raptures of the higher poetry a condition of exaltation to which they have no parallel in their own experience, besides the spurious resemblance of it in dreams and fevers, impute a state of dreaminess to the poet. But the true poet dreams being awake. He is not possessed by his subject but has dominion over it.'[2] 'The true poet dreams being awake'—in this phrase Lamb expressed a central truth about poetry and one that needs to be constantly reemphasized, especially in periods when men are unduly fascinated by the night-side of the soul. For the poet desires to attain that special kind of wakefulness, the sober certainty of waking bliss, as Milton called it, in which he may best command his poetic talent and summon into the light the poem that lies hidden in the darkness.

---

[1] *Seven Types of Ambiguity* (2nd ed.), p. 20.
[2] 'On The Sanity of True Genius'. Cited by Trilling, op. cit., p. 174.

Chapter Four

I HAVE suggested in previous chapters that inspiration is a reality; that a great many poets are endowed with an unusually powerful animal sensibility; and that certain stimulants or stimuli have the power of inducing in a poet a mood which is peculiarly favourable to the composition of poetry. Granted that these favourable conditions are present, we have to ask ourselves in what shape the poem will come to the poet. Will he be visited by an idea, or experience an emotion, or will the poem take its origin from a state of being in which neither ideas nor emotions are predominant? I do not believe that there is any one single answer to this question. However confidently we may use phrases such as 'the poetic mind' or 'the act of poetic creation', we must remember that the mode of composition varies from poet to poet and that the impressive-sounding phrases beloved of the critic who fancies himself as a metaphysician are nothing more than convenient shorthand formulæ. We might even go so far as to say that there is no such thing as poetry, and no such thing as the poetic mind: there are only poems and poets. Nevertheless, if we can show that a number of poets have had a similar range of experiences when composing a poem, we shall have acquired some valuable evidence about the nature of poems and of the process by which they come into being.

A great deal of nonsense has been talked about the magical sound of poetry, as though poetry were nothing but a meaningless rhythmical incantation vainly attempting to rival the achievements that lie within the compass of music. Yet such theories, however wild and unbalanced they may be, remind us of the close and subtle relationship that exists between music and poetry. We are, in fact, perfectly justified in speaking of the music of poetry, provided that we respect the identity of the two arts and do not pretend that the one subsumes the other. We shall, therefore, be prepared to find that a great many poems appear to originate in a musical or in a verbal phrase; that there are analogies between musical and poetic form; that a poet is remarkably sensitive to sound and to rhythm; and that this sensitivity may help to endow a poet with a sympathy and an insight that enable him to perform his peculiar task.

The famous aphorism that all art aspires to the condition of music is a bold attempt to solve the problem of the relationship between music and poetry, a problem that began to tease the minds of poets and of critics early in the nineteenth century. Shelley drew attention to the existence of such a relationship, without endeavouring to explain its nature: 'Sounds as well as thoughts have relation between each other and towards that which they represent, and a perception of the order of their relations has always been found connected with a perception of the order of the relations of thought.'[1]

It has become fashionable in recent years to minimize the bizarre, romantic elements in Baudelaire's poetry, and to insist upon the classical perfection, order, and discipline that give strength and durability to his verse. Whatever may be the truth about his poetry, his literary criticism reveals a profound dissatisfaction with the classical doctrines that had dominated French poetry for the previous two hundred years. From time to time, those who practise the art of poetry, like those who practise the art of war, appear to have reached an impasse. Part of the fascination exercised by the two arts lies in the challenge that both present to human ingenuity. Faced by the apparent impasse, soldiers and poets of genius invent new strategies or new tactics in their attempt to find a way of escape, so that once again the field may be open for the manœuvring, for the exercise of skill, that alone can preserve the vigour and the suppleness of the artistic tradition. Baudelaire realized, with the perception of genius, that the new musical forms and, in particular, the music of Wagner, could touch the human heart more deeply and more strangely than the mass of French classical poetry. He saw also that a more profound understanding of music might enable poets to develop the instrumental resources of language, and thereby to evoke a total response from the very depths of the soul. He believed that the closeness of the links between poetry and music had not hitherto been adequately recognized: 'La poésie touche à la musique par une prosodie dont les racines plongent plus

[1] *A Defence of Poetry.*

avant dans l'âme humaine que ne l'indique aucune théorie classique.'

In the later nineteenth century the unsystematic reflections of Baudelaire became the starting-point of a complex, recondite theory of poetry whose adherents were struggling to break away from the legacy of Romanticism and to combat the tenets of the Parnassian school. The story of Mallarmé, of Verlaine, and of the Symbolists, although properly belonging to French poetry, cannot be ignored by any reader of English poetry, for the past fifty years have witnessed the attempts of our most gifted poets to incorporate the heritage of Symbolism into the structure of their verse, to express the concepts of a European aesthetic revolution in the native accents of English poetic language. John Sparrow has described Mallarmé's intentions in the following words: 'Mallarmé . . . declared that his aim was to recover "un art d'achever la transposition, au Livre, de la Symphonie" and it was perhaps the same relation between the arts that Dryden had in mind when he said that music was "inarticulate poesy".'[1]

Such an aim was far removed from the conventional practice and theory of both Classicism and Romanticism. Hostile critics might deride the vagueness of Symbolist doctrine and quote the scornful lines of Pope to support their attack on the new theories:

> In the bright Muse, though thousand charms conspire,
> Her voice is all these tuneful fools admire,
> Who haunt Parnassus but to please their ear,
> Not mend their minds; as some to Church repair,
> Not for the doctrine, but the music there.

Nevertheless, the ideas and the emotional attitudes of the Symbolists began to percolate through the hard crust of literary orthodoxy, until the poetry of France, England, Germany, and Italy grew more fluid and subtle, less oratorical and hortatory, more akin to a musical composition in its modulations, shifts of emphasis, rhythmical patterns, and harmonic progressions. It is tempting to speculate on the effects produced upon English poetry by the simultaneous decline in the study of the Classics and the revival of the native musical tradition that had so long been lying dormant. Did both these movements lend an impetus

[1] *Sense and Poetry*, pp. 27–28.

to the attack upon rhetoric and to the exploration of the musical element in the arts that had begun in France some years before it started to leave its mark upon English poetry?

It is probably true that the theory of Symbolism, in so far as it laid stress upon the music of poetry, was less original than it appeared to be at the time. Whitman not only loved Italian opera but openly proclaimed the debt that he owed to the art of music: 'But for opera I could never have written *Leaves of Grass*.'[1] He did not mean simply that his powers of sympathy and of emotional apprehension had been aroused by the dozens of operas that he had attended in his youth, although no doubt they did awaken his sensuous faculties. He was referring to a more precise debt that he owed Italian opera, a debt that is visible in the structure of his poems, for, in the words of an anonymous critic, 'his poetry is designed to forms taken from operatic construction'.

Whitman was the only great poet of his time to be so profoundly influenced by music, although Browning's knowledge and love of music were probably greater than Whitman's.[2] Tennyson's inexhaustible search for metrical variety drove him to experiment with language, in an effort to achieve new and startling effects. He seems to have disliked music but to have realized, with characteristic shrewdness, that a skilled metrist could profitably study musical rhythms and reproduce in his verse some of the most striking discoveries that he chanced to make. The lyric 'Come into the garden, Maud', is based upon the rhythms of a mid-Victorian waltz, a device that is effective both lyrically and dramatically. More remarkable was his imitation of Hawaiian rhythms in 'Kapiolani' written at the beginning of the eighteen-nineties. Twenty-five years before, in 1865, Queen Emma of the Sandwich Islands had visited Tennyson at Farringford, accompanied by a small entourage, among whom were a Mr. and Mrs. Hoapili. They used to sit on the drawing-room floor, their hair wreathed with briony berries, chanting Hawaiian songs.[3] It has been remarked, unkindly, that all Tennyson's exotic

---

[1] Review of Robert D. Famer's *Walt Whitman and Opera* in *T.L.S.*, 29 Feb. 1952.

[2] Hopkins also was passionately devoted to music, and it is worthy of remark that he spoke of Whitman's mind as being 'more like my own than any other man's living'. *Letters*, i, p. 155.

[3] Charles Tennyson, *Alfred Tennyson*, pp. 358, 523.

landscapes are faintly reminiscent of the Isle of Wight and that his perception of the hot, vibrating quality of life in the tropics is sadly deficient. It is a trifle pathetic, yet endearing, to think that Tennyson's closest contact with one of these distant, romantic islands which nourished his imagination should have been limited to a visit from a dusky queen, and significant that the rhythms of Hawaii which once echoed in an English drawing-room should have remained for so many years in the mind of an English poet.

In the twentieth century, the relationship between music and poetry has become a little subtler. The influence of music upon the verse of the Sitwells has been considerable, yet it is not easy to lay one's finger upon any particular passages from their poetry and demonstrate the precise links between them and the piece of music which has inspired them. Dame Edith Sitwell has told us that 'Façade' may be regarded as the poetic equivalent of Lizst's Transcendental Exercises. This remark indicates one of the ways in which music may help to mould the verse of a poet who attempts to enlarge the range of his chosen medium by a study of a sister art. The example set by musicians may teach the poet to look upon language as an unrivalled instrument, enormously powerful and varied, but highly intricate, elaborate, and difficult to master. He may realize that, in order to obtain the finest orchestral effects from language, he must learn to command its full range of tone, its characteristic rhythms, and its harmonic capabilities.

Secondly, a particular composer may come to mean so much to a poet that the qualities which are found in the composer's music may be discernible in the poet's writings. Dame Edith Sitwell, quoting a line of her 'Dark Song' which forms one of the poems in 'Façade',

The brown bear rambles in his chain

adds a note that explains the origin of the line: 'This line and the two following lines came into my mind through hearing a song of Stravinsky's. I do not know its name and I only heard it once; but it contained lines rather like these.'

Sir Osbert Sitwell's autobiography gives ample proof of the admiration for Stravinsky's work that has always been felt by himself, his brother, and his sister. Is it fanciful to detect in the poetry of Dame Edith a technical brilliance, an elegance, a tenderness beneath the most highly-polished surface, and an ability to assimilate past styles into her own mode of expression, which are all present in the work of a composer with whom she has so many temperamental affinities? There is no question of her attempting to portray in verse the verbal equivalent of Stravinsky's music, or to write a tone-poem in reverse. The nearest parallel is with Whitman's debt to Italian opera. Even if it is not true to say that, without Stravinsky, her early poems could not have been written, they would, none the less, have been very different had the poet never known the rhythms of that strange, original, exotic music which seemed to capture the spirit of the early twentieth century and to become part of the very life of those who responded to its proclamation of new values, its revelation of new experiences.

A comparison has sometimes been drawn between the posthumous quartets of Beethoven and the last group of poems written by W. B. Yeats. It has seemed to some critics that, in both the music and the poetry, there are certain qualities which make it possible to recognize a kinship between the mind of the German musician and of the Irish poet, an intensity, an urgency, a clairvoyant perception which has freed itself from the obscuring film of conventional mediocrity that normally blurs our vision. It is true that there is in Yeats an absence of the utter tranquillity, the song of heavenly thanksgiving, that pervades the quartets; it is true also that Yeats himself never turned to Beethoven as a source of illumination. Nevertheless, the analogy between these two achievements of the human spirit is as close as any such analogy can be and it confirms the belief that, deep in the heart, like submerged islands beneath the sea, the territories of music and of poetry melt insensibly into each other.

It is curious to note that T. S. Eliot has hinted at a possible analogy between his aims and the final achievement of Beethoven. In an unpublished lecture delivered in New Haven, Connecticut, during the winter of 1933, he says that he has attempted 'to get *beyond poetry*, as Beethoven, in his later works, strove to get *beyond music*'.[1] An attentive reader of T. S. Eliot's prose can often gather hints about the type of poetry that he is intending

---

[1] Cited by F. O. Matthiessen, *The Achievement of T. S. Eliot*, 2nd ed., p. 90.

to write in the future, and he may also learn what Eliot thinks he has accomplished in the past. From time to time, in his critical writings, he talks about the relationship of music to poetry, the problem of sound, the meaning of such a phrase as 'the music of poetry'. We may, therefore, expect to find in his verse some trace of the preoccupation with music that has been displayed in his prose.

In his lecture on 'The Music of Poetry', given in 1942, Eliot reveals something of what he has learned from the practice of poetry, besides outlining a theory of poetic form which helps to explain the genesis of *Four Quartets*:

> ... The use of recurrent themes is as natural to poetry as to music. There are possibilities for verse which bear some analogy to the development of a theme by different groups of instruments; there are possibilities of transitions in a poem comparable to the different movements of a symphony or a quartet; there are possibilities of contrapuntal arrangement of subject-matter.

Such an idea was not unprecedented. We have already seen that Baudelaire and Mallarmé had long before hinted at the possibility of a poem which should produce an effect akin to that of a symphony. Sir Herbert Read had envisaged a poem on the analogy of the quartet in music and, early in the nineteenth century, Schiller had expressed a similar notion: 'The perception with me is at first without a clear and definite object; this forms itself later. A certain musical mood of mine precedes, and only after this does the poetical idea follow with me.'[1] Nor is it true that T. S. Eliot's later work is a repudiation of his earlier poetry and that he paid no attention to the musical quality of verse in his younger days. Like all great poets, he has constantly struggled to combine the colloquial ease of speech with the musical perfection of language, the *Four Quartets* being a consummation of his poetic career, rather than a departure from it. If one turns to *The Waste Land* with the same receptiveness that one brings to the poetry of a man long dead, one's overwhelming impression is of the complete mastery displayed by the poet in his use of language. There are passages in it as lyrical, as melting, and as exquisite as anything in *Lycidas*. The poem is a symphonic invocation of

[1] Cited by C. Day Lewis, *The Poetic Image*, p. 71.

London, past and present, of a stricken Europe, of the human situation. Music creeps by upon the waters, different kinds of music: the song of the Rhine-maidens, who are also the Thames-daughters; the song of Tristan; the water-dripping song of the hermit-thrush; the music that is heard in the pulsating life of London day by day, where the dead sound of a church clock mingles with the pleasant whining of a mandoline. It is, in fact, the sort of poem that might be written by a poet who was a master of technique and who had immersed himself in Wagnerian opera while the poem was germinating in his mind.

To deny that T. S. Eliot was the first poet to recognize certain analogies between music and poetry and to perceive that a poem might bear a formal resemblance to a symphony or to a quartet is not to belittle his achievement. No poet is ever entirely original or utterly alone, because dead poets are always there to help him, and no poetic problem is new, if only because the old ones, never having been solved, perpetually recur. Great artists seldom invent fresh modes of expression; their habit is to seize upon the ingenious notions of lesser men, to develop them in ways undreamed of by the originators of the idea, to change a freakish, erratic theory into a practical technique that enables other discoveries to be made. Eliot has not only written a masterpiece but has made it possible for his successors to produce long poems that will not appear to be uneasy imitations of nineteenth-century achievements. We cannot foresee how long it will take for this particular poetic form to grow oppressive and sterile, but its flexibility and subtlety are such that it may prove as fruitful and as stimulating as the sonata form has been to European musicians for the past two centuries.

It would be untrue to say that all poets have recognized the links between music and poetry, nor have all poets loved music, however inexpertly and uncritically. It might be thought that poets who, like Victor Hugo and Dr. Johnson, detest music will write verse more distinguished for its imagery or for its structural firmness than for its cadences, but the facts do not support such a neat theory. Few poets of the past hundred years have written verse more obviously musical than that of Swinburne, Tennyson, and Yeats, but all three of them were tone-deaf. Nor is a knowledge of prosody an essential part of a poet's technique.

W. B. Yeats was never able to recall the rules of prosody, and T. S. Eliot has admitted his incapacity to remember the elaborate regulations and codifications which eminent prosodists have sought in vain to impose upon the turbulent life of poetry. Prosody is, doubtless, an interesting study and, like all intellectual disciplines, is not to be despised, but an expert prosodist is no more fitted to write or to understand poetry than a distinguished phonetician. I am not denying the necessity of technical skill in any of the arts: the ballet dancer must be thoroughly versed in the basic steps of the dance; the musician cannot ignore the laws of harmony and of counterpoint; the painter must have at least a rudimentary acquaintance with the science of optics and with the properties of colour. Unfortunately, a thorough grounding in prosody and in phonetics in no way equips a poet to understand even the technique of his art. Such a bald statement needs, perhaps, to be explained and amplified, for if a poet may be indifferent to both music and prosody, whence can he derive his ability to write musical poetry and how can he acquire the technical skill that is the basis of every art?

The answer is that a feeling for the phrasing of words, for rhythm, and for cadence is the most vital technical gift of any poet. Although the prosodist may be able to classify the various metrical devices which have been successfully exploited in the past, he is unable to offer the poet any guidance in the matter of phrasing, without which the most ingenious handling of a metrical pattern degenerates into a barren, mechanical exercise. The phonetician, however accurately he may distinguish the sounds of different words, is not qualified to explain the means whereby sound, sense, and association of ideas miraculously combine to form a poem. A poet is a man whose feeling for language, and, in particular, for the rhythmical flow of speech, is more highly developed than is usual among his fellow men. It is probable that such a feeling is innate, or that it shows itself at an early age, although it can certainly be strengthened until it ceases to be a mere feeling and becomes a skill which enables a poet to employ words with delicacy, precision, and power. This skill is best acquired by constant study of the poetry written by other poets from the days of Chaucer onwards, rather than by perusal of treatises on prosody, for the history of poetry is, in part, the chronicle of the poet's struggle to record in permanent form the inflexions of the living speech of his day, and, as such, can both encourage and rebuke the contemporary poet. However mistaken Wordsworth may have been in his theory of poetic diction, he recognized the central truth that a poet is a man speaking to men. In all the finest poetry of the past we can discern, through the obscuring mists of obsolete grammar, outdated ideas, unfamiliar vocabulary, and outmoded allusions, the image of a man speaking to us in the authentic tones of a passionate, suffering human being.

Succeeding generations of English poets, glorying in the ever-varying burgeoning of our tongue, the shifts of meaning, the bewildering enrichment of the vocabulary, have relied on their native wits rather than on the codification of metrists, or on the stuffy restrictiveness of purists. All the finest English poets have been great readers of poetry; many have delighted in the lilt and tang of vigorous speech, in the raciness of local dialect, which has remained uncorrupted by the stale phrases of a newspaper-sodden urban proletariat: very few have had their enthusiasm kindled by a handbook on prosody. The only rules which merit attention are those which cannot be defied with impunity by a good poet.

Even those poets who have given time and thought to metrical analysis are not remembered chiefly for their technical innovations. Bridges and Campion hold an honoured place in English poetry through their ability to make music out of a living language and not because they attempted to resuscitate classical metres. The poetry of Barnes presents a trickier problem, for, despite his apparent naïvety, he was a deliberate craftsman who sought to introduce into English poetry elaborate stanzaic forms and metres which had been employed by the classical Persian poets. Even the use of the rustic Dorset speech was a premeditated device which he adopted after writing youthful poems in the standard English of his day, for Barnes, like Burns, was no ill-read peasant who chanced to sing like a nightingale, but a man who had read a great deal of poetry and whose simplicity is the last reward of highly deliberate art. Yet it remains true that Barnes's metrical virtuosity is almost as unimportant as his comical attempts to obliterate the vocabulary of ordinary, everyday speech and to replace it by an uncouth, barbarous lingo, designedly based upon an obsolete language which had ceased to flourish soon after the Norman Conquest. His claim to distinction is that he introduced into English poetry certain harmonies and cadences which were wholly original, and which remain inimitable because they vibrate with the individual tone of voice of a man who, at a particular moment in a particular place, had learned to assimilate the music of the language spoken daily around him and to make it the basis of a delicate poetry.

Hopkins may be regarded as an exception to the general rule that a mastery of the spoken language, rather than a profound knowledge of prosody, is the distinguishing mark of a poet. It is true that Hopkins made an exhaustive study of both prosody and diction; how exhaustive it was may be seen from a glance at W. H. Gardner's two learned volumes on the poet. Not content with investigating the properties of Logaoedic Rhythm, Sprung Rhythm, Running Rhythm, Rising and Falling Rhythm, Rocking Feet, and Outriders, Hopkins ceaselessly endeavoured to incorporate into English verse some of the more complicated patterns of metre and of rhyme that he had encountered in the obscure thickets of Greek, Hebrew, and Welsh poetry. Like Barnes, he found the vocabulary of the ordinary English poet woefully inadequate and impoverished, and viewed with disfavour the triumph of the Greco-Roman language over the pure Anglo-Saxon tongue. A study of Aeschylus suggested that compound epithets might lend to English verse a weight and a vividness which it so badly needed if it were not to die of pernicious anaemia. Old words might be used in new senses, or, if existing words were insufficient, the best solution might be to imitate the practice of Shakespeare, and to supplement the deficiencies of the current vocabulary by minting fresh words to meet the ever-increasing demands of the poet who finds the old coins worn thin and greasy from constant handling.

Yet even if we choose to judge Hopkins as an innovator in technique and as an influence upon poets of the past twenty-five years,[1] rather than as a great poet in his own right, we must still try to discover why he found it necessary to abandon the normal patterns of versification and the generally accepted diction that

[1] The influence of Hopkins on English poets in the years 1918–30 was negligible.

satisfied his contemporaries. Hopkins has given us the answer in a letter that he wrote about 'The Eurydice', a poem that seemed to its contemporary readers a wilful and perverse departure from orthodox prosody: 'When . . . I opened and read some lines, reading, as one commonly reads whether prose or verse, with the eyes, so to say, only, it struck me aghast with a kind of raw nakedness and unmitigated violence I was unprepared for: but take breath and read it with the ears, as I always wish to be read, and my verse becomes all right.'[1] If we bear this sentence in mind, we shall begin to grasp what Hopkins was trying to achieve and why he felt obliged to do such apparent violence to the English language and to the generally accepted principles of versification. Like Donne, he desired to say a great many harsh, passionate, agonized things and he discovered that the poetic conventions of his day did not permit him to say them. The structure of nineteenth-century prosody was too infirm to bear the onslaught of scalding words that clamoured to be uttered:

How to keép—is there ány any, is there none such, nowhere known some,
     bow or brooch or braid, or brace, láce, latch or catch or key to keep
Back beauty, keep it, beauty, beauty, beauty. . . .

Hopkins, commenting on these lines, remarked: '*Back* is not pretty, but it gives the feeling of physical constraint which I want.'[2] Always there is the same insistence on the importance of basing poetical language upon living speech. Poetical language, he wrote, 'should be current language heightened, to any degree heightened and unlike itself, but not an obsolete one'.[3] Herein lies the justification of all his innovations, the invention of new, farfetched words, the attempt to employ a kind of musical notation as an aid to scansion, the heavy alliterations, the merciless breaking-up of the smooth pattern of contemporary versification, the breathless, clogged, contorted movement of the verse. If, at times, we seem to be hearing the almost incoherent cries of a man who is being tortured on the rack, we must remember that it was spiritual agony which spurred Hopkins to write poetry and that a poet's tongue must try to convey as exactly as possible the ebb and flow of his mind:

---

[1] *Letters*, i, p. 79.   [2] Ibid. i, p. 162.
[3] Ibid., i, p. 89.

... birds build—but not I build; no but strain,
Time's eunuch, and not breed one work that wakes.
Mine, O thou lord of life, send my roots rain.

I am, therefore, in complete accord with F. R. Leavis when he writes of Hopkins: 'Paradoxical as it may sound to say so, his strength was that he brought poetry much closer to living speech.'[1] This, indeed, is his enduring legacy to those poets of the twentieth century who can be trusted to eschew his mannerisms and to grasp his revelation of the truths that a poet must be able to assimilate into his verse the full range and depth of the language of his day, and that the music of poetry must exclude no words in common use, however dissonant or unpoetical they may sound to the reader with a fixed idea of what a poetic vocabulary should be. He has taught us also that poetic rhythm must be flexible enough for the expression of concepts and states of feeling too subtle, recondite, passionate, and bewildering to be contained within the framework of regular syllabic versification. His eccentricities of rhyme, his theories about scansion, his attempts to impose the metrical schemes of other literatures upon the rhythmical flow of English poetry are, at worst, disfiguring tricks of style and, at best, mere by-products of his great achievement as a poet. In reading the finest poetry, we are conscious that we are listening to a man speaking to us in the tones and accents of perfect sincerity and, at the same time, we are aware that the musical potentialities of the language at that particular moment of its historical development are being realized to the full. At his most superb, in 'The Wreck of the Deutschland', 'Felix Randal', and the last sonnets, Hopkins conveys to us the double impression of terrible candour and of musical intensity that can be derived from none but a great poet. His verse is yet one more confirmation of the truth that a poet's stature depends above all upon his mastery of the poet's tongue.

Most people know the story of Mallarmé's reply to Degas, who was complaining about the difficulty he had experienced in writing a sonnet, although his head was full of ideas: 'But sonnets are made with words, not with ideas.' It is less generally realized that Mallarmé's remark would have been regarded as a common-

---

[1] *New Bearings in English Poetry* (1950), p. 160.

place three centuries before in Persian literary circles: '... the Art of discourse, whether in verse or prose, lies only in words, not in ideas ... ideas are common to all, and are at the disposal of every understanding to employ as it will, needing no art'.[1] The dangers inherent in such an attitude are too obvious to need stressing. Hopkins summed them up when he wrote that 'words only are only words', but he realized that one could not dismiss the whole question by an epigram. A passage from his notebooks gives us his considered views: 'Some matter and meaning is essential to poetry, but only as an element necessary to support and employ the shape which is contemplated for its own sake.'[2] This sentence throws some light upon another passage in Hopkins that helps us to understand the whole purport of his work: 'But as air, melody, is what strikes me most of all in music, and design in painting, so design, pattern, or what I am in the habit of calling "inscape" is what I above all aim at in poetry. Now it is the virtue of design, pattern or inscape to be distinctive.'[3]

Just as sculptors are fascinated by the very feel of the raw material from which they shape their work, so most poets delight in the sound and shape of words, in exploring the sensuous pos-sibilities of their chosen medium. Hamlet is usually considered to be, of all Shakespeare's characters, the one most akin to his creator, the man who is, potentially, a poet even though we are not specifically told that he has written a line of verse. It is inter-esting to note that one of Hamlet's most striking characteristics is his tendency to play with words. From his first appearance in the play until the final scene, he is continually scrutinizing every word uttered by others or by himself, intent upon extracting an equivocal meaning from the most harmless or conventional phrase. He can take nothing at its face value, but must investigate the meaning beneath the meaning, discovering the various shades of implication that lurk in an apparently harmless remark. His very first sentence is a pun; he contrives to convert the mono-syllabic replies of Ophelia into an obscene dialogue; and, finally, he forces the poisoned wine down the throat of his murderer with a grim, contemptuous play upon the word 'union'. Hamlet's play upon words has indeed little in it that is joyful or frivolous;

[1] Ibn Khaldun, cited by Grigson, *The Harp of Aeolus*, p. 114.
[2] *Note-Books*, p. 249.   [3] *Letters*, i, p. 66.

it is, rather, the brilliant, terrifying sport of a man who is intent upon finding in language the same ever-widening treachery that he has discovered in life. The other characters in the play hear nothing but wild and whirling words, failing to recognize the unifying obsession that controls even the most outrageous bursts of invective and the most riddling of utterances. One of the most curious contradictions in the play is that, although we feel Hamlet to be an essentially noble character, almost every single one of his actions is bad. His behaviour shows him to be morbid, irresolute, cruel, rash, crafty, pitiless, and revengeful, a man who inflicts pain upon those who love him most, and who involves friend and foe alike in destruction. It may be that Shakespeare is trying to demonstrate how the noblest qualities will, when corrupted by a tincture of rottenness, breed a hideous type of evil. If this is true of Hamlet's actions it is true also of his words. He is obviously fascinated by the latent ambiguity of language, and is more than usually responsive to the sensuous and to the intellectual reverberations of meaning that emanate from the spoken word, but the malady that infects his spirit prevents him from realizing his potentialities as a poet. For whereas the poet plays with words in a spirit of joy and of love, using his special, individual gift to communicate with his fellows, Hamlet twists new, dark significances out of words in order to lay bare the ulcerous sore beneath the smooth, white surface and to emphasize his own isolation in a world of corruption. What, in the poet, is a shaping spirit of imagination, becomes, in Hamlet, a demoniacal energy that moulds and distorts human speech into queer and disturbing patterns.

If words are of such prime importance to a poet, and if the shape and the sound of words have for the poet a significance almost as great as that provided by their overt meaning, we shall not be surprised to find that a great many poets have displayed a marked sensitivity to the spoken word at an early age. Burns has left two accounts of the process by which the seeds of poetry were implanted in him. In the first account, he describes a bewitching creature, a fellow harvester, whom he met in his fifteenth autumn: 'Among her love-inspiring qualities she sung sweetly, and it was her favourite reel to which I attempted giving an embodied vehicle in rhyme. Thus with me began love and poetry.'[1] There is no reason to doubt the accuracy of the poet's recollection, nor need we dispute the fact that the words and the music of the song, coupled with the attractiveness of the singer, impelled the adolescent boy to express his confused feelings in verse, but we may suspect that the true origin of the poetic impulse has its roots in some experience other than the troubled stirrings of the adolescent heart. Burns himself has indicated the nature of this formative experience: 'In my infant and boyish days too, I owed much to an old woman who resided in the family. She had, I suppose, the largest collection in the country of tales and songs concerning devils, ghosts, fairies, brownies, witches, warlocks and other trumpery. This cultivated the latent seeds of poetry.'[2]

Robert Louis Stevenson would listen, enraptured, to his nurse as she recited, by the hour, the fierce psalms and prayers of Scottish Calvinism, whose rhythms fell with compelling force upon the impressionable mind of the child, and left their trace upon him long after he had forgotten the words themselves. Wilfred Owen is another poet who, when young, listened to the pattern of sound underlying the overt meaning of the words and needed to hear this pattern before his satisfaction was complete. Sir Osbert Sitwell has rightly drawn our attention to a remark made by Mrs. Owen, the poet's mother: 'As a little child his greatest pleasure was for me to read to him, even after he could read himself.'[3] W. B. Yeats spent his early years in Ireland eagerly listening to the racy talk of peasants whose language had not been flattened out by the compulsory study of standard English. Throughout his life, Yeats never forgot the turns of phrase that he had heard in childhood, just as he never forgot the values rooted in a way of life to which English industrialism, protestantism, and democracy appeared in the guise of alien, ignoble intruders. His mature poems are remarkable both for the individuality of their diction and for their distinctively bold rhythms which, at times, recall the rhythms of ballads and of nursery songs. It is probable that these twin characteristics derive from the same source—childhood memories.[4] We have seen that Yeats

---

[1] *Letters*, cited in *Burns* (edited by Meikle and Beattie, Penguin Poets series), p. vi.
[2] Ibid., p. v.   [3] *Noble Essences*, p. 93.
[4] John Clare also became familiar with poetry at an early age. He learned scores of

loved the company of countrymen whose vocabulary was rich and full of sap; he enjoyed also the fierce rhythms of heroic songs. Early in life, he would spend hours in a stable-loft while a stable-boy read Orange ballads to him, and, later on, his father used to read aloud the long poems of Macaulay and of Scott. W. H. Auden's suggestion that a poet is a person who enjoys playing with words needs to be supplemented by the corollary that a poet is a man who is, by nature, peculiarly responsive to the cadences of words, and who is moved by certain phrases even before he is fully aware of their meaning.

I have already indicated that this sensitivity to the lilt of words may display itself at a comparatively early age. Sir Harold Nicolson has shown how Tennyson's finest poetry springs directly from his childhood days when he listened in terror to the sounds that came to him across the fens, and how the repetition of certain phrases appeared to satisfy some emotional longings of his inmost nature: 'As a small child he would rush about shouting Tennysonian formulae such as "far, far away", and "I hear a whisper in the wind". . . . From very early years he was puzzled by the problem of personality, and would sit upon the damp moss of Holywell Glen saying, "Alfred, Alfred", to himself, and again "Alfred", until every thing became poignant, mystical and hazy.'[1]

A similar kind of self-hypnosis was practised by W. B. Yeats when he was a child. As a little boy, with no knowledge of Latin or of Greek, he loved to repeat the phrase 'Magna est veritas et praevalebit' and, in the summer of 1879, he went around for days saying over and over again the phrase which he had heard from a village boy, 'I saw thee and the little brothers and the maids at church'. This habit of repeating isolated words or sentences remained with him all through his life. For long periods he would be obsessed by a single recurring phrase which haunted him, as if to demand that it be included in a poem. He frequently composed his poems aloud, the very sound of one line releasing other lines which had, until then, remained imprisoned in the dark places of his mind.

A third example may be quoted of the power of a single line

ballads and traditional songs from his father and from an illiterate old woman called Granny Bains. [1] *Tennyson*, p. 46.

or phrase to influence profoundly a mind that is responsive to poetry. When Sir Edmund Gosse was eleven years old, his father repeated from memory the first of Virgil's bucolic poems, and Gosse, like Yeats, discovered that a sonorous Latin phrase, barely understood, might linger on persistently in the memory: 'As I hung over the tidal pools at the edge of the sea, all my inner being used to ring out with the sound of *formosam resonare doces Amaryllida silvas.*'[1]

In the light of these facts we can begin to understand that the genesis of a poem may be a single word, a group of words, a phrase, or even a particular rhythm in which no individual words are clearly distinguishable. Such an idea is, indeed, quite incomprehensible if we think that a poem is the translation of a thought or of an emotion into words, but there is a great deal of evidence which suggests that this process of translation does not always take place and that a poem may unfold like a flower from the bud of a solitary word.

Wordsworth, in describing the origin of 'The Idiot Boy', makes it clear that the whole poem grew from a phrase rather than from an idea: 'The last stanza "The Cocks did crow to-whoo, to-whoo, And the sun did shine so cold"—was the foundation of the whole.' 'The Charge of the Light Brigade' originated when Tennyson heard the chance remark 'Someone had blundered', and 'The Hunting of the Snark' pieced itself together at odd moments in the course of a year or two after a single line had come into Lewis Carroll's head as he was walking alone on a hill-side on a bright summer day: 'For the Snark *was* a Boojum, you see.'[2] Housman has told us how, on occasions, a line or two, or even a stanza, of verse would flow into his mind, as a prelude to the writing of a poem.[3] Paul Valéry remarked that the inspiration for 'Le Cimetière Marin' came to him in the form of a rhythm and that the whole poem was an exercise in constructing a particular stanzaic pattern. We have it on the authority of the poet himself that Cecil Day Lewis's fine sonnet which begins:

Children look down upon the morning gray

sprang out of one line that was given to him in an instant:

[1] *Father and Son.*   [2] Cf. Rosamond Harding, op. cit., p. 59.
[3] *The Name and Nature of Poetry,* p. 49.

The flags, the roundabout, the gala day.[1]

Everything else in the poem flowered unerringly from that single phrase, with true poetic logic, supporting, developing, illuminating it and, at the same time, deriving from it strength, cogency, and luminosity. Those poets who rely upon a word or a phrase upon which to build their poems are faced with certain dangers that do not menace a poet who is granted an idea or an image as the starting-point of his composition. The chief of these dangers is that the associative and the emotive value of words may be so heavily overstressed that words and meaning become divorced. In extreme cases the rational content of words may be thrown overboard and we are left with nothing but 'trans-sense', a mode of expression favoured by the Russian poets Anton Lotov and Alexander Kruchenykh.[2] Aldous Huxley's young poet in *Crome Yellow* resembled Stephen Spender in his reliance upon the appearance of a key line in an active, male, germinal form,[3] but the results were not invariably happy. He was given, by some mysterious agency, the phrase 'Passion carminative as wine', and, immediately, there flooded into his mind the traditional characteristics associated with love and wine, powerfully reinforced by the hint of scarlet conveyed by the word carminative, so clearly derived from the adjective carmine. It was not until he had looked up the meaning of carminative that he decided to proceed no further with the poem.

A second and allied danger is that a poet may be tempted to discover a meaning, where none exists, in the sound-values of words. The belief that certain vowels are invariably charged with an emotional significance, that certain consonants or groups of consonants have a particular connotation and that phonetic values determine meaning cannot be maintained, despite the ingenious pleas of those who cling to the theory that poetry is a species of magical incantation.[4]

Nevertheless, there is a relationship between sound and sense which poets have recognized and utilized to enrich their verse.

[1] *Poetry For You*, pp. 35–39.

[2] C. M. Bowra, *The Creative Experiment*, pp. 11–15.

[3] Cf. *Poet*, pp. 64–65, where Stephen Spender describes how he is visited by inspiration.

[4] Cf. Bateson, op. cit., pp. 19–30, and Robert Graves, *The Common Asphodel*, p. 73.

The principal uses of rhyme are to recall the sound and the meaning of preceding lines, to help the poet and the reader in the delicate task of exploring the associative connotations of words, and to contribute to the total harmony of the whole poem by emphasizing its musical unity. Secondary merits of rhyme are the pleasure which it gives to the reader by its repetition of the sounds that have been heard before, and the discipline which it imposes upon the poet by restricting his choice of words and by forcing him to work within the limits of a pattern. Alliteration, internal rhymes, assonance, repetition of words, and word-play are other devices which may be used to replace or to supplement the more common employment of end-rhymes. Hopkins is a great master of all these devices, although he occasionally staggers from one word to another simply because of an accidental similarity of sound between them, thereby divorcing sound from sense and diminishing the force of these twin elements that give a poem its strength and beauty. At his finest, he commands a tremendous orchestral range which both compels the attention of the reader and drives home the total meaning of the words:

> Flesh fade, and mortal trash
> Fall to the residuary worm; | world's wildfire, leave but ash:
> In a flash, at a trumpet crash,
> I am all at once what Christ is, | since he was what I am, and
> This Jack, joke, poor potsherd, | patch, matchwood, immortal diamond,
> Is immortal diamond.

The ending of 'Felix Randal' is perhaps an even better example of Hopkins's power to convey the full implication of his meaning by his deployment of the full musical resources of the language:

> This seeing the sick endears them to us, us too it endears,
> My tongue had taught thee comfort, touch had quenched thy tears,
> Thy tears that touched my heart, child, Felix, poor Felix Randal;
>
> How far from then forethought of, all thy more boisterous years,
> When thou at the random grim forge, powerful amidst peers,
> Didst fettle for the great grey drayhorse his bright and battering sandal.

Only by reading aloud the whole poem can we fully appreciate the tremendous impact of the final line. The first thirteen lines of the sonnet have at least one break apiece, a break dictated by punctuation, by sense, or by physical necessity. Daniel Webb, in 1762, noticed that in Hamlet's line

> And in this harsh world draw thy breath in pain

'the breast actually labours to get through this line'.[1] In Hopkins's sonnet, the sense of physical suffering, frightened bewilderment, and bodily dissolution is made almost palpable by the broken, crowded, irregular movement of the verse. Finally, in order to emphasize the magnificence of the body and the glory of animal existence in their unflawed prime, Hopkins extricates the last line from the toils of the struggling rhythms in which the opening thirteen lines have been caught, and sets it free to reach a climax of mounting splendour.

Some of the implications of relying upon words as the starting-point of a poem have been discussed by an anonymous critic in an article on *Europa and the Bull* by W. R. Rodgers:

> As M. Picasso is said to have endeavoured to transfer his emotions directly to the canvas, so the new romantic transfers his emotions to the page by an alchemy of spitting or singing words. He creates in the reader a heady emotional effect by the subtlety of his connotations and the dexterity of his ambiguities. . . . Mr. W. S. Graham, when pressed for an 'explanation' of his poems, is reported to have said: 'I build my poems with words as a house is built with bricks'.[2]

This critic goes on to describe the effect produced upon the reader by the highly individual way in which W. R. Rodgers handles the English language. He notes the fondness of the poet for 'wry or bedevilled word-play', for 'impish punning', but he does not fully appreciate that Rodgers employs the pun less in the manner of Hood than in the style of Hamlet. For Rodgers, like Hamlet, uses the pun to bring out the contradictions, the paradoxes, and the odd inter-relationships that underlie our apparently rational life, but whereas Hamlet discovered beneath the surface nothing but darkness, W. R. Rodgers stands amazed, though never speechless, at the bewildering light and beauty of it all.

The writer of the article has placed his finger upon one quality that distinguishes the poems collected in *Europa and the Bull*—

---

[1] Cited by F. W. Bateson, op. cit., p. 32.   [2] *T.L.S.*, 29 Aug. 1952.

the sense of joy implicit in every phrase: 'The poem wears the suspicion of a smile. It is all fire and fun. Pebbly words splash in the pool of the imagination, the phrases gather a harvest of echoes.' The title-poem glows with an incandescent Mediterranean light and with a sense of joy and richness that lives in the words of the poem as the sap dwells within the tree. In this poem, all the traditional devices of poetry are used to enrich the texture of the verse. It is a mark of the poet's skill that the heavy alliteration and the dazzling metaphors, tropes, and word-plays in which the poem abounds are felt to be integral parts of the verse. There are times when the poet's verbal ingenuity leads him into danger, but he is saved from the trap of empty word-spinning by the vivid sensuousness that we have already noted as the hallmark of the poet. The word-play that glitters, like the most brilliant metaphysical conceit, in the following lines is, perhaps, too far-fetched for an austere taste, but, to my mind, the puns are so deeply rooted in sensuous reality that they ride triumphantly on the wave of the verse, and pulsate with a Baroque energy:

> On all sides
> The tall cliffs rose like sighs; and far below,
> Grotesticled and still, like long-ago-ness,
> The cold sea wrinkled languidly and
> Wrangled roundly in its orchid coils.
> Still through all these eel-and-alley-ways of water
> The wakeful bull wove on to where the lost wave
> Wept and slept away to land.

Two further examples may suffice to give some idea of the way in which the words of the poem clash against one another to produce the flame that leaps from the verse. The first is taken from the climax of the poem and conveys, in its piling-up of extravagant metaphor, the overwhelming nature of the experience described:

> Here on the sill
> Of silence and assent
> She waited wordless, though her body spoke.
> As trundling thunders pause
> And pitch their lightning tents upon the hush,
> Or as the darkling bird
> Crowds all its longings into one last rush, so

Her backward breasts like trumped-up charges rose
And brazened out his coming.[1]

The second comes from the closing lines of the poem:

O, as grass amasses grass,
May sleep after sleep, loved over by leaves,
Engross those two, house them and hush them
In arms of amaranth,
And may the nodding moth of myth
In every mouth take breath and wing now,
And dance these words out in honour of that wedding.

Every poetic method is fraught with its own particular danger, and a severe critic might bring against W. R. Rodgers the accusation that was levelled at Hopkins a generation ago: 'His worst trick is that of passing from one word to another, like the Jewish admirer of Mr. Jaggers in *Great Expectations*, merely because they are alike in sound. This at its worst produces the effect almost of idiocy, of speech without sense and prolonged merely by echoes. . . .'[2] Rodgers handles language with such assurance that he seems able to bridge gaps which normally yawn between words and to discover logical or emotional links which have not hitherto been suspected. His poems are carried along irresistibly by the momentum which gathers its force from the dance of the words, and the dance is governed by the counterpointed music that Rodgers extracts from the ever-moving pattern of sound and meaning.

Poets of earlier times have recognized the truth that the sounds of words, by their powers of suggestion, may aid the process of composition. They have also paid tribute to the disciplinary function of rhyme, although they have not always realized that alliteration and similar devices may be just as efficacious. Dryden, writing in 1664, after listing two or three minor virtues of rhyme, declares: 'But that benefit which I consider most in it, because I have not seldom found it, is, that it bounds and circumscribes the fancy. For imagination in a poet is a faculty so wild and lawless, that like an high-ranging spaniel, it

---

[1] Cf. Tennyson's remarkable image of a waterfall:
A thousand wreaths of dangling water smoke
That like a broken purpose waste in air.

[2] *T.L.S.*, 9 Jan. 1919.

must have clogs tied to it, lest it outrun the judgment.' Rhyme, in Dryden's opinion, is 'that which most regulates the fancy, and gives the judgment its busiest employment'. He is, however, insistent that the poet must confine 'his sense to his couplet, and must contrive that sense into such words, that the rhyme shall naturally follow them, not they the rhyme'.[1]

Such a proviso may sound eminently sensible, but the logic of poetry is something other than prosaic reasonableness, and a great many poets have refused to be bound by the dictates of Dryden's massive common sense. A poet must learn to trust words, to respond to their promptings, and to commit himself to the element wherein he displays his mastery. More than one poet has discovered that the configurations of his verse have been largely determined by the imperious demands of rhyme. Shelley's reliance upon the suggestive power of rhyme appears, on occasion, to have been excessive: 'In *Epipsychidion*, for example, the original draft has many lines that are completely blank except for the rhymes.'[2] It seems as if Shelley allowed himself to be led by the reverberations that arose from the rhymes, and that his remarkable grasp of the relationship between sound and thought enabled him to respond unerringly to the most tenuous intimations of the words.

Cecil Day Lewis reminds us of Paul Valéry's admission that the need for a certain rhyme altered the whole course of one of his poems, and quotes an admirable passage from Coventry Patmore's essay on William Barnes. Patmore speaks about 'the *curiosa felicitas* . . . which means the "careful luck" of him who tries many words, and has the wit to know when memory, or the necessity of metre or rhyme, has supplied him unexpectedly with those which are perhaps even better than he knew how to desire'.[3]

More sweeping and rhetorical than this moderately-phrased and sensible description of the way in which the poet learns to co-operate with his chosen medium is Poincaré's oracular pronouncement that 'the accident of a rhyme can call forth a system. I would add, sometimes a planetary system.'[4] Perhaps the most

---

[1] Epistle Dedicatory of *The Rival Ladies*.
[2] F. W. Bateson, op. cit., p. 43, footnote.
[3] Cited by C. Day Lewis, *The Poetic Image*, p. 71.
[4] Cited by Edith Sitwell, 'On My Poetry', in *Orpheus*, ii, p. 105.

beautiful and subtle description of the germinating powers of rhyme is that given by Whitman in his Preface to *Leaves of Grass*, a preface which recognizes that a poem moves with something of the power and grace that inform the motions of an animal, and invites us to discover in a poem a bloom and a perfume analogous to the sensuous properties of a flower:

> The profit of Rhyme is that it drops seeds of a sweeter and more luxuriant rhyme; and of uniformity, that it conveys itself into its own roots in the ground out of sight. The rhyme and uniformity of perfect poems show the free growth of metrical laws, and bud from them as unerringly and loosely as lilacs or roses in a bush, and take shapes as compact as the shapes of chestnuts and oranges and melons and pears, and shed the perfume impalpable to form.

We have seen how a phrase, a single line, or an isolated word may prove to be the starting-point of a poem. The genesis of a poem may be something still more evanescent and insubstantial than a solitary phrase—a poem may come to the poet in the form of a rhythm devoid of words. T. S. Eliot has described his experience of this phenomenon: 'I know that a poem, or a passage of a poem, may tend to realise itself first as a particular rhythm before it reaches expression in words, and that this rhythm may bring to birth the idea and the image.'[1]

Eliot has never had an unqualified admiration for Goethe, and it is curious to note that Goethe, like Eliot, confessed that, with him, the rhythm sometimes came into existence before the text. As the nineteenth century wore on, Baudelaire and his successors laid an ever-increasing emphasis upon the musical elements in poetry and, consequently, upon the significance of rhythm. Swinburne listened for weeks to the rhythms thundering in his head and waited for the appropriate words that would fit the imperious sounds. In this he seems to have resembled Mallarmé whose technique of composition was described by Arthur Symons in his book *The Symbolist Movement*, published in 1899 and read by T. S. Eliot in 1908. One sentence in particular merits our attention: 'But guided always by the rhythm, which is the executive soul, . . . words come slowly, one by one, shaping the message.'[2] In the twentieth century poets have come to recognize

---

[1] *The Music of Poetry*, p. 28.
[2] Cited by J. Isaacs, *The Background of Modern Poetry*, p. 21.

that rhythm, even when it is unaccompanied by intelligible words, may largely determine the way in which a poem develops. Stephen Spender, in 'Poet', describes how he sometimes becomes aware of 'a rhythm, a dance, a fury, which is as yet empty of words', and Robert Graves goes even farther than Spender in his emphasis upon the formative power of rhythm, asserting that 'the nucleus of every poem worthy of the name is rhythmically formed in the poet's mind, during a trance-like suspension of his normal habits of thought, by the supra-logical reconciliation of conflicting emotional ideas'.[1]

This formative rhythm is clearly associated with the night-side of the mind, with sleep, darkness, dreams, and memories that are both deep and far away. We are in the world of childhood, perhaps the childhood of the human race, in which the rocking of a cradle or the beating of a drum evoke an immediate and overpowering response. We are, in short, being led back to the great ocean of primitive feeling which lies far away from the landlocked continent of scientific rationalism in which we habitually pass our lives.

As long ago as 1918, in the September issue of *The Egoist*, T. S. Eliot declared that 'the artist is more *primitive*, as well as more civilised, than his contemporaries'.[2] He has invented the term 'auditory imagination' to describe the part played in poetry by the obscure rhythmic impulse which animates the movement of the verse, and he believes that this faculty enables a poet to explore the primitive and inchoate thoughts and feelings which lie submerged in the depths of our nature.

Confirmation of such views is to be found in Vico and in Valéry, both of whom stress the fact that poetry links man to the primitive, ancestral world by its quality of incantation. For, says Vico, 'Man, before he has arrived at the stage of forming universals, forms imaginary ideas. Before he reflects with a clear mind, he apprehends with faculties confused and disturbed: before he can articulate, he sings: before speaking in prose, he speaks in verse.'[3] Valéry echoes this opinion: 'I find a very ancient man in every true poet; he still drinks at the source of language; he

---

[1] *The Common Asphodel*, p. 1.
[2] Cited by F. O. Matthiessen, *The Achievement of T. S. Eliot* (2nd ed.), p. 94.
[3] Cited by Herbert Read, *Collected Essays in Literary Criticism* (2nd ed.), p. 42.

invents "verses"—just as the most gifted primitive man had to invent "words" or the ancestors of words.'[1] In an eloquent passage, Valéry rightly insists upon the power of language to move us by its extra-logical qualities:

> What is sung or articulated in the most solemn and the most critical moments of life; what we hear in a Liturgy; what is murmured or groaned in the extremity of passion; what calms a child or the afflicted; what attests the truth of an oath—these are words of a particular tone and expression which cannot be resolved into clear ideas, nor separated out without making them absurd or silly. In all these cases, the accent and inflection of the voice outweigh anything intelligible conveyed to us: it is our life rather than our mind which is addressed—I would say that such words incite us to *become* rather than to understand.[1]

It would, however, be dangerous to use this passage in support of any theory which exalts the pure music of words at the expense of their meaning. Even the emotions aroused by the words of a liturgy or by the murmurs that we hear in the moments of passion, have power to move us only because they are heard in the appropriate context, in the splendour of a church, or in the presence of the beloved. The sounds are but a secondary element in the ritual of faith or of love. Moreover, without some knowledge of the meaning of the ritual, the uttered sound has little effect upon us: the chanting of the liturgy awakens no response in a Hindu standing outside the tradition of Christendom, just as the nasal intonation of South Indian *ragas* soon becomes wearisome to the untrained ear of the European. It is one thing to assert that inflexion, accent, expression, tone, and stress enrich poetry and greatly influence our response to it; it is quite another to claim that the sounds of words and the cadences of verse have a significance divorced from their context.

A poem, unless it is a verse-play, is not aided by being set in a context whence it can derive emotional support; it has nothing but its words to sustain it. Furthermore, whereas the cadences of a liturgy point to the meaning of the ritual but do not constitute it, the meaning of the poem resides within the cadences themselves. The poem is a network of cadences and of meanings, a moving pattern rather than a mechanical unity, but unless the meanings arise from the cadences, as the flower buds from its

---

[1] Cited by Read, op. cit., p. 97.

roots, the poem will be nothing but a series of unconnected sounds. The analogy sometimes drawn between a poem and a liturgy is imperfect and, therefore, likely to be misleading. Similarly, the incoherent murmur of passion is as far removed from poetry as the song of a bird, since the distinguishing mark of poetry is its absolute coherence and precision.

Bearing these considerations in mind, we may glance at two pronouncements about cadence and sound which, to my mind, ignore the true nature of the way in which rhythm operates in English poetry. The first, and more famous, is Ezra Pound's set of instructions to the neophyte who desires to be a poet. After stressing the degree of technical proficiency which the poet should strive to attain, Pound gives detailed advice on how best to attain it: 'Let the candidate fill his mind with the finest cadences he can discover, preferably in a foreign language, so that the meaning of the words may be less likely to divert his attention from the movement.' Pound permits the neophyte to study poems in the English language, e.g. Shakespeare's songs, provided that he rigorously shuts his ear to their meaning. Before scrutinizing this advice, let us look at a second passage complementary to the first:

Far more words are onomatopœic in origin than is generally realised, their roots sunk deep in the remote times when prehistoric man began to evolve a language from sounds that were suggestive of the thing described or of the thought or emotion they struggled to express. Certain sounds, and combinations of sounds, therefore, must have an elemental significance of which we are not consciously aware, sounds which are echoed and partially reproduced in words like *lie, light, foam, sea, beat, grave, stone, day, glory.* I am suggesting that as there is a visual symbolism in dreams there is in language an aural symbolism lying deep in the unconscious, and fully operative and evocatory only when experienced in the semi-hypnotic condition induced by verse, and to a lesser degree by rhythmical prose such as that of the Bible and Sir Thomas Brown.[1]

Taken in conjunction, these two passages suggest the main elements of a theory of poetry based upon the sound-values said to be inherent in words and in cadences. Certain words are reputed to have an elemental significance incapsulated in their sound; a sequence of these words forms a cadence which, by means of onomatopœia, melopœia, and hypnotic rhythm,

---

[1] F. E. Halliday, *Shakespeare and his Critics.*

produces the required emotional effect in the reader; a series of these cadences makes up a poem.

Phoneticians, I believe, still differ about the origin of language and about the degree to which words owe their present form to onomatopœia or to gestures made by lip and tongue. Even if they were unanimous about these matters, their conclusions would be of comparatively little use to readers of poetry, for the connexion between man's first gropings towards articulate speech and the fully-developed language of the civilized poet must always remain tenuous and speculative. Burke remarked, two hundred years ago, in his essay *On the Sublime and the Beautiful*, that 'words undoubtedly have no sort of resemblance to the ideas for which they stand', and the importance of this truth has been re-emphasized by Dr. I. A. Richards.[1]

Constable once said that he never saw an ugly thing in his life, and no words, for the poet, are too ugly to be used in a poem, although they may, for a variety of reasons, be inappropriate in a given context. When men complain of an ugly word, they are not, in fact, objecting to its sound. Critics of music who protest against the introduction of German jargon-terms into the vocabulary of English criticism may claim that these words are ugly, whereas it would be more accurate to say either that they are hard to pronounce, or that we have good English words which are just as precise and which are hallowed by usage. A great many people dislike to hear a woman undergraduate described as an undergraduette. The cadence of undergraduette is, surely, more delicate and feminine than the cadence of under-graduate; the valid objection to it is that it is a bastard word, formed on a false analogy and suggestive of such words as usherette. Similarly, if to call a rat-catcher a rodent operative is an abuse of language, we may inquire why this is so. Neither rodent nor operative is an ugly word; both have their legitimate uses in a zoological or in an industrial context. Rat-catcher is a better expression than rodent operative for reasons unconnected with the sound of the words. It is a plain, exact, vivid description of a man who carries out a traditional occupation. We know where we are with him and with the pretty little rat-catcher's daughter. A rodent operative is a cosmopolitan abstraction, a

[1] *Practical Criticism*, pp. 363–4.

rootless figure from the twilight world of displaced persons, undesirable elements, and political reconditioning centres, in which a cloud of poisonous verbiage hides the pain of real men. The objection to such words as undergraduette and rodent operative is primarily a grammatical, intellectual, and moral objection, although we may sum up our dislike for the offensive phrases by saying that they sound hideous.

Few readers of poetry nowadays are naïve enough to admit that they don't give a fig for the sense of a poem, so long as the music of the words gives them a thrill, although a glance at the protocols collected by Dr. I. A. Richards might suggest that this kind of naïvety is more widespread than one likes to admit. There are, however, numerous readers who tend to over-emphasize or to misconstrue the part played by the sound of words in poetry; who talk about the magical quality of words or (if they are more sophisticated) about tonal values inherent in certain vowel-sounds; who appear to think that Milton's greatness as a poet lay in his ability to roll out a fine-sounding list of proper names.

A few moments' reflection should convince us that the mental reverberations occasioned by a word or by a line of verse are far more significant than the physical properties of sound inherent in the words themselves. A Russian, who obviously cared more for sound-values than for sense, affirmed that the most beautiful word in the English language was coal-scuttle. Conversely, I understand that the name Raskalnikov, which falls upon our ears with a romantic, albeit sinister, cadence, is no more pleasing to a Russian than the name Higginbottom is to an Englishman. Wordsworth's line:

> Spade! with which Wilkinson hath tilled his lands

is comic for reasons which have nothing to do with the sound of the words. Indeed, the alliteration and the internal rhyme make the line move with a pleasing melodiousness which is, unfortunately, spoiled by the bathetic pomposity of the invocation to the spade and by the inappropriateness of the name Wilkinson, which is redolent of urban shopocracy and thus out of place in an idyllic picture of a noble yeoman cultivating his small-holding. The line

> I am Lord Mayor of Birmingham

is, it will be agreed, less satisfactory than Swinburne's

> I am the Queen Proserpina,

although it would be hard to show wherein its vowel music and
cadence are less exquisite. Swinburne's line evokes pleasure because it occurs in a poem about dead queens renowned for their
fatal beauty, and because the whole context of the poem has
aroused in us a mood of nostalgia and regret. Add to this the
associations connected with the rape of Proserpina, and the
Swinburnian conjuring-trick reaps its reward.

Sacheverell Sitwell begins his poem *Agamemnon's Tomb* with
two highly evocative lines:

> Tomb
> A hollow, hateful word

and it is tempting to say that the long-drawn vowel-sound is, of
itself, suggestive of deep despair. It is more probable that the
effectiveness of the lines springs from the associations produced
by the word *tomb*, and from the similarity of sound which it
bears to words and phrases such as the gloom of approaching
death, the doom of all mankind, and the uncreating womb of
humanity. The effect of the long vowel-sound does not
invariably arouse feelings of despondency. When Charles
Trenet sings

> Boum! why does my heart go boum?

or when a music-hall comedian bellows

> Ta-ra-ra-*Boom*-de-ay!

the effect is one of gaiety.

If it should be objected that such examples are trivial and unfair
we may turn to a line from *Macbeth* that has been universally
admired:

> To-morrow and to-morrow and to-morrow

We are told by some critics that the very sound of this line, with
its repetition of the *o* and the *r*, is evocative of the leaden despair
which has taken possession of Macbeth. F. W. Bateson has
demonstrated the weakness of such a theory,[1] and we may follow
his example by constructing a piece of doggerel in which the

---

[1] *English Poetry*, p. 26.

sound and the movement of this very line, in a new emotional and rhythmical context, unmistakably convey an impression of a devil-may-care insouciance and of irresponsible flippancy and jauntiness:

> Why am I gay? Because day after day
> I borrow and I borrow and I borrow.
> 'When will you pay?' all my creditors say
> —To-morrow and to-morrow and to-morrow.

What, then, is the explanation of the undeniable potency which resides in this line when we hear it in *Macbeth*? Part of its power to move us comes from the context in which it is set, especially when a skilled actor, by gesture and by tone, can communicate to the movement of the line something of that deadly weariness which has usurped the place of feeling in the exhausted tyrant. Furthermore, the rhythm of a line or of a poem must be capable of bearing the weight of intonation and of feeling which is laid upon it by the thought and by the emotion inherent in the situation. Unless there is this perfect correspondence, we get incongruous lines of poetry in which the rhythm appears to be thumbing its nose at the emotion:

> The monkey doesn't jump about since little Willy died.

One of the marks of Shakespeare's genius is his unfailing ability to create rhythms that are dramatically and emotionally appropriate to the situation.

> Keep up your bright swords, for the dew will rust them.

> Remorseless, treacherous, lecherous, kindless villain.

> Eros—I come my queen!—Eros!—Stay for me.
> Where souls do couch on flowers we'll hand in hand
> And with our sprightly port make the ghosts gaze.

In the line from *Macbeth*, we ascribe to the words a rhythm which reflects the movements of our mind, and the basic structure of the line is perfectly adapted to receive that rhythm. There is one further point which may help to explain the tremendous effectiveness of this line. When Macbeth first meets Lady Macbeth after the battle and announces Duncan's approaching visit, the following dialogue occurs:

Macbeth.	My dearest love
	Duncan comes here to-night.
Lady Macbeth.	And when goes hence?
Macbeth.	To-morrow,—as he purposes.
Lady Macbeth.	O never
	Shall sun that morrow see.

It may be that we are meant to recall that early fragment of dialogue, to contrast the significance of the word *tomorrow* for Macbeth, as he was, with the significance which it holds for him now. Once, tomorrow offered glory and honour or shame and an act too horrible to contemplate. Now, tomorrow can bring nothing, except tomorrow. Such an interpretation may be considered fantastic, but we have to realize that Shakespeare habitually uses recurrent themes and images in his plays to convey a musical and an emotional pattern, and this reappearance of the word *tomorrow* at a crucial moment in the dramatic action is the kind of symphonic variation of which Shakespeare is a master.

Although Professor Livingston Lowes has demonstrated that *Kubla Khan* is a gigantic criss-cross of memories and of associations, some people are still under the impression that the poem derives its potency from the magic of its sound and that it is a piece of nonsense set to ravishing music. We cannot hope to write a second *Kubla Khan* but we may attempt to reproduce the music:

> In Bakerloo did Aly Khan
> A stately Hippodrome decree
> Where Alf the bread delivery man . . .

If readers of this version decide that it is inferior to the original, they may explain its inferiority by saying that the associations connected with Bakerloo, Aly Khan, and Alf the bread delivery man are ludicrous and incongruous. This may well be so: but once it is granted that associations aroused by words determine our response to a poem the theory of pure sound has been tacitly abandoned. Advocates of this doctrine may grimly decide to fall back upon a second line of argument, the nature of which has been indicated by I. A. Richards. He produced a meaningless set of syllables which were recognizably near in sound to Milton's ode 'On The Morning of Christ's Nativity'. His comment on the person who 'affirms that the mere sound of verse has *indepen-*

dently any considerable aesthetic value' is applicable also to the imaginary reader of my verse, *mutatis mutandis*:

> He will *either* have to say that this verse is valuable . . . *or* he will have to say that it is the differences *in sound* between this purified dummy and the original which deprive the dummy of poetic merit. In which case he will have to account for the curious fact that just those transformations which redeem it as sound, should also give it the sense and feeling we find in Milton. A staggering coincidence, unless the meaning were highly relevant to the effect of the form.[1]

Analysis of those Miltonic passages which are popularly supposed to resemble organ music would show that Milton's cunning lay in his manipulation of associations no less than in his mastery of vowels. Sir Alan Herbert's delicious parody of Henry V's rousing battle-speech is an acute comment upon the theory that an inherent nobility resides in the mere sound of proper names, however resonant they may be:

> Lancaster, York, great Salisbury and Monmouth,
> Hereford, Leicester, Northumberland and Kent,
> King's Cross, St. Pancras, Euston, Waterloo—
> All noble-sounding and capacious words.[2]

In the same way, an analysis of the verse written by any of the great masters of sound would reveal how much of its efficacy depends upon the layers of meaning sunk deep beneath the surface of the poetry. We may, if we choose, talk about word-magic so long as we remember that the sounds of a word's letters seldom imitate its meaning and, consequently, are, poetically, of minute significance. I. A. Richards, while admitting that there is 'a peculiar quasi-magical sway of words in the hands of a master', correctly attributes their power over our minds to 'the collocations of emotional influences that *by their very ambiguity* they effect'.[3]

That miraculous line of Tennyson's:

> And after many a summer dies the swan

loses all its radiance, as Aldous Huxley once remarked, if for *swan* we substitute the word *duck*. The word *swan* conjures up a visual image of exquisite whiteness, luminosity, and grace,

---

[1] Op. cit., p. 232.
[2] *Two Gentlemen of Soho.*　　　　　　　[3] Op. cit., p. 364.

whereas the vision produced by the word *duck* is of a small, waddling creature devoid of dignity and of pathos. But over and above the purely visual representation of the swan and of the duck, we are conscious of a host of associations which influence our responses to these words. Out for a duck, a dying duck in a thunderstorm, a man with ducks' disease—such are the associations which are likely to present themselves to the average reader. The swan brings with it an aura of mystery and of beauty as it sails down the reaches of the mind, recalling the silver-throated swans of the madrigalists and of Spenser, the swan which caressed Leda, the swans which haunt some of Yeats's finest poems, and those living birds which still glide unruffled on the Backs at Cambridge. Tennyson's swan dies against the traditional background of English poetry, amid the lamenting music of five centuries.

We may now consider the implications of Ezra Pound's advice which I quoted a few pages back. Pound once waged a long and vituperative campaign against Milton, and I find it a shade ironical that Milton is one of the few people whom we know to have put Ezra Pound's precepts into practice. He made his daughters read aloud Greek and Latin verses, but steadfastly refused to let them learn these ancient languages. There is no evidence to suggest that they enjoyed listening to the cadences which they were forbidden to understand, nor does the movement of the verses seem to have helped them to become poets.

One of the more obvious flaws in Pound's thesis is that sense and context play a large part in determining the rhythmical movement of a poem.[1] The music of a phrase or of a line is determined by the music of the words which precede and follow it. The neo-Swinburnian line:

> I am Lord Mayor of Birmingham

can be scanned in four distinct ways, according to the pattern of the stanza in which it is set, and according to the emphasis demanded by the sense of the passage:

> Í am Lord Máyor of Bírmingham
> Í am Lórd Mayor of Bírmingham

---

[1] Pound himself insists upon this elsewhere: 'Rhythm MUST have meaning'—*The Letters of Ezra Pound*, p. 91.

I ám Lord Máyor of Bírmingham
I am Lórd Mayor of Bírmingham

Another example may be cited. The line so often chanted at Sunday-schools:

Count your blessings name them one by one

is, rhythmically, of unusual interest. The first half may be scanned: Cóunt your bléssings (a simple injunction to look on the bright side of things), or: Cóunt yóur bléssings (laying stress upon the number of blessings to be reckoned). The second half may be stressed: Náme them óne by óne (give them a name) or: Náme them óne by óne (name them individually). The difference in rhythm, which is considerable, is a direct consequence of the shift in sense.

The seventh line of 'Spring and Fall' is a nice example of the way in which sense points the rhythm:

And yet you will weep and know why.

I. A. Richards, in submitting the poem to his guinea-pigs, omitted the accent-mark which Hopkins had placed on 'will'. Without this guiding mark, the reader can take this word to be the future tense sign. Given its accentual mark, it can be read as the present tense of the verb 'to will'. Similarly, the reader can stress either the word 'and' or the words 'know why', the first reading giving the meaning that Margaret will one day know the cause of what is now blind grief, the second giving the meaning that she persists in demanding why the leaves fall and why she grieves.[1]

William Empson came across a line of poetry in *Punch* which he misread as:

Queen-lily June with a rose in her hair

and found it delightful. On looking at it again, he discovered that it should read:

Queenlily June with a rose in her hair

and, immediately, the charming image of June personified as the

[1] Op. cit., pp. 83 and 89.

most beautiful of lilies was destroyed.[1] There is a further point to be noted, which Empson does not stress. Technically, the two versions of the line may have to be scanned alike, but anybody sensitive to those minute variations of speech-rhythm which are the life of poetic music will recognize that the rhythm of the second is ruined by the word 'queenlily', whereas the rhythm of the first is both delicate and subtle. The sense of the words controls the rhythm as rigorously as it controls the images suggested by the noun 'queen-lily' and by the adverb 'queenlily'.

Even without such examples, we might have suspected that the music of poetry was largely determined by meaning if we had remembered that such music has survived all kinds of changes in pronunciation and in speech-rhythms. Our pronunciation of Latin is different from that taught in Victorian England, and Virgil's contemporaries would scarcely recognize either Gladstone's or T. S. Eliot's recitation of the *Aeneid*, yet its ocean-roll of rhythm, like the surge and thunder of the *Odyssey*, continues to impress itself upon our ears and upon our minds. We know, also, that Sir John Gielgud's interpretation of Shakespeare is, musically, vastly different from Burbage's or Garrick's, but Shakespeare's verse, surviving all superficial changes in pronunciation and in phonetic sound, remains incomparably the finest poetic music in our language. As Dr. Johnson declared, 'it is scarcely to be doubted that on many occasions we make the music that we imagine ourselves to hear'.

In the best poetry the music is complex, and this is true of even those short and apparently simple lyrics which appear to be as unpremeditated and as pure as a bird's song. The music of poetry is, almost always, made up of a counterpointed pattern, varying in complexity and subtlety, but implicit in the movement of the verse. There is, first, the regular pattern of the metre, together with the tiny modifications from it which good poets have always delighted to employ, in order that the reader, while recognizing the basic rhythmical pattern of the verse, may take pleasure in the almost insensible variations from it introduced by the poet. Parallel with the metrical pattern runs the pattern of ordinary speech rhythm. T. S. Eliot has suggested that, in certain epochs, poets are deeply concerned with subduing normal speech

[1] *Seven Types of Ambiguity*, p. 65 (2nd ed.).

rhythms and making them into verse patterns, while, in other epochs, their prime concern is with the elaboration of an intricate musical pattern which tends to grow more and more unlike the pattern of common speech. It is possible to trace in any given poem something of the conflict between the demands of speech that it should not be distorted and the pleas of musical pattern that it should not be ignored. In a successful poem, the resulting tension is a source of vitality and the twin rights and duties of speech and musical pattern are reconciled in a harmony of movement. Deeper still than these counterpointed rhythms, there lies yet another music, difficult to describe, yet instantly apprehended by those who know that the surface meaning and the overt metrical pattern of a poem bear to the poem the same relation that the glittering waves of the sea bear to the underlying swell of the ocean. Landor spoke of 'an undersong of sense, which none beside the poetical mind, or one deeply versed in its mysteries, can comprehend',[1] and those who read poetry attentively learn to recognize that a poem may have a total unity of form, meaning, and music, impossible to define, yet undeniably present. Certain theatrical producers interpret a complete play by Shakespeare, Strindberg, or Chekhov in terms of music, because only by some such analogy can they reproduce the curve and sweep of the drama.

It would be pleasant to conclude this chapter with a rhetorical flourish or with a dogmatic statement to the effect that rhythm is invariably determined by meaning. Unfortunately, the relation between rhythm and meaning is so delicately poised that it is not easy to define it with any precision. I have quoted four examples of verse whose rhythm is controlled by the sense, and, to redress the balance, I must give some examples of poetry in which the rhythm modifies the meaning or (and this is even more significant) in which the rhythm determines the quality of the meaning.

My first example is taken from 'Spring Quiet' by Christina Rossetti:

> Full of fresh scents
> Are the budding boughs
> Arching high over
> A cool, green house . . .

[1] *Imaginary Conversations*: 'Aeschines and Phocion'.

Here dwell in safety,
Here dwell alone
With a clear stream
And a mossy stone.

As one of the students tested by I. A. Richards was quick to point out, a clumsy and mechanical stressing of these lines totally ruins the meaning of the poem, although it may not distort the prose sense of the words.[1] To read the first stanza as:

Fúll of frésh scénts

Áre the búdding bóughs

Árching hígh óver

A cool gréen house

is to murder the delicate airiness of the rhythm which is a constituent part of the poem's meaning and a guide to its emotional implications. Furthermore, if one accents the word 'green' one tends to think either of a greenhouse or of a house painted green, whereas the mind ought to dwell upon the coolness of the space beneath the trees. In the second stanza, the wrong accenting of the lines would lead to a similar misinterpretation of the poet's intention:

Wíth a cléar stréam

Ánd a móssy stóne

besides being rhythmically disastrous, makes comparative nonsense of the meaning by suggesting that if you dwell among the trees you must have a clear stream with you and a mossy stone as well.

Even if the rhythm of a poem has no direct bearing upon its prose meaning it may still determine the quality of that total meaning by which a poem is judged. I came across two lines which seemed to me admirable in both rhythm and meaning:

Magnificent, out of the dust we came
And abject, from the Spheres.

The slight pause after 'magnificent' and again after 'abject' took almost all the stress off the words 'out' and 'from', so that the lines

[1] Op. cit., pp. 38–39.

moved with a sombre, majestic rhythm which served to underline the paradox of man's dual nature. Later, I discovered the whole poem from which these lines were taken, and realized that I had misinterpreted the movement of the lines which I had read in isolation:

> We are children of splendour and flame,
>   Of shuddering also and tears.
> Magnificent out of the dust we came,
>   And abject from the Spheres.[1]

The heavy, swinging rhythm of this stanza is, to my ear, distinctly inferior to the grave music which I had ascribed to the last two lines out of their context, and, in some strange way, the emphatic rhythm which hammers home the trebly-repeated paradox of our destiny brings out the commonplace nature of the antithesis and turns the stanza into a piece of inferior Swinburnese.

These two examples suggest that our response to the meaning of a poem may be profoundly modified by the rhythm of the words, and it raises the question of the inherent character of certain sounds and rhythms in the English language. Are there, in fact, certain rhythms which, by their very nature, destroy the meaning of the poem in which they occur, or, at least, limit the range of emotions which can be expressed in that rhythmic pattern?

Such an idea, however far-fetched it may seem, deserves our consideration since it poses several relevant questions. Is it possible, for example, to write a tragic poem in the form of a limerick, or a clerihew and, if not, why not? Could one compose a serious poem in the rhythmical pattern of:

> I love little Pussy, her coat is so warm

to the strains of Gilbertian comic-opera patter, or to the lilt of:

> There's a one-eyed yellow idol to the north of Khatmandu

and, if not, why not? Are certain rhymes, of necessity, comic or ludicrous, so that even from Hopkins we cannot swallow the rhyme of *Communion* and *boon he on*?[2] A. E. Housman drew attention to the existence of such problems in his famous lecture

[1] Sir William Watson, *Ode in May*.
[2] W. H. Gardner, in his *Gerard Manley Hopkins*, i, p. 149, says that Bridges, in calling this rhyme hideous, 'is not defending an absolute canon of taste but is merely expressing a conservative opinion'. My opinion is equally conservative.

on *The Name and Nature of Poetry* but, unfortunately, failed to give his views on them:

> I mean such matters as these: . . . the reason why some lines of different length will combine harmoniously while others can only be so combined by great skill or good luck; why, while blank verse can be written in lines of ten or six syllables, a series of octosyllables ceases to be verse if they are not rhymed . . . why, of two pairs of rhymes, equally correct and both consisting of the same vowels and consonants, one is richer to the mental ear and the other poorer; the office of alliteration in verse, and how its definition must be narrowed if it is to be something which can perform that office and not fail of its effect or actually defeat its purpose.[1]

I confess that I am by no means sure of the answers to the problems which I have raised. I suspect that it would not be possible to write a serious poem in metres which are traditionally associated with ribald verses. W. H. Auden, in his 'Christmas Oratorio', employs such a metre, but does so in order to achieve a contrast to the prevailing mood of the poem and to emphasize the slick futility of our age:

> Come to our jolly desert
> Where even the dolls go whoring;
> Where cigarette ends
> Become intimate friends
> And it's always three in the morning.

A meditative poem in such a metre is unthinkable.

Granted that this is so, we still have to decide whether the intrinsic nature of certain metres and rhythms precludes the expression of certain ranges of thought and feeling, or whether it is our association of ideas which makes these rhythms unsuitable. No poet would begin a poem in honour of Saint Theresa with the line

> There was a young saint named Theresa

because the minds of his readers would be flooded with highly unsuitable reminiscences of young girls and young ladies from Baroda, Birmingham, Cape Cod, and those other places made so familiar by anonymous stockbrokers and by major Victorian Bards in their unpublished works. Yet I am not certain that the rhythm of the line, impartially judged, is so grossly unsuited to its theme: in practice, we cannot hope to judge impartially, because

---

[1] p. 8, footnote.

we know too much about English poetry to rid our minds of preconceptions. We cannot, in short, judge the music of a poem without scrutinizing the total meaning of the poem, and the poem itself lives and moves in the wider context of poetry.

There is one tiny piece of evidence which suggests that no metre or rhythm is necessarily unsuitable for use in a serious poem. I used to think that it would be impossible to write any poem, except a Rabelaisian ballad, to the rhythm of:

It was Christmas day in the workhouse, the night of all the year,
The inmates' hearts were full of joy and their bellies were full of beer.

It seemed to me that the rollicking beat of the verse rendered it unsuitable for use in serious poetry, and it was with something of a shock that I discovered how, in Blake's hands, it had already been used, with perfect appropriateness, in a grave and charming song:

Upon a holy thursday, their innocent faces clean,
The children walking two and two in grey and blue and green.

I have said enough to show that, in a good poem, there should be a perfect marriage between meaning and rhythm. Meaning insensibly, but firmly, moulds the rhythm, shaping our response to it, and, simultaneously, the rhythm enlarges and clarifies the meaning, bringing out the shades and the tones which otherwise might have remained hidden. It is no accident that the two most musical poets in the language, Shakespeare and Milton, should also be the two poets whose meanings are the most complex, rich, and inexhaustible. Edgar Allen Poe, on the contrary, who sought at all costs to be musical, paid the penalty of his obsession and, in his frantic search for musicality, abandoned sense without gaining a compensatory melodiousness. A poet may, like Carroll and Lear, outrage meaning and, by cutting across all logical associations, deliberately produce a mirror world where meaning cuts fantastic capers to an absurdly endearing accompaniment of music. He can scarcely hope to ignore meaning, to treat it as irrelevant, or, if he persists in doing so, in the vain pursuit of the music of words, the music itself will elude him, obstinately refusing to divorce itself from the meaning.

Aldous Huxley's comments on Poe are especially illuminating.[1]

[1] *Vulgarity in Literature*, pp. 26–36.

Poe's choice of heavy emphatic rhythms, dactylic permanent waves, as Huxley calls them, tends to coarsen the meaning of the poem and to make it difficult for him to escape from the reiteration of the crudest emotional platitudes. The rhythms tyrannously insist that the meaning shall be shovelled into the highly efficient conveyor-belt of sound and swallowed up in the machine-produced music of Poe's factory. Not content with choosing the lush dactylic music, Poe delights in adorning his poems with high-sounding proper names, and in so over-working them for their romantic, euphonious qualities that they cease to be even musical. To make matters still worse, he uses disyllabic proper-names as end-rhymes, thereby emphasizing still more their rich, fruity splendour of sound. Thus we have Dead D'Elormie rhyming with 'bore me' and 'before me' and the couplet:

> I have reached these lands but newly
> From an ultimate dim Thule.

Alliteration is liberally sprinkled over Poe's verse, in order to make certain that we shall not miss the musicality of the lines:

> The skies they were ashen and sober;
>   The leaves they were crisped and sere—
>   The leaves they were withering and sere;
> It was night in the lonesome October
>   Of my most immemorial year;
> It was hard by the dim lake of Auber,
>   In the misty mid region of Weir—
> It was down by the dark tarn of Auber
>   In the ghoul-haunted woodland of Weir.

The insistent dactylic rhythm, the rhyming of 'Auber' with 'October', and the alliteration of m's and w's combine to produce a distressing jangle in which the last vestige of meaning is ruthlessly obliterated. The next stanza surpasses even its predecessor in its lush chromaticism and in its yeasty musical swell:

> Here once, through an alley Titanic,
>   Of cypress, I roamed with my soul,
>   Of cypress, with Psyche my soul.
> These were days when my heart was volcanic
>   As the scoriac rivers that roll—
>   As the lavas that restlessly roll

> Their sulphurous currents down Yaanek
> In the ultimate clime of the pole—
> That groan as they roll down Mount Yaanek
> In the realms of the boreal pole.[1]

It is hard to comprehend why Baudelaire, Mallarmé, and Valéry should have regarded Poe as a major poet. Unable to grasp those elusive but all-important undertones of meaning which cross and unite in English words, they failed to recognize the flashy jauntiness of tone and gesture implicit in Poe's verse. Nor did they sense that the rhythms weigh down the meaning under a heavy load of tawdry opulence. Poe wrote two or three beautiful lyrics, 'The City in the Sea', 'To Helen' and, finest of all, 'Romance'. It is significant that in all these poems he chose unemphatic rhythms which left the meaning free to counterpoint its own melody against the formal melody of the metrical pattern. Poe's finest music emerges when he ceases to strain after musical effects, when he shuns word-magic, high-sounding proper names, disyllabic rhymes, and when the falsetto of the virtuoso gives place to the voice of the man. Those who persist in admiring Poe's musicality are recommended to study the verse of Thomas Holley Chivers, where they will find an even more luscious music and an even weaker dilution of meaning than in Poe, with reminiscences of Shelley added for good measure:

> Many mellow Cydonian suckets,
> Sweet apples, anthosmial, divine,
> From the ruby-rimmed berylline buckets,
> Star-gemmed, lily-shaped, hyaline:
> Like the sweet golden goblet found growing
> On the wild emerald cucumber tree,
> Rich, brilliant, like chrysoprase glowing,
> Was my beautiful Rosalie Lee.

It is not wholly fanciful to see, in the nemesis of musicality, a type of that nemesis which awaits all philosophies that confuse ends and means. Those who worship material prosperity, scientific progress, and complete personal liberty, dismissing things of the spirit as subjective fantasies, commonly end by making a society which, even on the material plane, is poverty-stricken, obscurantist, and tyrannical. Despising all that is spiritual, they

---

[1] 'Ulalume'.

destroy their one chance of attaining the objectives which they have erected into absolute ends. Even so, the poet who makes an idol of musicality, ignoring or depreciating meaning, will end by writing poetry whose very music will be trite and thin. In poetry, as in all things, disaster awaits those who, through ignorance or pride, set out to reverse the scale of values which man is meant to observe. There is, in poetry, no less than in other spheres of action, a compelling *ordo amoris*.

Having cited examples of verse which ignore the due relationship between meaning and rhythm, I propose to end this chapter by quoting some passages in which these elements are perfectly interfused. In all these passages, the rhythm and the meaning are so interdependent that the attempt to separate them must inevitably appear clumsy, and any comments upon them can only serve to emphasize that the true purport of the lines resides in their movement and not in the prose explanation of how they move:

> Beauty is but a flower
> Which wrinkles will devour;
> Brightness falls from the air;
> Queens have died young and fair;
> Dust hath closed Helen's eye;
> I am sick, I must die—
> > Lord, have mercy on us.
> > > Nashe

The apparent simplicity of these lines conceals a rhythmical subtlety which is the final reward of consummate technical skill. The placing of the stresses varies from line to line, yet this variety of emphasis lends a miraculous unity to the whole stanza. The heavy emphasis on 'beauty', 'brightness', 'queens', counterbalanced by the stresses laid upon 'wrinkles' and 'dust', reinforces the weight of sickly oppression which broods over the poem. Then comes the flat, despondent, monosyllabic recognition of mortality:

> I am sick, I must die—

followed by the quiet prayer of resignation and of hope.

Although I have criticized certain lines of Poe for their too insistent alliteration, a skilful use of this device may enrich the music of a poem and clarify its meaning:

Heavily hangs the broad sunflower
  Over its grave i' the earth so chilly;
Heavily hangs the holly-hock,
Heavily hangs the tiger-lily.

Tennyson

As down the steep of Snowdon's shaggy side
He wound with toilsome march his long array.

Gray

It is instructive to compare these lines with Poe's 'my most immemorial year' or with his 'ghoul-haunted woodland of Weir', or even with his most famous alliterative *tour de force*, 'the viol, the violet and the vine'. Poe's employment of alliteration gives one a certain pleasure, but the rhythm and the total music of the poem are in no way strengthened by this decorative use of sound, and the inward ear, which is undeceived by mere sound, however mellifluous, reserves its praise for a deeper kind of music. Both Tennyson and Gray use sound and rhythm to point their meaning. The movement of Tennyson's lines helps to emphasize the rotten air of dankness which hangs like a cloud over the sick-bed of the dying man. Gray's lines, as a reading of them aloud will show, convey exactly the length and the wearisomeness of that long, serpentine descent through hostile country. Such a functional use of sound is in a different category of merit from a mechanical and purposeless tintinnabulation.

Donne's music, at its best, has a perfection and a subtlety of movement unsurpassed by any poet in our tongue. Nowhere is this better illustrated than in the following stanza:

Study me then, you who shall lovers bee
At the next world, that is at the next Spring:
   For I am every dead thing,
   In whom love wrought new Alchemie.
    For his art did expresse
A quintessence even from nothingnesse,
From dull privations and leane emptinesse:
He ruin'd me, and I am re-begot
Of absence, darknesse, deathe; things which are not.

The opening lines, with their quick, challenging rhythm, the solemn pace of the third line, and the level tone of the sixth, seventh, and eighth lines correspond to the varying emotions which ebb and flow in the poet's mind, now rising, now falling,

139

and now flowing undisturbed by the eddyings of passion. The last line, with its heavy stresses, and the long, solemn, funereal monosyllables which conclude it, falls upon our ear like a passing-bell. The second line, which is made up entirely of monosyllables, moves at a much greater speed than the last line, although both lines are composed of ten syllables, and although the metrical basis of both is the same. It is worth comparing the contrasting ways in which Donne uses monosyllables to achieve utterly dissimilar ends, the resulting music being less the product of sound than of meaning interfused with sound.

I propose to give two more examples of verse which seems to me to display the marriage of music and sense that marks the successful poem. The first is a comparatively unfamiliar fragment by Kingsley:

> They drift away. Ah, God! they drift for ever.
> I watch the stream sweep onward to the sea,
> Like some old battered buoy upon a roaring river,
> Round whom the tide-waifs hang—then drift to sea.
>
> I watch them drift—the old familiar faces,
> Who fished and rode with me, by stream and wold,
> Till ghosts, not men, fill old beloved places,
> And, ah! the land is rank with churchyard mold.
>
> I watch them drift—the youthful aspirations,
> Shores, landmarks, beacons, drift alike.
>   .   .   .   .
>
> I watch them drift—the poets and the statesmen;
> The very streams run upward from the sea.
>   .   .   .   .
>
> Yet overhead the boundless arch of heaven
> Still fades to night, still blazes into day.
>   .   .   .   .
>
> Ah, God! My God! Thou wilt not drift away.

Kingsley's rank as a poet is not high, but these particular lines seem to me admirable and moving. His normal verse style is conventional, competent, and straightforward, unremarkable for passion, for perceptive imagery, or for rhythmical subtlety. He cared, above all things, for social justice, cleanliness, public decency, and honourable manliness; verse-making was a fine, healthy activity of which he approved, unless it led to the contemptible effeminacy that he had so roundly condemned in

Keats. Such views, and such gifts as he possessed, led him to produce a body of verse that was pleasant, talented, and, fundamentally, of no significance. W. B. Yeats said that profound philosophy must spring from terror, and he might have added that great poetry, also, has its origin in those moments of terror when all familiar certainties are shaken. In this fragment, Kingsley seems to have experienced, with overwhelming force, the conviction that public health, cricket on the village green, the daily life of social activity, all the concepts of good citizenship, were mere defences and distractions which conceal from us the immense fact of death. Deprived of the habitual excitements and consolations of daily life, Kingsley speaks, in this poem, like a man who, for the first time, perceives the truth behind the flimsy screens of illusion. The conventional metrical form vibrates with the rhythm of anguish. In the third line, the rhythm conveys, with unusual skill, the fury of the irresistible flood which sweeps all to oblivion, and the tenth line moves haltingly and irresolutely in tune with the poem's mood. After the wild flow of the rhythm in the first twelve lines, comparative tranquillity descends upon the poem, the music grows quieter, until, in the last line, which is half affirmation, half desperate plea, the heavily emphasized 'Thou' rises like a rock in the midst of swirling waters.

My final example is drawn from *The Waste Land*, a poem which, as we have seen, is the earliest example of T. S. Eliot's work wherein the analogy between the structure of a piece of music and the shifting moods of a poem is tentatively suggested and adumbrated. The typist, her clerk having groped his way downstairs, puts a record on the gramophone, and a new theme enters:

> 'This music crept by me upon the waters'
> And along the Strand, up Queen Victoria Street.
> O City city, I can sometimes hear
> Beside a public bar in Lower Thames Street,
> The pleasant whining of a mandoline
> And a clatter and a chatter from within
> Where fishmen lounge at noon: where the walls
> Of Magnus Martyr hold
> Inexplicable splendour of Ionian white and gold.

This passage, although not one of the most elaborately musical in *The Waste Land*, nevertheless demonstrates how closely the rhythm and the music of poetry are linked with the sense, and how numerous are the interlocking elements which are moulded into unity by the esemplastic power of the poet. The opening two lines remind us of *The Tempest*, of the enchanted island where music out of the thin air stole upon the sense. Then, by a sudden modulation, we are back again in twentieth-century London, in the poor quarters of the metropolis. The gentle, sliding rhythm of the first line changes into the flat banality of the fourth, which, in its turn, gives way to the onomatopœic description of the noises coming from the public house. The slack uneven movement of:

> Where fishmen lounge at noon: where the walls
> Of Magnus Martyr hold

prepares the way for the magnificent concluding line. One must, when reading it aloud, pause for a moment after the word 'hold' if the full effect of the final line is to be experienced. After the irregular movement of the preceding lines, the spacious majesty with which the last line solemnly moves clinches the whole passage and shapes the total melody. The contrasting *i* and *o* sounds which alternate in this line may be taken to correspond with the white and the gold which adorn the walls of Magnus Martyr, a vowel-contrast repeated in the words 'inexplicable splendour'. The effect of these lines is similar to that produced by the superb final chorus in *Samson Agonistes*:

> Oft he seems to hide his face,
> But unexpectedly returns
> And to his faithful Champion hath in place
> Bore witness gloriously; whence Gaza mourns

in which the long final line, with its open vowels, rings out triumphantly, in contrast to the broken rhythm of the first three lines that serves to underline the uncertainty of the apparently forsaken servants of God, and so to prepare the way for the tremendous reaffirmation of His power. In *The Waste Land*, the aimless noise of London back-streets, which has replaced the music of Prospero's isle, finally yields to the luminous peace of Magnus Martyr.

I have tried, in this chapter, to indicate that the origin of a poem may lie in a verbal phrase or in a particular rhythm wherein no words are distinguishable. Furthermore, I have suggested that the analogies between music and poetry are worth studying and that T. S. Eliot's *Four Quartets* may prove as fruitful for poets as the invention of sonata form has been for musicians. I have also drawn attention to the intricate relationship between rhythm and meaning, to the extraordinary complexity of the musical element in poetry, and have given my reasons for agreeing with I. A. Richards that 'what criticism most needs is less poeticizing and more detailed analysis and investigation'. In all the welter of confusion and of mumbo-jumbo about the magic of poetry, one fact is clear: no man can be a poet unless his ears are attuned to the most delicate inflexions of living speech, for the music of poetry is rooted in the actual language of men, language which is ever-changing and which moves with an elemental power beyond the wit of man to fathom or to control. A great poet may, for an instant, impose his own harmony upon the tidal flow of language, but his momentary conquest, though it may serve to encourage those who come after him, is but a perpetual reminder that each generation of poets must find its own music in the language of its own day. For the music of poetry is not to be discovered in arcane researches into vowel-sounds or into metrical patterns: it can be won only by a long apprenticeship to the study of language, a patient acceptance of human experience, and a tireless exploration of the harmony that lies hidden in the flux of created things.

Chapter Five

WE saw in the last chapter that a poem may originate in a single word, or in an isolated phrase, or even in a wordless rhythm, particularly if the poet is more than usually sensitive to the subterranean links between sound and meaning. There are, however, some poets whose command of imagery is far stronger than their auditory imagination and a poem may enter their field of consciousness in the guise of an image. Just as Leonardo da Vinci constructed his pictures by gazing at the stain-marks fortuitously scattered upon a wall and reducing them to well-conceived forms, even so the poet may build up his poems from a series of fragmentary and evanescent images.

There are certain writers whose imagination is primarily visual, and this fact has led some critics to suppose that one of the chief functions of the poet is to paint a vivid picture in words. This misconception is based upon the erroneous belief that all poets conform to one physiological and psychological type and upon the mistaken notion that all images are visual. This second error goes back at least as far as Addison, who wrote: 'We cannot indeed have a single image in the fancy that did not make its first entrance through the sight';[1] and it has been repeated, in varying forms, by divers critics, for two and a half centuries. Even so acute a writer as Remy de Gourmont appears to have regarded the non-visualizer as an inferior type of artist whose imagination is necessarily impoverished by his regrettable inability to conjure up a vivid mental picture. His contention is invalidated by his failure to realize that there is no justification for elevating one method of composition above another. Robert Graves, for instance, relies very largely upon his sense of touch in his dealings with the external world and his method of apprehending sensual reality is, poetically, as valid as any other. The republic of the five senses admits no king.

A good poet should, indeed, be a master of imagery, but imagery is something more complex and elaborate than a series

---

[1] *The Spectator*, No. 411 (1712). Cf. Michael Roberts, *Critique of Poetry*, pp. 45–57.

of unambiguous pictures. A distinction must be drawn between a visual image, which evokes a clear picture of an object, and a symbolic image, which arouses a network of associations. The word 'aspidistra' will call up, for some people, the exact, photographic image of this small domestic flower. The non-visualizer will be unable to describe an aspidistra with any precision, or to recall what it looks like, yet the word may evoke a stream of mingled pictures, associations, and reminiscences—a Victorian drawing-room cluttered with furniture, the smell of leathery arm-chairs, the distant lineaments of a world that was full of confidence and of purposeful energy. In the same way, while the visualizer who is confronted with the word 'olive-tree' may see in his mind's eye a precise image of its slender form, the non-visualizer will be stirred, by a whole complex of emotions, to recall the landscape, the light, and the unique beauty of that ancient Mediterranean region whose civilization still rests upon the olive and the vine. Coming nearer home, those who are visualizers will, on hearing the word 'sun-dial', have a clear picture of a round piece of metal or of stone let into a wall or resting upon a stone plinth. The minds of the non-visualizers will recollect, perhaps, a sun-dial inseparably linked with a particular place, a garden or a college quadrangle, and may recall, also, a host of associations newly awakened by this single word. They may experience a memory of things past, of a vanished way of life centred round a walled garden or a sunlit courtyard, of an epoch which was not enslaved by the insistent demands of a mechanical clock, of a world which moved to an older and more fundamental rhythm than the one to which we so frenziedly agitate ourselves. The image of the sun-dial may have power to arouse a range of concepts and a host of intimations divorced from geography and from history—the sense of sad mortality and of empty desolation. For the sun-dial can symbolize, among other things, the passing of the hours, and man's brief enjoyment of life in the sun. It is a symbol that points to the dead:

> . . . and with them Time
> Slept, as he sleeps upon the silent face
> Of a dark dial in a nameless place.

Hood's dark dial speaks to all our senses, not to our eyes alone, as

eloquently as the dial which Donne enshrined in his verse to
remind his mistress that her beauty was not immutable:

> And all your graces no more use shall have
> Than a Sun dyall in a grave.

This distinction between the two main types of imagery is so
clear that the failure of critics to recognize it is incomprehensible.
Even in the eighteenth and nineteenth centuries there were a few
writers who realized that Addison's dictum was completely inadequate and misleading. Burke reminded his readers that poetry
'does not in general produce its end by raising the images of
things but by exciting a passion similar to that which real objects
will excite by other means',[1] and G. H. Lewes warned his readers
not to make 'the grand mistake of supposing that *all* images in
poetry must be addressed to the eye',[2] thereby anticipating the
contention of Michael Roberts that 'the poet, unlike the painter,
is not compelled to express the perception of all his senses through
imagery derived from one'.[3] Lewes, while insisting that images
in poetry need not be designed for the eye, was not thereby
countenancing any sloppy imprecision and smudginess: 'An
image that is addressed to the *eye* should of course be clear and
defined.'

Clarity alone is not enough, for imagery must be subordinate
to the total design of the poem, and one of the marks of a poet's
skill is the tact with which he handles imagery: in particular, he
must ensure that the images which are meant to achieve their
effect by appealing to all our senses and by evoking a series of
associations are not rendered ludicrous by an intrusive and inappropriate mental picture. *The Song of Solomon*, fully visualized, would become an incoherent kaleidoscope of Surrealist
images, but even the most persistent visualizers are persuaded by
the poet's command of language to respond to the erotic images
with the sensual imagination. The following couplet by George
Herbert illustrates how a poet who fails to observe the distinction
between visual and non-visual images may come a cropper:

> Christ left his grave-clothes that we might, when grief
> Draws tears or blood, not want an handkerchief.

---

[1] *On The Sublime And The Beautiful.*
[2] *Inner Life Of Art.*
[3] Op. cit., p. 56.

The force of the metaphysical conceit is impaired by the distract-
ing visual image of the handkerchief, and Herbert is unlucky in
that the rather trivial contemporary connotations of the word
'handkerchief' help to spoil his image for twentieth-century
readers. This last consideration may remind us that often the
fault may lie with the reader, or with the passage of time that
distorts the meaning of words and phrases, rather than with the
poet. As a small boy I used to sing a hymn which contained the
lines:

> And the heart of the Eternal
> Is most wonderfully kind.

I found these lines disquieting, since we had a bathroom geyser
upon which was inscribed 'The Eternal', and whenever we sang
this hymn I saw the geyser in all its coppery ugliness. The writer
of this hymn could not be blamed for my private aberration, but
sometimes it is difficult to apportion the blame between the poet
and the reader. When we read Vaughan's enthusiastic declaration:

> How brave a prospect is a bright backside

it is as if we were listening to a solemn lecture by a man whose
trousers are whisked away unexpectedly. An element of farce has
irretrievably ruined a serious discourse. We may decide that
Vaughan is merely a victim of misfortune in that the meaning of
backside has endured a miserable decline and fall in the past three
hundred years, but as long ago as 1541 it bore the meaning of a
privy and as far back as 1500 it was used as a colloquialism for
the posterior. Even a poet and a mystic must take into account the
vulgar connotation of the phrases that he employs; indeed a poet
ought to be more deeply aware than anybody else of the manifold
implications of his words.

We may acquit Coleridge of carelessness in writing the line

> As if this earth in fast thick pants were breathing

since the use of pants as a vulgar abbreviation for pantaloons was
unknown until 1846. Francis Thompson, however, seems to me
guilty of a lapse in tact when he writes of

> Panting red pants into the West

and in poetry, no less than in life, a deficiency in tact points to an emotional clumsiness or crudity which we rightly condemn as a flaw.

These examples illustrate the confusion that may arise when a shift in a word's meaning allows a ludicrous visual image to disturb the gravity of the proceedings. Sometimes the poet cannot even plead that he has been betrayed by an unfortunate linguistic development; there are lines which have always been ridiculous and which will always remain so:

> Hope kicks the curl'd heads of conspiring stars.
>
> Crashaw[1]

> No more will I endure Love's pleasing pain,
> Nor round my heart's leg tie his galling chain.
>
> Anon.

> Love's feet are in his eyes.
>
> Anon.

> I dream'd a banish'd Angel to me crept:
> My feet were nourish'd on her breasts all night.
>
> Meredith

The usual explanation of the grotesqueness of such lines is that mixed metaphors are inevitably confusing and almost invariably comic. This statement is untrue, for mixed metaphors can both enlarge our understanding of a situation and, strange as it may seem, clarify our apprehension of its significance:

> Was the hope drunk
> Wherein you dress'd yourself? hath it slept since
> And wakes it now, to look so green and pale
> At what it did so freely?
>
> Shakespeare

Hazlitt singled out a distinctive feature of Shakespeare's style when he drew attention to his repeated employment of mixed metaphors, a characteristic which Lamb also had noticed: 'His language abounds in sudden transitions and elliptical expressions. This is the source of his mixed metaphors, which are only abbreviated forms of speech. These, however, give no pain from long custom. They have, in fact, become idioms in the language.' This defence of Shakespeare's poetic method is singularly lame,

---

[1] Cited by D. B. Wyndham Lewis and Charles Lee, *The Stuffed Owl*, p. 1.

for it suggests that we tolerate it only because we are so familiar with the Bard's peculiarities that we are prepared to overlook his little faults. Middleton Murry puts the matter in a truer perspective when he reminds us that 'we have not, and we are not intended to have time to unfold his metaphors. . . . His success, when we examine it, is not really so surprising, for the extent to which images are discordant depends upon the extent to which we unfold them, and that is wholly within the great poet's control, for it in turn depends primarily upon the rhythm and tempo of his writing.'[1] I think that the vital point is not so much the extent to which we unfold a metaphor as the degree to which we visualize an image that is meant to be primarily symbolical and non-visual. If Shakespeare's lines from *Macbeth* awakened a series of visual images in our minds they would leave us befuddled and bewildered. In fact, we grasp the implication of each succeeding metaphor without being disturbed by irrelevant mental pictures, and the cumulative weight of the passage stamps its meaning indelibly upon our receptive mind. Shakespeare, by his art, has compelled us to respond to his images in precisely the way that he intends, like a great lawn-tennis player who dictates the pattern of every rally.

Contemporary poets occasionally exhibit a similar mastery of mixed metaphors. W. H. Auden uses one to convey the sweep and the fury of history:

> And all sway forward on the dangerous flood
> Of history, that never sleeps or dies,
> And, held one moment, burns the hand

Dylan Thomas, in one of his finest poems, employs this device with great daring and with complete success:

> The hand that signed the treaty bred a fever,
> And famine grew, and locusts came;
> Great is the hand that holds dominion over
> Man by a scribbled name.
>
> The five kings count the dead but do not soften
> The crusted mound nor pat the brow;
> A hand rules pity as a hand rules heaven;
> Hands have no tears to flow.

---

[1] The quotations from Hazlitt and from Middleton Murry are taken from F. E. Halliday, *Shakespeare And His Critics*, pp. 131–2.

Mixed metaphors, then, are often extremely beautiful and appropriate provided that the poet does not permit incongruous mental images to thrust themselves upon our attention. Crashaw's Hope is ludicrous because we cannot help visualizing her as high-kicking like a chorus-girl, whereas Shakespeare's hope remains uncontaminated by the all too active picture-making faculty of the normal reader.

Even when there is no question of a mixed metaphor the poet must control the deployment of his imagery with unremitting watchfulness. In a previous chapter I cited the line

> The monkey doesn't jump about since little Willy died

as an example of how a serious meaning could be corrupted by an inappropriate rhythm, and I quote it now to show how a line can be ruined by the poet's insensitivity to the function of imagery in poetry. The mention of little Willy, though meant to be tender and moving, irresistibly reminds us of one of those melodramatic Victorian death-bed scenes which, according to Oscar Wilde, only those with hearts of stone can read without laughing. Furthermore, the monkey is, in this context, a purely comic figure reminiscent of those mischievous little creatures who perform such outrageous feats in the zoo. The conjunction of little Willy and the monkey is irresistibly funny, a burlesque of the solemnity of death.

Tennyson occasionally commits a similar error of taste and allows an unseemly image to obtrude itself upon the reader. In describing the martyrdom of St. Stephen, he lapses into a wooden laboriousness of utterance which compels us to visualize the scene, instead of apprehending it with our understanding:

> But looking upward, full of grace,
> He pray'd, and from a happy place
> God's glory smote him in the face.

Such intrusive visual images are liable to slip into poetry unperceived, especially when the poet's concern is with things so lofty that he forgets his earthy humanity and the ever-present menace of the trivial and the ludicrous. The verse of Charles Williams, though it rises at times to a harsh magnificence, is all too often disfigured by a striving after impressiveness, and by a humourless insensitivity to the grotesque implications of the eccentric imagery with which it is crammed. When he speaks of

> The web of the net of the imperially bottomed glory

we can scarcely avoid catching a glimpse of a portly dowager displaying the brave prospect of a bright backside. The last four lines of 'On Leaving Church', though less crude, are even more insidiously risible, because of the emotional disequilibrium which they reveal:

> The noises of the world's concern
>   And the high sun break through:
> I rise, I genuflect, I turn
>   To breakfast and to you!

It is, of course, only fair to say that breakfast, in its original sense, had a religious connotation, and that even today we refer to a wedding breakfast, which should follow a nuptial mass. It is just possible to argue that the reference to breakfast, properly interpreted, is perfectly in order and that we must read a poem with sympathetic understanding if we are to judge it aright. Nevertheless, I believe that these lines conjure up a series of inappropriate visual images which completely wreck the poet's meaning and evoke in his readers a series of responses which he did not intend to arouse. For the word 'breakfast' immediately suggests sizzling bacon or a plate of cereals, and the coupling of 'breakfast and you' is a piece of bathos whose enormity is stressed by the exclamation mark with which the poem closes. Again, although the action of genuflexion is a natural gesture of piety, the word itself smacks of ritualism, and the combination of genuflexion, breakfast, and you! suggesting as it does the Oxford Movement, muscular Christianity, and healthy sex is enough to ruin a poem more robust than 'On Leaving Church'. Had Lytton Strachey employed this collocation of words, he would have been accused of facile irony; Charles Williams's moral earnestness and the sincerity of his attempt to fuse the commonplace and the supernatural are not in question, but his disregard of the way in which imagery functions has, in this poem, brought him to the edge of disaster.

Two quotations from Dylan Thomas may serve to reinforce my contention that a poem's success or failure often depends

upon the poet's ability to control the way in which we respond
to his imagery and, in particular, upon his power to prevent us
from visualizing an image which is meant to be non-visual. The
last section of *Twenty-five Poems* consisted of a sonnet sequence,
designed to be part of a work in progress, although the work
was never completed. Image upon image, religious, sexual, and
psycho-analytical, tumble over one another in priapic revelry
and confusion. The undeniable force of these images is often
misdirected, and not infrequently chaotic, mainly because the
sequence of pictures which assaults the eye fails to make any
coherent impression upon us, despite its nightmarish intensity.
Indeed, the ferocity of the onslaught launched by these visual
images renders us incapable of deriving any illumination from
them; their visual clarity is so blinding that their meaning is
obscured. When we read lines such as:

> The bagpipe-breasted ladies in the deadweed
> Blew out the blood gauze through the wound of manwax

we can scarcely help visualizing these grisly harpies and, in so
doing, we linger upon the picture conjured up by the lines to
the detriment of the poem as a whole. Instead of enjoying the
poem as a harmonious unity, we are alternately worried and
fascinated by a succession of dismembered images.

The last poem of the sequence is, however, more balanced and
coherent than some of its predecessors. It ends with a reference to

> that Day
> When the worm builds with the gold straws of venom
> My nest of mercies in the rude, red tree.

If we were to visualize the sequence of images which lie folded
in these lines the effect would be inept and even ridiculous, since
worms do not build nests, straws are not made of venom, and a
rude red tree is unknown to botanical science. We are not, in
practice, troubled by such considerations, because this type of
legalistic and literal interpretation is clearly out of place and
utterly irrelevant, belonging to the category of objections
levelled by Rymer against *Othello*. As G. S. Fraser has pointed
out,[1] these lines contain a beautiful and complex undercurrent
of meaning, which is gradually apprehended as we permit the

---

[1] *New Statesman and Nation*, 29 Nov. 1952.

ambiguity of the associations implicit in the images to work upon our minds and our senses. It is plain from their context that these lines refer to the Day of Judgement, and that Thomas is drawing upon that relationship between Adam's temptation and Christ's crucifixion which exercised the imagination of medieval writers and which provided both Donne and Herbert with a congenial theme. Donne treated it with his customary ingenuity and fervour:

> We thinke that *Paradise* and *Calvarie*,
> *Christs* Crosse and *Adams* tree, stood in one place;
> Looke Lord and finde both Adams met in me;
> As the first *Adams* sweat surrounds my face
> May the last *Adams* blood my soul embrace.

Herbert achieved an intensity and a tender gravity, which even he rarely surpassed, in *The Sacrifice*, a long meditation on Christ's passion, beautiful alike in its imagery and in its slow lamenting rhythm:

> Oh all ye who pass by, behold and see;
> Man stole the fruit, but I must climb the tree,
> The tree of life, to all but only me,
>   Was ever grief like mine?

G. S. Fraser is probably correct in taking the word 'venom' as a reference to the poison with which the serpent mortally wounded Adam and Eve, although I confess that the poet has compressed his meaning here so tightly that it is not easy to unravel it. It is, however, clear that the rude, red tree is both the tree of Paradise and the cross of Christ, and that death which brings the worm that never dies brings also the mercy won for man by Christ's blood. The conjunction of gold and straws, counterpointing against each other the ideas of indestructible precious metal and worthless trash, is reminiscent of the paradox which Hopkins handled with supreme virtuosity:

> This Jack, joke, poor potsherd, | patch, matchwood, immortal diamond,
>   Is immortal diamond.

There is, of course, an element of visual imagery in Thomas's lines and, indeed, it is the sensuous vividness of the gold straws and of the red tree which stings us into responding to the challenge of the verse. My point is that these visual images have not been permitted to run riot, but have been employed in order to clarify and to intensify the total design of the poem.

The degree to which visual imagery occurs in poetry will vary, depending partly on the temperamental affinities of the poet and partly on the effect which he desires to produce in any given poem. In some verse, the imagery is predominantly visual; in some, the visual element is deliberately eliminated since its intrusion would be highly unwelcome; often, the imagery is neither wholly visual nor entirely symbolic but a fusion of pictorial images with sensuous and intellectual associations. It is not always easy to analyse a poet's images and to decide the precise extent to which they are meant to be visual, since our response to them will be influenced by our own physiological make-up. We can, nevertheless, make a fairly accurate distinction between the three main types of images to which I have drawn attention.

Some of the most beautiful images in English poetry are predominantly visual, appealing almost exclusively to the one sense and scarcely calling upon the other senses to reinforce their effect upon the mind's eye:

> Doth not a Teneriffe, or higher hill
> Rise so high like a rock, that one might think
> The floating moon would shipwreck there and sink?
>
> Donne

> Her rising Breasts are white as polish'd Shells,
> And in each part a different Beauty dwells.
>
> Diaper

> All in a hot and copper sky,
> The bloody Sun at noon,
> Right up above the mast did stand,
> No bigger than the moon.
>
> Coleridge

> You found he ate his supper in a room
> Blazing with lights, four Titians on the wall
> And twenty naked girls to change his plate.
>
> Browning

> Out in the dark over the snow
> The fallow fawns invisible go
> And the fallow doe

154

And the winds blow
Fast as the stars are slow.
Edward Thomas

Above the quiet dock in midnight,
Tangled in the tall mast's corded height,
Hangs the moon. What seemed so far away
Is but a child's balloon, forgotten after play.
T. E. Hulme

The North Wind rose: I saw him press
With lusty force against your dress,
Moulding your body's inward grace
And streaming off from your set face;
So now no longer flesh and blood
But poised in marble flight you stood.
O wingless Victory, loved of men,
Who could withstand your beauty then?
Robert Graves

We are meant to visualize these images as clearly as if they had been depicted by a painter, and the effect is so vivid and pleasing that we are tempted to think that all images ought to be visual. We should remember that an equally fine effect may be secured by the deliberate suppression of the visual element in imagery, or by toning it down almost to vanishing-point, the supreme example of this technique being *The Song of Solomon*. Lorca employs a similar device in his poem on Thamar:

> Thamar, in your high breasts
> are two fishes that call me,
> and in the tips of your fingers
> a message of the cloistered rose.

This remarkable image of the fishes, which might be considered ludicrous by a persistent visualizer, seems to me triumphantly successful. It conveys something of the cool, smooth, silvery beauty of Thamar's breasts, the salt tang of desire, the deep mystery of passion wherein we drown as if in a sea, the separateness and the uniqueness of love, symbolized by the non-human 'otherness' of fishes which live a life so remote from ours, the evasiveness of sexual pleasure, which slips away from our grasp as a fish glides away into the sea-bed, and, perhaps, the cold-blooded sexuality which Thamar has the power to awaken. The image of the rose, though more commonplace, is designed to evoke a set of emotions that will supplement and extend the range of sensations aroused by the image of the fishes.

The most effective erotic poems are those in which the physical charms of the lovers and the pleasures of love itself are obliquely conveyed by images which appeal to our five senses and to our memories:

> Where is my golden palace,
> Where my ivory bed?
> Where the joy of my morning hour?
> Where the sons of eternity singing
> To awake bright Urizen my King,
> To arise to the mountain sport,
> To the bliss of eternal valleys;
> To awake my King in the morn.
> To embrace Ahania's joy
> On the breadth of his open bosom?
> From my soft cloud of dew to fall
> In showers of life on his harvests. . . .
>
> Blake

> That night I rode
> the best of all roads,
> astride a pearly mare
> without bridle or stirrups.
>
> Lorca

> Happy indeed who never misses
> To improve that precious hour,
> And every day
> Seize her sweet prey,
> All fresh and fragrant as He rises
> Dropping with a balmy shower
> A delicious dew of spices.
>
> Crashaw

Precious metals, smooth, gleaming surfaces, valleys, harvests, clouds, dews, and spices—such are the symbols which these poets adopt to evoke a sensation which steals upon all our senses. A simple visual image would, by its very exactitude, eliminate a whole range of experience which these complex images so potently suggest.

So far we have considered two of the three main types of imagery commonly found in poetry—imagery that is purely visual, and imagery that is designed to exclude, as far as is practicable, all visual elements and to permit the reader's imagination to roam at will among its sensuous memories. The type of imagery most commonly found in English poetry is, simultaneously, descriptive and emotive, combining a pictorial representation of an object with an evocation of its latent significance. Ezra Pound's definition of such imagery has not been excelled: 'An "image" is that which presents an intellectual and emotional complex in an instant of time. . . . It is a vortex or cluster of fused ideas and is endowed with energy.' We can lay it down as a general rule that the intellectual and emotional complex will tend to be elaborate and far-reaching in its implications whenever the visual element in the image is small and that, conversely, a clearly defined visual image will limit the field in which the associative faculties of the reader are free to operate. We shall also discover that an image which appears to be primarily visual may owe its effectiveness to the non-visual associations which have been attracted into its orbit. In the couplet:

> Like cats in air-pumps, to subsist we strive
> On joys too thin to keep the soul alive

the mental picture of cats in air-pumps is not altogether pleasing and may indeed be disquieting to those who are old-fashioned enough to find cruelty to animals distasteful. The delight we feel in reading the couplet springs from our admiration at the conjunction of incongruous notions, the comparison drawn between cats and the soul, between the air in air-pumps and joys. We are under the spell of comedy, which converts all that is painful and degrading into an elegant dance of ideas whose pattern is our delight.

We may profitably compare the lines from Mandeville's 'A Description of the Morning' with a famous conceit by Cleveland. Mandeville presents us with an ingenious comparison, a delightful example of Fancy in the Coleridgean sense:

> Dame Earth pull'd off her Mask to Sol,
> As Strumpets do to Sentinels;
> Whose Red Coat, in St. James's Park
> From every Face dispels the dark.

These lines charm us by their clever play upon words and by the consciously artificial nature of the comparison drawn between

Dame Earth and the Strumpet and between Sol and the red-coated sentinel. Its main weakness is that there are no reverberations of meaning or of associations in these lines, no undertones or overtones in which a richly comic significance perpetually wells up and overflows. The very brightness of the image has for ever transfixed the meaning of the lines into a posture of complete rigidity. Cleveland, on the contrary, presents us with a whole world of wit and impropriety miraculously concentrated into a couple of lines, in his query to his coy mistress:

> Why does my she-advowson fly
> Incumbency?

The dexterity with which he sets in motion the interplay between visual imagery and the non-visual connotations of the words repays careful study. The terms 'advowson' and 'incumbency' transport us to a world of clerical patronage, of fat slumbers and comfortable livings where all is bland and decorous. Against this background the reluctance of the young woman to become the poet's mistress is, somehow, more amusing than in a more conventional setting, partly because jokes about clergymen and adultery are part of our humorous tradition. The expression 'she-advowson' is particularly apt and witty, suggesting to perfection the demureness of the young woman who displays the modesty normally expected of future incumbents. The play upon the technical and the root meanings of incumbency is sharpened by the hint of two visual images—the parson being inducted with due solemnity and the girl hesitating before her initiation into the rites of Venus. This brilliantly equivocal use of language and of imagery is a perfect example, in miniature, of the way in which a poet who knows his job will employ visual and non-visual images in the correct proportion, using the visual to focus more sharply the complex of experience which he is presenting, but permitting the ripples of meaning to extend into the farthest reaches of our minds.

Donne's image of the twin compasses, which seems predominantly visual, proves, on closer examination, to be compounded of both visual and symbolic elements, the latter, although less obvious, being even more significant and essential than the former. He is meditating upon the eternal problem of lovers, the separateness of two beings who would be one:

If they be two, they are two so
   As stiffe twin compasses are two,
Thy soule the fixt foot, makes no show
   To move, but doth if the other doe.

And though it in the center sit,
   Yet when the other far doth rome,
It leanes and hearkens after it,
   And growes erect, as that comes home.

Such wilt thou be to mee, who must
   Like th' other foot, obliquely runne;
Thy firmness makes my circle just,
   And makes me end, where I begunne.

These lines are deeply satisfying, but I doubt whether many readers see in their mind's eye every stage of the geometrical operation which Donne has chosen to depict. The purpose of the imagery is to introduce us to the perfect world of mathematics, that world into which Wordsworth in the 1790's sought to escape, since in it 'the disturbances of space and time find no admission'. Seventeenth-century poets frequently employ the image of the circle as a symbol of completion, and Donne's object is to make us aware of the union that can exist between lovers who find, in complete mutual sympathy, a self-sufficient world where all is harmony. Luckily for Donne, the fact that we still use compasses in our mathematical lessons enables us to take the image in our stride, and our attention is not distracted by our having to look up an illustration of an obsolete piece of equipment in order to get the drift of the passage. We are, therefore, free to concentrate upon the meaning of the lines which lies beneath the decorative ingenuity of the image.

A quatrain by Isaac Watts may be compared with the opening lines of a poem by George Herbert, both passages being examples of the way in which an apparently visual image conceals a multiplicity of symbolic meanings:

Why should we tremble to convey
   Their Bodies to the Tomb?
There the dear Flesh of Jesus lay
   And left a long Perfume.
                        Watts

I got me flowers to straw Thy way,
I pluck'd me boughs off many a tree,
But thou wast up at break of day,
And brought'st Thy sweets along with Thee.
                                        Herbert

Without the images of the Flesh, the Tomb, the flowers, and the boughs the lines would not vibrate with the warmth and light that animate them, yet all these images are meant to point beyond themselves to a state of apprehension in which mental pictures are drowned in the great flood of awareness that bathes our whole being.

Robert Browning, at his best, is a master of significant imagery which is both exact yet allusive:

Only, one little sight, one plant,
    Woods have in May, that starts up green
Save a sole streak which, so to speak,
    Is spring's blood, spilt its leaves between,—

That they might spare; a certain wood
    Might miss the plant; their loss were small:
But I,—whene'er the leaf grows there,
    Its drop comes from my heart, that's all.

The vivid picture of the green leaf streaked with blood is both an exquisite piece of descriptive writing and a beautifully appropriate symbol of Browning's grief for the friend who had died in the previous spring. Even the spring sheds its blood, for pain accompanies growth, and Browning has chosen his imagery to make us aware of the sadness which is inseparable from joy, of the unsuspected affinities between contraries which are hinted at in the title of the poem, 'May and Death'.

Tennyson achieved a tremendous degree of concentration in the line:

Now lies the earth all Danaë to the stars

and it is tempting to regard this line simply as a visual image of unusual brilliance. It is, in fact, not altogether satisfactory if we insist upon visualizing it with literal exactitude, since the metaphor is not, pictorially, beyond reproach. Danaë was a young girl confined within a tower by her father, and is not an entirely suitable pictorial equivalent for earth, which cannot be confined in a tower and which is seldom visualized as a young girl. Yet all such trifling objections are swept away by the overpowering force of this image. Wherein does its potency reside?

Tennyson seems to have been fascinated by the idea of a woman waiting to be possessed by her lover, and by the emotional tension which is generated in an atmosphere of expectancy. The coming of dawn, of death, of a lover, excited his senses to a pitch of remarkable acuteness, inspiring him to write with unusual poignancy and perceptiveness. The image of Danaë conveys, with matchless skill, the warm passiveness of a summer's evening which seems to sink deep into the veins of a girl whom love has softened and awakened, and whose being is irradiated by the light of the stars. I suspect, also, that Tennyson's Danaë sprang from a memory buried deep in the poet's mind. Titian's Danaë sums up in herself the full opulence of Renaissance sensuality, and part of Tennyson's nature longed passionately for the untrammelled splendour of paganism. There was an even more personal reason why the image of Danaë should recur to the poet; Hallam's last letter to his friend had referred to Titian: 'I wish you could see his Danaë. Do you just write as perfect a Danaë.' We cannot tell whether Tennyson remembered his friend's injunction, but the image of Danaë is so laden with tenderness and passion that he may well have been inspired to create it by the memory of his friend, the beauty of the figure from classical legend and Renaissance art acquiring a deeper import as it ceased to be a myth from a book and became a living presence that recalled the most profound emotional experience in the poet's life.

A skilful poet will employ colour imagery either to sharpen the outlines of what he is trying to depict or to evoke a set of responses heavily charged with emotion. W. B. Yeats's commentary on two lines by Burns is not invalidated by the fact that he slightly misquotes them:

> There are no lines with more melancholy beauty than these by Burns—
>> The white moon is setting behind the white wave,
>> And Time is setting with me O!
>
> and these lines are perfectly symbolical.[1] Take from them the whiteness of

---

[1] The lines should read:
> The wan moon is setting ayont the white wave,
> And time is setting with me, oh!
>
> 'Open the Door to Me, Oh.'

the moon and of the wave, whose relation to the setting of Time is too subtle for the intellect, and you take from them their beauty. But, when all are together, moon and wave and whiteness and setting Time and the last melancholy cry, they evoke an emotion which cannot be evoked by any other arrangement of colours and sounds and forms.[1]

More than one poet has found in the colour white a symbol of loneliness and separation, of infinite remoteness tinged with bewilderment:

> Nurse, O my love is slain, I saw him go
> O'er the white Alps alone
>
> > Donne

> O dear white children, casual as birds,
> Playing among the ruined languages.
>
> > Auden

> Shower down thy love, O burning bright! for
> > one night or the other night
> Will come the Gardener in white, and
> > gathered flowers are dead, Yasmin!
>
> > Flecker

> When cometh Jack Frost? the children ask.
> Shall they clasp a comet in their fists?
> Not till, from high and low, their dust
> Sprinkles in children's eyes a long last sleep
> And dusk is crowded with the children's ghosts
> Shall a white answer echo from the rooftops.
>
> > Dylan Thomas

In all these examples we both perceive with our eyes and understand with our hearts the whiteness and the melancholy which inseparably cling to the image raised up before us.

Once we have grasped the double nature of the image we shall begin to understand that, for some poets, it may be the germinating seed from which a poem buds and flowers, just as, for poets more richly endowed with the auditory imagination that is fired by a single phrase or by a half-heard rhythmical dance and fury empty of words, the origin of a poem may lie in a sentence or in a cadence divorced of meaning.

Edwin Muir has told us how his poem 'The Riders' first came into his mind:

---

[1] *Ideas of Good and Evil.*

THE FIRE AND THE FOUNTAIN

> At the dead centre of the boundless plain
> Does our way end? Our horses pace and pace
> Like steeds forever labouring on a shield,
> Keeping their solitary heraldic courses.

These four opening lines suddenly presented themselves to him and the whole poem was built around the central image of the horses:

> The Horses, as I see them, are an image of human time, the invisible body of humanity on which we ride for a little while.... Yet the steed—mankind in its course through time—is mortal and the rider is immortal. I stated this belief tentatively in the poem, because it was written in a mood of unusual dejection. The painful emotion in the poem comes from a simultaneous feeling of immortality and mortality; and particularly from the feeling that we, as immortal spirits, are imprisoned in a very small and from all appearances fortuitously selected length of time.... I was not aware, or at least fully aware of all these implications when I wrote the poem.[1]

The last sentence is of particular interest, for it suggests that an image may develop according to its own inner logic and that, like the Angels who guided Blake, it may gradually take charge of the poem, compelling the half-reluctant poet to utter the words that demand to be spoken. Even when the poet begins to write a poem with a clear idea of what he wants to say, he may discover that the image which he has summoned to aid him insists upon taking control of the entire operation, much as the barbarian chieftains called in by unwise kings to act as mercenaries save the threatened kingdoms but depose the monarchs. W. B. Yeats began to write a poem about the inevitability of a violent annunciation that would usher in a new era now that liberal democracy was exhausted. He started to play with the metaphor of Leda and the Swan, but while he was writing the poem the image banished the politics, and the result was that masterpiece of sensual prophecy, 'Leda and the Swan'.

Goethe said that 'one must allow the images to form with all their associations before one criticises', and the wise poet knows that only after permitting the images to pass to and fro, weaving what patterns they will, does he begin tentatively to fashion his poem and to move 'the sleeping images of things towards the light'.[2]

Some writers have maintained that all true poems grow organically from images, and that images are never to be used merely as

<hr>

[1] Gwendolen Murphy, *The Modern Poet*, pp. 168-9.   [2] The phrase is Dryden's.

a decoration of a theme already chosen. Dryden's account of the poetic process, with its implicit division of form and matter, is dismissed as offensively crude: 'Expression is, in plain English, the bawd of her sister, the design . . . she clothes, she dresses her up, she paints her, she makes her appear more lovely than she is.'[1] Sir Herbert Read goes so far as to assert: 'It is not a case of the mind in need of expression choosing between two ways—one poetry, the other prose. There is no choice for the particular state of mind in which poetry originates.'[2] This is plainly untrue: poets as diverse as Virgil, Jonson, Pope, Goldsmith, Coleridge, Tennyson, Browning, Rossetti, and Yeats have all drafted a prose version of what they wanted to say and have later set it out in a metrical pattern. Even Hopkins, who, on one occasion, deplored what he called the Castalian or Parnassian style, 'that is the language of poetry draping prose rhetoric', toyed with the idea of making prose drafts, as Virgil had cast the *Aeneid*, 'to help on my flagging and almost spent powers'.[3]

Our contemporary interest in the unconscious mind, in Freudian symbols and in Jungian archetypes, leads us to place a disproportionate emphasis upon the dialectical interplay of images, for the unconscious regions of the mind express their intimations in symbolical pictorial forms. The cult of imagery among poets and critics during the past twenty-five years has grown increasingly perfervid, rarefied, and unbalanced. Kathleen Raine, for instance, believes that the highest type of poetry must, like the later poems of Blake, concern itself with the 'pre-verbal interplay of symbol and the personified potencies of the eternal human archetypes'.[4] She admits that in order to appreciate such poetry we must lay aside the poetic habits of the last two thousand years. Before we jettison all verse from Homer to Yeats we may be permitted to ask whether poetry, which is necessarily composed of words alone, can depict any kind of pre-verbal interplay; and we may legitimately doubt whether poetry is concerned solely, or even primarily, with eternal human archetypes or with the primordial aspects of symbolic forms. It is equally concerned with the actual world of incarnate human beings who live and

---

1 Cited by W. H. Auden, *The Enchafèd Flood*, p. 47.
2 *Collected Essays in Literary Criticism* (1951), p. 42.
3 *Letters*, i, pp. 159 and 170.
4 *William Blake*, p. 29.

move and suffer in historical time. The illumination of this world, 'the outer life of telegrams and anger', as E. M. Forster calls it, the transmutation of ordinary feelings into poetry, and the passionate exercise of sinewy, conscious reason are as much the task of poetry as the exploitation of the obscure states of being that lie concealed in the recesses of the psyche.

Our contemporary demand for lyrical intensity and for imagery that shall be complex, powerful, and evocative, rather than for the leisurely unfolding of a theme, is responsible for our tendency to regard imagery as the mainspring of all poetry and to misrepresent the way in which it functions. We stress the infinite resonance of Blake's images in:

> Ah, Sunflower! weary of time

but forget that his address 'To Mercy, Pity, Peace and Love' is pure philosophical argument that dispenses almost entirely with imagery. We rightly admire the superb assurance with which T. S. Eliot concentrates an epic theme into the kaleidoscopic images of *The Waste Land* but fail to observe that in the Dantesque encounter with the ghostly figure before dawn in *Little Gidding* the Symbolist technique is discarded and the bare bones of statement replace the musical suggestiveness and the imagistic logic of the earlier work. In some of Hardy's best poems there are no vivid images that play upon our nerves; instead, we are given a series of flat, almost banal, utterances in a calm, neutral tone of voice.[1] Such imagery as Hardy employs, far from being the germinal seed from which the poem grows, serves merely to illustrate the theme that he has chosen as the starting-point for his meditations:

> A cry from the green-grained sticks of the fire
>   Made me gaze where it seemed to be:
> 'Twas my own voice talking therefrom to me
> On how I had walked when my sun was higher,
>   My heart in its arrogancy.

Then follows the poet's humble recognition of his own failure and inadequacy, the poem ending with a quiet, unaffected confession of a truth so commonplace and time-honoured that few living poets would have the courage to avow it in such naked simplicity:

[1] Cf. Cecil Day Lewis's analysis of Hardy's poetry in *The Poetic Image*, pp. 150–3.

'You taught not that which you set about',
  Said my own voice talking to me;
'That the greatest of things is Charity. . . .'
And the sticks burnt low, and the fire went out,
  And my voice ceased talking to me.

Robert Graves is another contemporary poet who, on occasions, uses imagery with the utmost economy, relying upon other poetic devices for his effects. In one of his most ingenious and beautiful poems, *The Thieves*, he sets his witty reflections dancing to a gay and delicate music:

Lovers in the act dispense
With such meum-teum sense
As might warningly reveal
What they must not pick or steal,
And their nostrum is to say:
I and you are both away.

The remaining stanzas continue to play with such concepts, the dry, quasi-legal phrases glowing with warmth, wit, and tenderness, but of imagery there is little trace.

Nevertheless, we may readily admit that the command of imagery, whether visual or non-visual, is one of the distinguishing marks by which we can recognize a poet. We have learned, moreover, that the germinating properties of images are considerable and that they rival the seminal powers of rhythm. We can even say, with some confidence, that the origin of most poems worthy of the name will be either in an image or in a rhythm, rather than in a concept, a thought, or a feeling. Can we explore the genesis of the poem still more deeply, venturing into the regions where the image and the rhythm which determine the shape of the poem themselves have sprung? It is worth making the effort to penetrate the obscurity which shrouds them, since, if we can discover something of the nature of these images and rhythms which mould the poem, we may understand the nature of the poet's task as he struggles to subdue those intimations which have come to him, and which torment him until he has obeyed them. Only then, like the Furies which haunted T. S. Eliot's most tragic hero, will they reveal themselves as the bright angels.[1]

---

[1] Cf. *The Family Reunion*.

Chapter Six

WHEN we first plunge into the world of imagery it is as though we were in a luxuriant tropical forest, where myriads of flowers, trees, and tangled vegetation threaten to overwhelm us with their dazzling colour and heavy perfume. Gradually, however, we begin to distinguish a pattern in the forest, to recognize the members of the same species of flowers, to separate the freakish growth from the normal plant, to appreciate the minute variations in texture and in shade which distinguish one blossom from another. In short (to drop the metaphor), we can hope to study images in poetry with a fair chance of discovering their origin, their nature, and their inter-relationships. We can reasonably ask such questions as: why do certain images recur in poetry, century after century; why are some images used extensively for a decade or two, only to lapse into oblivion; is there any common source of images upon which all poets can draw, or is an image the expression of a poet's private sensibility?

Pick up any collection of Elizabethan love-lyrics and you will notice that the same images are repeated *ad nauseam* in the poets' description of their mistresses. The simple explanation of this wearisome repetition of conventional epithets is that literary fashion, then as now, dictated the type of imagery most congenial to the poetry-reading public of the day, and to the most influential patrons of the Elizabethan poets. John Hoskins, writing about 1599, put the matter succinctly: 'It is true that we study according to the predominancy of courtly inclinations: whilst mathematics were in request, all our similitudes came from lines, circles and angles; whilst moral philosophy is now a while spoken of, it is rudeness not to be sententious.'[1] We tend to ignore such robustly cynical explanations, partly because we consider them too facile to account for the proliferation of complex imagery, but still more because we are reluctant to admit that anything so trivial as fashion can determine the course of poetic development, forgetting that fashion is very strong and that poets, like other

[1] Cited by F. W. Bateson, *English Poetry*, p. 150.

men, want to be in the swim. It is difficult to resist the lure of slang in, say, a Mess or a school, and the lingo affected by literary men, chic and sophisticated as it will often be, is likely to prove irresistible to poets who want to be in the fashion or who, to put the matter less crudely, desire to show their awareness of contemporary sensibility.

Every age has its own fashion in poetic imagery and in poetic form. The Elizabethans laboriously constructed their centuries of sonnets, sugaring their verse with images derived from Ovid and from the more luscious portions of the Old Testament. The Jacobean preoccupation with skulls, charnel-houses, and decomposition gave way to the Metaphysical fondness for imagery which drew upon scholastic learning and the new science in equal proportions. It would be wearisome to plod through English literary history in an effort to discover which set of images was dominant at any given period, and it is enough to note briefly the rapidly changing fashions of the past century and a half. The new range of imagery explored by the first Romantics quickly became part of the poetic landscape, only to be superseded by a more startling mode of expression. Mario Praz has analysed this necrophilous mania, which produced a crop of highly coloured but fundamentally boring images, in his book *The Romantic Agony*, a mania which spread from France to England, appearing in a less virulent form in the poetry of the eighteen-eighties and nineties, only to expire when, after the trial of Oscar Wilde, the cosier aspects of nature began to gain in popularity at the expense of marionettes, skulls, painted harlots, and flagellated nuns. The prickly landscape of T. S. Eliot's waste-land ousted the lusher pastures of the Georgians, remaining fashionable until the early nineteen-thirties. Apart from a few daring images, smuggled into English poetry from French Surrealist verse and the paintings of Dali, the new set of images was primarily industrial, clinical, and avowedly contemporary, designed to illustrate the pathological aberrations of a dying capitalistic order, rapidly disintegrating beneath the threat of war and the compulsions of its own neurotic longings. The verse of the thirties is full of pylons, arterial roads, frontiers, laboratories, machinery, and the paraphernalia of a cosmopolitan, unhealthy culture. H. G. Porteus satirically jotted down a series of fashion notes on the trend of poetry in the thirties: 'Verse will be worn longer this season and rather red. More vocatives will be used, with verbs invariably imperative. Articles definite and indefinite will be almost entirely dropped.'[1] Inspired by the powerful genius of Dylan Thomas, the next generation of poets crammed their verses with the juice and joy of heady images—blood, loins, sinews, elemental symbols, and Freudian allusions, an olla podrida where sexuality and religiosity simmered and spluttered.

It would be foolish to suppose that fashion and conscious imitation, by themselves, account for the characteristic imagery of any given period. Even if we assume that fashion in poetic images is a mere replica of fashion in dress we are not much farther forward in our inquiry. Fashion in dress is directed by professional designers; it does not grow of itself; it reflects the ever-varying contours of economics, politics, morality, aesthetic taste. To point to fashion is to pronounce a word but to evade an explanation.

Fashions in poetic imagery become widespread in one of two ways. A great poet, or a dominant figure who has the power of impressing his contemporaries, adopts a number of images which seem to him appropriate for conveying what he has to say. His disciples persuade themselves that these images in some way represent the age and express the central truths of the times, or, more simply, realize that they can be employed as sophisticated clichés to smarten up their somewhat threadbare poetic offerings. Dylan Thomas lets off a fusilade of fireworks which emblazon upon the sky the portrait of the artist as a young dog and, within a few years, we are asked to admire the antics of his fleas. Occasionally, a minor poet, or a group of minor poets, hits upon a set of images which are then taken up by the generality of poets. A few Elizabethans delve into the erotic passages of the Scriptures which have so conveniently been translated for the edification of Protestants, and a new array of exciting images is at once available to aid the poets in their exploration of that elaborate sensuality which the Renaissance had depicted and to which the Elizabethans responded with untrammelled vigour. A great poet writing in an era when a particular vogue in imagery becomes extensive may deliberately go against the stream and deride the

[1] Cited by Michael Roberts, *Critique of Poetry*, p. 222.

mode. Shakespeare, obviously wearied by the cloying similes automatically churned out by his versifying contemporaries, gives us, contemptuously, a catalogue of clichés:

> My mistress' eyes are nothing like the sun;
> Coral is far more red than her lips' red:
> If snow be white, why then her breasts are dun;
> If hairs be wires, black wires grow on her head.

In his later plays he seems mistrustful of all commonplace images, and dislocates language in order to rescue it from the flabbiness inseparable from conventional image-making. When he wishes to portray the desirability of a woman, he deliberately avoids the use of a descriptive simile and gives us a searing image:

> ... let not the virgin's cheek
> Make soft thy trenchant sword; for those milk-paps,
> That through the window-bars bore at men's eyes,
> Are not within the leaf of pity writ.

Some great poets, on the contrary, pick up the current coin of imagery and stamp it with the impress of their own burning force and integrity. Pope drew upon the Augustan commonplaces, which he then transformed as completely as Mozart transfigured the unremarkable themes which were floating about the musical world of his day. Baudelaire made use of the common properties available to any fashionable writer in the Romantic swim, and gave to the symbols which he acquired a tragic import.

No matter whether the originator of a fashion in imagery be a major or a minor poet, we still have to discover both why he selected this particular type of imagery and why it impressed itself so vividly upon his contemporaries. Similarly, we must attempt to account for such changes in poetic form as the rise of blank verse, its decline, its surrender to the heroic couplet, and its subsequent return to favour when the heroic couplet has been discarded. Faced by such problems, and realizing that any explanation which attributes fundamental revolutions in poetry to the caprice of fashion must be superficial, some critics have maintained that the imagery and the rhythms of poetry are determined by the spirit of the age. Marxist writers, more radical and more precise, attempt to correlate the changing forms of poetry with the varying pattern of economics and politics, regarding the characteristics of verse at any one moment as symptoms of the morbid condition of society.

The spirit of the age is one of those convenient abstractions without which we should be unable to disguise our ignorance and bewilderment. Asked to account for the rise of Counter-Reformation piety, the style of Baroque art, and the savagery of the Thirty Years War, we can explain that they are all diverse manifestations of the spirit of the age. It is only when we try to trace the precise relationships of these historical phenomena to one another and to their supposedly common source that we begin to discover unexpected complications, awkward facts, fortuitous events, and inexplicable sequences of events that make nonsense of our symmetrical generalizations. We may even come to doubt whether the spirit of the age is not the name that we give to a complex of forces too subtle for us to analyse. Nor have we the right to assume that poetry and the other arts passively reflect current events and preconceptions. Roger Fry warned us that the relationship between Art and Life was less simple than it appeared to be on the surface. Baroque art, we are told, may be regarded as the visible expression of Counter-Reformation piety, but it is equally legitimate to hold that this piety was partly induced by a contemplation of that Baroque art which sprang inevitably from the flowering of certain elements latent in the painting and in the architecture of the Italian Renaissance. One of the earliest examples of Czech Baroque, the Church of Our Lady of Victory, in the Lower Town, Prague, was originally built in 1611–13 for German Lutherans and dedicated to the Holy Trinity. To imagine that the spirit of the age determines the forms of art is to forget that these very forms are part of the infinitely complex and elaborate patterns of behaviour, thought, and feeling which constitute this spirit, and that without these minute particulars the abstraction would never have been conceived.

Moreover, it is all too easy to claim that a poet is conveying the spirit of his age when he is merely flattering the self-esteem of his contemporaries by reproducing their superficial ideas and titillating their emotions. A commentary in verse upon men's current interests, peppered with slick and modish imagery, stands a fair chance of being hailed as brilliant contemporary poetry.

G. W. Stonier put his finger on the weakness common to all those who desperately strive to be contemporary, when he criticized the imagery that was flaunted by a bunch of war-poets: 'For them a primrose isn't a yellow primrose, but an early shell-burst in the spring offensive.'[1]

Having expressed our scepticism about the influence of the spirit of the age, we can the more readily admit that the force of an image or of a rhythm may be fully experienced only if we understand the historical context in which it is set. Donne's rapturous invocation of his mistress:

> O my America, my new-found Land

loses its significance unless we apprehend what America stood for in the late sixteenth century, unless we can recapture the excitement aroused by the tales of a fabulous land glittering with gold and redolent with spices. Shakespeare's reference to

> Bare ruin'd choirs where late the sweet birds sang

takes on a richer poignancy when we reflect that the England of his day was strewn with the wrecks of abbeys and of monasteries, their inhabitants martyred, or comfortably ensconced in fat livings, their altars desolated, their music silenced. W. H. Auden uses a remarkable image to portray the neuroses by which men of the twentieth century are haunted:

> Loss is their shadow-wife, Anxiety
> Receives them like a grand hotel.

The associations aroused by the image of a grand hotel in our day serve to emphasize the terrible emptiness and impersonality which are laying waste the world. For the grand hotel is the meeting-place of rootless cosmopolitans, of business executives making a round trip, of innumerable sub-committees engaged in abortive conferences, of international organizations trying to cope with that perfect symbol of twentieth-century man—the refugee. The image of the grand hotel both illuminates the contemporary situation and draws sustenance from it.

T. S. Eliot's earlier poems attempt to evoke, by means of cunningly chosen images and rhythms, the state of Western civilization in the Jazz Age, with its vulgarities, its nostalgia, its

[1] *New Statesman and Nation*, 31 July 1943.

frantic seeking after novelty that sprang from a sense of frustration and insecurity. In *Four Quartets* the effectiveness of the imagery and the rhythm no longer depends upon our awareness of contemporary modes of thought and feeling, even the references to the London tubes and to the raiding bombers being cloaked in shadowy periphrases. These great poems are, in a sense, meditations upon the age-old elements of Air, Earth, Water, and Fire, the recurring imagery and the deep rhythms of the verse designedly leading us away from a contemplation of the world ruled by clocks and chronometers to an exploration of a timeless state of being. These quartets belong indisputably to our period, are, indeed, the crown of its poetic achievement, but their imagery does not reflect the spirit of the age. This fact may embolden us to go one step farther and declare that the relationship between poetic images and the spirit of the age cannot be adequately described by any simple formula; that the spirit of the age, though a useful concept, is no more than a convenient shorthand term for a bewildering variety of phenomena and that the poet in his quest for images will seek them and accept them wherever they are to be found. The myth that the poet is the servant of the timeless Muse liberates us from the stultifying provincialism which would make of him a superior journalist, dependent upon the contemporary situation for his material and for his imagery.

We may now consider the Marxist attempt to correlate a poet's imagery and rhythm with the condition of society at a particular moment in the historical process. Marx himself once stated that 'certain periods of highest development in art stand in no direct connection with the general development of society',[1] but the orthodox Marxist teaching about the arts postulates a direct connexion between the structure of society and the artistic products of the time, regarding the latter as symptomatic of the particular stage which society has reached in the dialectical process. Marxism endeavours to explain every activity of human life by relating it to the class-structure and to the necessities of the class-struggle. Poetry is valued and appraised as a pointer to the underlying reality, much as a patient's temperature chart is studied as an indication of the course which his disease has run.

---

[1] Cited by Edmund Wilson, *The Triple Thinkers*, p. 190 (1932 ed.).

Of small value in itself, it confirms the diagnosis and adds to our knowledge of the cycle through which the disease has passed. The Marxist attempt to apply its philosophy of history to all phenomena has enabled it to offer a salutary challenge to older and more complacent interpretations of poetry, painting, and the other arts. It has compelled non-Marxists to abandon the idea that the development of poetry can be studied without reference to the changing modes of thought and behaviour in society, just as it has forced philosophers to examine afresh the relationship between the elaboration of a metaphysical system and the pressure of economic necessity upon the structure of society. The strength of Marxism as an intellectual weapon lies in its power to make sweeping generalizations which appear to give meaning to a vast array of facts hitherto unrelated and unexplained. A theory that can throw light upon genetics, poetry, chess, and women's fashions has an obvious appeal for all those who desire assurance that everything can be explained by reference to one overriding cause. The Marxist creed is more dogmatic than Catholicism, more pervasive and minute in its application to daily life than Hinduism, more exciting in its apocalyptic message than the wildest revelations of British Israelitism. Its weakness is that, like all dogmas which seek to find one simple cause for a variety of complex phenomena, it ignores or deliberately brushes aside all those little inconvenient facts that do not fit into the preconceived pattern. Darwin used to note down every fact which appeared to invalidate any of his hypotheses, recognizing that human fallibility and impatience will contrive to push awkward considerations out of the way, corrupting even the memory so that it loses what the scheming brain does not wish it to retain. Marxism regards such a scrupulous perusal of evidence as typical bourgeois liberalism, a vain pursuit of academic truth, no less ridiculous than bourgeois conceptions of impartial justice or bourgeois preoccupation, in the arts, with a sterile formalism. Sir George Clark has shown the consequences for historical thinking of applying Marxist technique to the study of that Scientific Movement which was the great contribution of seventeenth-century England to European thought and behaviour.[1] Our present concern, however, is with the Marxist

[1] *Science and Social Welfare in the Age of Newton.*

endeavour to account for the efflorescence of poetry, and for the changes in style, in rhythm, and in imagery which it undergoes, by reference to the fundamental alterations in society which occur from time to time.

Robert Graves, though never a Marxist, advanced a Marxist argument in an essay on *The Future of Poetry* (1926). After contrasting the two systems of prosody most commonly found in English poetry, he endeavours to show their relationship to the political systems from which they are deemed to have sprung:

> Syllable-counting is a principle of Continental prosody imposed upon English by the Norman-French invaders; in the earlier native prosody the metre was determined by the stress-centres of the line and the time-intervals between them. This earlier prosody has never been abandoned by popular poets and is frequently used by poets of culture. Its most familiar use is in nursery rhyme and country ballads. . . . The two principles of prosody correspond in a marked way with contrary habits of life and political principles: the calm, feudal principle of pre-ordained structure, law and order, culture spreading downward from the King and peers;—the communal principle, threatening the feudal scheme from below—impulsive, emotional, headless, unforeseeable. . . . The future of English prosody depends on the political outcome of the class warfare now declared.[1]

We may be grateful for the new light thrown upon English prosody by this generalization without accepting Graves's theory in its entirety. The revolt of Hopkins against the limitations imposed on poetry by conventional metres was not an outcome of his impulsive, emotional, headless, unforeseeable insurrection against a hierarchical social system. His whole life was one long sacrifice to the principle of Catholic order, and he regarded his metrical innovations as a recall to a stricter art of poetry, and as a protection against licence in versification. He felt that certain revolutionary changes in prosody were essential if the poetic language of his day were to be rescued from deteriorating into artificiality and triviality. Changes in prosody depend less upon the outcome of class warfare than upon the measures taken by poets to preserve the vitality of a language which it is their duty and their privilege to guard.

The most learned and thorough-going advocacy of Marxism as the key to a true understanding of poetry is to be found in Christopher Caudwell's *Illusion and Reality*. All changes in the

---

[1] Reprinted in *The Common Asphodel*, pp. 52–54.

formal pattern of verse and in the imagery employed by poets in different epochs are directly related to the varying manifestations of the class struggle which never sleeps or dies. In order to emphasize his thesis he draws up a comparative table in which, side by side with a summary of the successive phases of the historical process, he epitomizes the technical characteristics of the poetry written in each phase, and indicates how these stylistic features are derived from the underlying reality of the economic death-grapple. His dogmatism enables him to present his conclusions with supreme assurance. Elizabethan blank verse is depicted as the inevitable mode of expression of poets living in a brilliant society, where the Renaissance Prince, surrounded by a dazzling court, governed as a tyrant conscious of his strength and nobility: 'The iambic rhythm, expressing the heroic nature of the bourgeois illusion in terms of the ancient world, is allowed to flower luxuriantly and naturally.' The squalor of the Jacobean age is immediately reflected in the verse of Shakespeare's successors: 'Blank verse (Webster) portrays the decline of princeliness and loses its noble undertone.' Finally, in the late seventeenth century, the shift in political alignments causes a fundamental change in poetry in which blank verse is superseded by a new form: 'There is an alliance of the bourgeoisie with the aristocracy instead of the people; and the court returns, but no longer in the form of the absolute prince. The prince is now subject to "reason". . . . Poetry indicates its readiness to compromise by moving within the bounds of the heroic couplet.'[1]

The relationships between the prince, the people, the aristocracy, and the *bourgeoisie* in the seventeenth century are still being investigated by historians. Similarly, there is no simple equation by which we can illustrate the interaction of such diverse forces as Puritanism, Capitalism, and the Scientific Movement. Crude references to alliances between the *bourgeoisie* and the people are, as an explanation of seventeenth-century history, as much a caricature of the truth as *Little Arthur's History of England*. Even assuming that Caudwell's summary of a century of bewildering change is valid, can we accept the conclusions which he draws from it about English poetry?

The chief objection to his method is that it tells us nothing

---

[1] Caudwell op. cit., p. 127.

about poetry that we really want to know. The iambic rhythm of Elizabethan blank verse is said to express the heroic nature of the late sixteenth-century bourgeois illusion, just as Webster's blank verse portrays the Messianic Prince in his decline from glory. A cursory study of blank verse from 1550 to 1620 reveals that, far from its being a static form corresponding to an unchanging bourgeois illusion, every decade witnesses a significant variation in the music and the movement of blank verse. The early stiffness gradually gives way to a new suppleness; Marlowe learns how to make the unrhymed iambic pentameter flow with a musical grace reminiscent of the cadences in Spenser; Shakespeare produces, in the space of twenty-five years, a cycle of plays in which he executes almost every conceivable variation upon the basic form within which he chooses to work. After his death, blank verse as a dramatic form begins to disintegrate, but there are important differences in the styles of Webster, Massinger, and Tourneur which forbid us to lump all Jacobean verse under one heading and to ascribe all its characteristics to one simple cause. Unless we can point to specific changes in the political and economic structure of Elizabethan England and demonstrate how blank verse reflects them, Caudwell's thesis helps us neither to understand nor to enjoy the poetry of that epoch.[1]

The prime defect of Marxist literary criticism is its failure to perceive, or unwillingness to admit, that poetry buds and flowers according to its own inner necessity. If we seek to discover the reasons for the rise and fall of a verse form, or for the employment by poets of a particular set of images, we shall not gain much enlightenment from a perusal of sociological trends. We shall have a better chance of understanding such questions if we examine the curve of poetic tradition and seek to estimate the way in which it modifies the direction of the poet's individual talent.

Poets, like statesmen, can neither choose the moment of their birth nor select the problems which confront them as they attain maturity. They have to make the best of a more or less bad job,

---

[1] There was a minor Industrial Revolution in Elizabeth's reign which Caudwell might have mentioned, but it is an impossible task to correlate this movement with the development of blank verse.

fighting against unpropitious circumstances and accepting, if need be, a barren legacy from their predecessors. Since their perennial concern is with language, their style will be partly determined by the state and by the resources of the language at the particular moment of history when they begin to write. We cannot hope to understand a poet's use of language unless we try to imagine the specific urgent tasks and problems with which he is faced at the time of composition. Poetry is a difficult game which, like other games, must be perpetually renovated by new tactics if it is not to grow cumbrous and ossified; and, like every human activity, it has its proper rhythm. This rhythm of question and answer, challenge and response, unswervingly obeys its own laws, moves at its own speed, is unique in each one of its manifestations, and cannot be explained by reference to any external historical process.

We may now consider the way in which a poetic form or a set of poetic images comes to be adopted by a poet, or by a whole generation of poets. There arrives a moment in the history of the language when poets find that the current modes of expression are no longer adequate. The orange is sucked dry, the soil is exhausted, the parrot's cry has become unbearable—employ what metaphor you will to express the discontent and nausea which overcome the poet when he tries to work in the stale atmosphere of the prevailing forms. Donne, stifled by the insipid Petrarchian convention, not only stuffs his verse full of the invigorating new images pilfered from the scientific hypotheses of his day, but invents over forty stanzaic forms, driven on by the compelling need to obey the new, furious impulse which has animated the rhythm of English poetry. Verlaine revolts against Parnassian marmoreal dignity and Tennysonian flatulence—'When he should have been heartbroken he was full of reminiscences'— because there is nothing more to say in the style perfected by his immediate predecessors. T. S. Eliot turns to Laforgue and to the Jacobeans in an endeavour to find a way through the blank wall of blank verse, and destroys a set of heroic verse couplets when Ezra Pound reminds him that there is no point in doing again what Pope has done once and for all. There must be a breaking-up of perfection by violence, as Hopkins saw; new poetry shocks us, in the words of Eliot, 'by its syntax more than by its sentiments', for versification 'is essentially a disturbance of the conventional language'.[1]

The poet seizes upon the new form, plays with it, holds it up to the light, experiments with it, and, finally, exhausts all its possibilities. The rate of development varies: the rondeau, the rondel, the villanelle, and the triolet cannot be exploited for long, whereas blank verse seems to yield something new and valuable for every generation. Comic verse forms appear to be subject to a similar law of decay, the limerick proliferating into fantastic shapes, until general weariness supervenes, and a nimble wit, tired also of turning out ballades, invents the clerihew which, after forty years' prosperity, shows signs of flagging vitality.

The development of blank verse from the middle of the sixteenth century onwards is a typical example of the way in which a verse form is explored by practitioners of the art of poetry. Marlowe and Shakespeare enlarged its range, Webster and the other Jacobeans stretched its resources to the very limits, until, by the reign of Charles I, it was no longer capable of responding to the efforts of any poet to whip it into life again. Other verse forms had to be sought if a dead end was to be avoided, forms which still retained their suppleness and vigour. Shakespeare himself could handle the heroic couplet with considerable skill (he puts a set into Iago's mouth), but was so busy finding out what he could do with blank verse that there was no temptation for him to conquer new territories. The later seventeenth-century writers, compelled by the logic of their art to abandon blank verse, searched for a new mode of expression to match their fresh range of interests and looked to France for guidance. Versailles, under its Catholic, absolutist prince, was, politically, economically, and socially, a far cry from bourgeois, Protestant, scientific London, but English poetry, at that particular stage of its development, needed the help of the French literary tradition to guide it out of an impasse. Freedom is, for the poet, the recognition of poetic necessity, and poetic necessity is not conditioned by

[1] F. O. Matthiessen, op. cit., p. 86. Victor Hugo boasted that he had dislocated the great ninny of an Alexandrine. He felt compelled to commit this outrage upon the classical Alexandrine because the time had come to destroy a magnificent form which, by its very perfection, was choking the growth of new poetic forms. Hugo was, as it happens, a political as well as a poetical revolutionary, but his onslaught upon the classical Alexandrine was in obedience to *poetic* logic.

economic determinism. Marxism, in its tortuous efforts to explain poetry in terms of bourgeois illusion, ignores the truth that poetry is not subservient to sociology but is governed by its own laws. This inner logic, which is extremely complex in its operation, is difficult to fathom but impossible to disregard if we desire to understand the nature of poetry. It springs from a series of tensions, from the interplay between the personal and the communal, the poet's temperamental affinities and the poetic tradition of his day, the imagery and the rhythms embedded in his own nature, and the archetypal images which persist in the order of the universe. Destroy this sense of tension and of paradox, as the Marxists desire to do, and you make nonsense of the complex pattern which we call poetry.

Some critics, reacting violently against the provincial superficiality of Marxist exegesis, have attempted to divorce poetry almost completely from sociology, removing it from the confines of historical time into the realms of eternal myth. G. M. Young has shown how 'themes float and drift from one age and language to another, and Nature contrives these correspondences'.[1] The suggestion is that certain themes continually recur because the universe and the human psyche have a structure which persists, unalterably and eternally, though superficial alterations in social and political forms may cloud our vision and prevent us from perceiving the unchanging reality. Some years before Jung had outlined his concept of archetypal patterns, W. B. Yeats spoke of a great memory which brings to men's minds profound images and enables our limited, shallow understandings to glimpse the source of all truth:

Any one who has any experience of any mystical state of the soul knows how there float up in the mind profound symbols, whose meaning, if indeed they do not delude one into the dream that they are meaningless, one does not perhaps understand for years. Nor I think has any one who has known that experience with any constancy, failed to find some day in some old book or on some old monument, a strange and intricate image, that had floated up before him, and to grow perhaps dizzy with the sudden conviction that our little memories are but a part of some great memory, that renews the world and men's thoughts age after age, and that our thoughts are not, as we suppose, the deep but a little foam upon the deep.[2]

[1] *Daylight and Champaign*, p. 275.
[2] *Essays*, p. 96. This passage, written in 1901, is cited in Hough, *The Last Romantics*, p. 229.

Jung's account of the process is more elaborate and systematic, but it does not differ essentially from Yeats's intuitive conviction that we are able to draw upon a great memory in order to enrich our insignificant personal memories. Jung believes that there exists a collective unconscious, in which great constellations of primordial images and of ancestral patterns of experience are for ever preserved. The poet who responds to the promptings of this collective unconscious is able to tap deep emotional sources, inaccessible to those unaware of the timeless archetypes that lie buried in the recesses of our mind.

Nor is it Jung alone who suggests that certain images possess an unchanging validity and significance capable of awakening emotional responses in men and women of all epochs. Freud's theories point to the existence of myths and of symbols which illuminate the universal structure of the human psyche. His emphasis is upon the individual rather than upon the collective unconscious, but, like Jung, he postulates the existence of certain recurring themes heavily charged with emotional significance.

If such speculations are valid, if, indeed, mysterious imprints and influences can be apprehended by poets of all ages, we may begin to understand why themes float and drift through time and space, awaiting the poet who shall embody them in the words of his poem. We shall recognize that such figures as Orestes, Oedipus, Hamlet, Faust, and Don Juan have the power to stir generation after generation because they are archetypal figures, mythical beings incorporating in their persons the basic truths of the human situation.

. We may go even further and claim that a similar truth resides in certain images, even, it may be, in certain rhythms, which correspond to the physiological nature of man and of the universe. C. S. Lewis reminds us that a metaphorical use of language will, if pursued to its logical conclusion, involve us in metaphysical speculation: 'It does follow that if those original equations (metaphors and images) . . . were from the beginning arbitrary and fanciful—if there is not, in fact, a kind of psycho-physical parallelism in the universe—then all our thinking is nonsensical.'[1] Those who believe in the theory of archetypes, like those who accept the Freudian interpretation of images, hold that the images

[1] *Rehabilitations*, p. 158.

of poetry, far from being arbitrary and fanciful, are chosen by inescapable necessity. Followers of Jung would claim that the poet is recognizing the racial memories, the personified potencies, and the visionary forms which lie submerged in the collective unconscious; Freudians would emphasize the compelling power of the images which stream through the obscure depths of every individual's mind.

Such concepts throw light upon the recurrence in poetry of themes and of images, and relate the pattern of images to the configurations of our mental existence. They explain why the images of Dali and of Surrealist poetry bear such a striking resemblance to the pictorial images by which the painter Bosch was obsessed. For, as Caudwell pointed out, the conviction held by Surrealists that they alone are completely free is a pathetic illusion, since the dictatorship of the unconscious mind is utterly rigid and constricting, and the range of images which it permits to emerge from its imprisoning darkness is distressingly limited. Certain kinds of mental aberration and of sexual disequilibrium appear to express themselves in a few, repetitive symbols, as if they were bound to these images by some inexplicable elective affinities. W. H. Auden has revealed the significance of such primordial images as the Sea, the City, and the Desert, a significance which is discovered by poets rather than invented by their idiosyncratic use of language.[1] When Auden himself writes the line:

> Rise in the wind, my great big serpent

he is employing an image whose sexual connotations, emphasized by Freudians, have long been recognized. Eve's temptation by the serpent has its parallel in the seduction of Persephone by Jupiter in the guise of a serpent; Apollo destroyed the serpent personified by Python; Saturn was depicted as a serpent biting its own tail. In Jewish, Greek, and Mexican mythology the serpent was used as a symbol of fire, death, time, sex, and generation.[2]

Similarly, the images of roses, apples, lilies, spices, and water continually recur, bearing an unequivocal significance:

---

[1] *The Enchafèd Flood.*

[2] Sir Herbert Read has called attention to Shelley's fondness for the image of a serpent interlocked with an eagle, and suggests that it may indicate the presence of some form of castration complex. *The True Voice of Feeling*, p. 251.

Cherries kissing as they grow
  And inviting men to taste,
Apples even ripe below,
    Winding gently to the waist:
      All love's emblems, and all cry:
      'Ladies, if not plucked, we die!'

                Fletcher

Fair is my love that feeds among the lilies,
The lilies growing in that pleasant garden,
Where cupid's mount, that well-beloved hill is,
And where the little god himself is warden.

See where my love sits in the bed of spices,
Beset all round with camphor, myrrh and roses.

         Bartholomew Griffin

The naked virgin then
Her roses fresh reveals,
Which now her veil conceals.
The tender apples in her bosom seen;
And oft in rivers clear,
The lovers with their loves consorting were.

                 Anon.

      . . . taste the ripened cherries,
The warm, firm apple, tipped with coral berries.
Then will I visit with a wandering kiss
The vale of lilies and the bower of bliss.

                 Carew

'Mother, I'll throw them apples down,
  I'll fetch them cups of water'.
The mother turned with an angry frown,
  Holding back her daughter. . . .

'There is no water can supply them
  In western streams that flow;
There is no fruit can satisfy them
  On orchard-trees that grow.

'Once in my youth I gave, poor fool,
  A soldier apples and water;
And may I die before you cool
  Such drouth as his, my daughter'.

             Robert Graves

183

Here he will then, here he will the fleet
Flinty kindcold element let break across his limbs
Long. Where we leave him, froliclavish while he
    looks about him, laughs, swims. . . .
What is . . . the delightful dene?
Wedlock. What is water? Spousal love.

                         Hopkins

It is clear that the theories of both Jung and Freud about the nature and the origin of images enable us to detect a logic in the poetic employment of imagery which might otherwise have escaped us. We shall not fall into the error of regarding imagery as a mere decorative pattern upon the surface of the poem, since we have come to recognize that poetic images are the means by which a poet conveys his vision of central truths inherent in the nature of things. Nevertheless, we cannot accept uncritically the extreme claims of those who interpret all poetic imagery as an emanation of a changeless archetypal pattern.

We may legitimately doubt whether the concept of archetypal patterns is more than the ingenious verbal elaboration of the simple truth that the best poetry is written upon a number of basic themes—birth, death, love, the changing seasons, man's struggle with natural forces, and his efforts to live in society with his fellow men. Poetry, like the other arts, probably began as collective ritual, designed to propitiate demonic forces and to secure a fertile harvest. Man inherits traditions from his ancestors which exert over him a deep and powerful influence, so that he feels himself part of a great community in which the living and the dead are inextricably linked. If, as Jack Isaacs says, 'it seems as though the history of poetry in all ages is the attempt to find new images for the moon',[1] we need not assume that the moon is an archetypal image. We can say, in simpler language, that men from remote times have been fascinated by the moon and that something of the awe which it engenders has been passed on from one generation to the next. The postulate of racial memory is unnecessary, and the existence of archetypal patterns embedded in that memory is purely speculative. As Caudwell pointed out, emotions generated by collective experience have the power to move us, but we must not confuse the accumulated weight of

---

[1] J. Isaacs, *The Background of Modern Poetry*, p. 30.

human history with a timeless absolute, removed from the sphere of history to the world of myth.

I have given my reasons for rejecting the Marxist attempt to explain poetic imagery and rhythm in terms of sociological tension. It is only fair to record my belief that a quasi-Marxist critique of the theory of archetypal patterns exposes the flimsy basis upon which it rests. We may question whether some of these eternal patterns are, in fact, eternal, and inquire whether they are found universally, or solely in certain types of societies at a particular stage of development. It is worth noting that Auden's examples are almost all drawn from nineteenth-century Romantic writers to whom the Sea, the City, and the Desert had a connotation of which eighteenth-century writers were ignorant.[1] Nor does the image of the *femme fatale*, which appears to be archetypal in its scope and range in the period of the Romantic agony, have any deep significance in Elizabethan or in Augustan literature. Even such great archetypes as Oedipus and Faustus may personify certain traits and aspirations of Greek and of German civilization rather than unalterable truths about human psychology. Blood guiltiness, which colours the whole of the Oedipus legend as we now know it, is a comparatively late idea in Greek mythology: 'In the earliest version of one of their favourite legends Oedipus killed his father and married his mother, and even after he had made these two dire discoveries was allowed to continue living among his fellow-men and to go on ruling over Thebes.'[2]

The interpretation of so-called archetypal images will vary from age to age, according to the predispositions of the period and the imaginative genius of individual writers. The sea, which does not have any profound emotional significance for Elizabethan or for Augustan writers, suddenly takes on a fresh import in the Romantic epoch. Byron, Tennyson, Arnold, Baudelaire, and Rimbaud find in the sea a symbol of death, of immensity, of eternity, the outward projection of the great Romantic desire to escape. This way of regarding the sea is perfectly legitimate, provided we recognize that the Romantic exaltation of the ocean corresponded to the configurations of the Romantic temperament,

[1] *The Enchafèd Flood.*
[2] Zimmern, *The Greek Commonwealth*, p. 308.

and that it has no permanent validity.[1] Arnold imagined that Sophocles reacted to the Aegean much as a nineteenth-century poet, torn by intellectual and spiritual disquiet, responded to the melancholy, long, withdrawing roar of a northern sea. It is more probable that a fifth-century Greek, lacking the nostalgic uncertainty and the half-formulated aspirations of a Victorian Romantic, was not tempted to make of the sea an archetypal symbol of man's deepest longings.

The image of Perseus and Medusa has appeared to some poets to be of permanent symbolic value but, significantly, they find in it a meaning which reflects their own preoccupations. Cecil Day Lewis considers that it throws light upon the way in which a poet 'may focus reality for the sword-thrust of his imagination'.[2] Robert Graves takes it as a symbol of the way in which, for the Greeks, the poetic drama was a rite of spiritual cleansing.[3] Louis MacNeice employs the figure of Perseus confronted by Medusa as an image of petrification, symbolizing mental illness and mental deficiency.[4]

Even when an image has, for centuries, borne one traditional significance, a change in men's basic assumptions may lead them to interpret the image in completely new terms. Whales, like other monsters of the deep, were traditionally held to be a symbol of rebirth and of resurrection, moving in the depths and the darkness beneath the face of the waters. The imaginative force of Melville's novel, *Moby Dick*, and the obsession of twentieth-century man with sexual experience, to the detriment of religious meditation, have combined to give the image of the whale a new significance:

So he (Ahab) encounters Moby Dick and loses a leg . . . this is a castration symbol. . . . It is possible to attach too much importance to this as also to the sexual symbol of the Whale as being at once the *vagina dentata* and the Beast with two backs or the parents-in-bed. The point is that the sexual symbolism is in its turn symbolic of the aesthetic, i.e. the Oedipus fantasy

[1] Compare Louis MacNeice's use of the archetypal image of fire in his poem, 'Brother Fire', with T. S. Eliot's employment of this symbol in *Four Quartets*. Their metaphysical predispositions determine their response to the archetypal image and to the incendiary raids on London which brought home to men of the present age the destructive power of this element.

[2] *The Poetic Image*, pp. 99–100.

[3] *The Common Asphodel*, p. 3.

[4] 'Experiences With Images', *Orpheus*, ii, p.129.

is a representation in aesthetic terms of the fantasy of being a self-originating god, i.e. of the ego (Father) begetting itself on the self (Mother), and castration is the ultimate symbol of aesthetic weakness, of not being an aesthetic hero.[1]

A great many images which are said to be archetypal can be more accurately regarded as products of a definite phase in a civilization. The necrophilous imagery of the Jacobeans almost certainly reflects the spiritual perturbation of the age, and the poets of the time may well have derived some of their gloating obsession with physical decay from their contemplation of the terrible ravages of syphilis in the early seventeenth century. And the free play of mind which Surrealists advocate as a means of discovering significant images is, in part, a desperate attempt of artists, entirely divorced from any relation with the society of their epoch, to assert their own unconditioned freedom. In this sense, the images of Surrealism are the symptoms of a diseased society very near its final dissolution.

Unless we study the background of the society in which a poet works, we cannot hope to appreciate the significances of his imagery or of his rhythms. Sometimes it is clear that a poem is a direct reflection of the contemporary scene: the poets of the early seventeenth century, like the poets of the nineteen-thirties, attempted to incorporate into their verse the new scientific discoveries and the bewildering philosophical concepts which were troubling men's minds. Occasionally, the relationship between a poet's imagery and rhythms and the changing pattern of life is almost too subtle to express in words. Tennyson and his contemporaries shared a fondness for images drawn from a minute study of nature, which is partially explicable as the protest of sensitive men against the encroachments of an ugly, urban, industrial civilization upon the peaceful countryside.[2] The tempo of modern life may have altered our total response to poetry far more fundamentally than any specific political events. On the surface, the most striking effects of modern life upon poetry, in the verse of the inter-war years, were revealed in the images drawn from the darkening international scene which it became

---

[1] *The Enchafèd Flood*, p. 115. Cf. D. H. Lawrence's poem, *Whales Weep Not!*
   And over the bridge of the whale's strong phallus, linking the wonder of whales,
   the burning archangels under the sea keep passing, back and forth.
[2] G. M. Young's Warton Lecture on Tennyson, reprinted in *To-Day and Yesterday*.

fashionable to employ—pylons, frontiers, spies, refugees, exiles, the unemployed—but a more profound revolution of sensibility was taking place, unsuspected even by those whose modes of apprehension were being transformed: 'The great architect, Monsieur Le Corbusier, said that as the result of the Machine Age, "new organs awake in us, another diapason, a new vision". He said of persons listening to the sound of certain machinery that "the noise was so round that one believed a change in the acoustic function was taking place". It was therefore necessary to find rhythmical expression for the heightened speed of our time.'[1] T. S. Eliot made a similar observation in his introduction to his mother's dramatic poem *Savonarola*: '. . . perhaps the conditions of modern life (think how large a part is played in our sensory life by the internal-combustion engine!) have altered our perception of rhythm'.[2]

So far we have sought to trace the origin of a poet's rhythms and images in the world outside the poet's own sensations, in literary fashion, in sociological tensions, and in archetypal patterns. It is time now to ask ourselves whether we ought not to study the poet himself, not simply his mind or his consciously formulated beliefs, but the man as he is, body, brain, and glandular secretions. Carlyle made a sardonical observation on this matter in *Signs of the Times*: 'Thought, he [Dr. Cabanis] is inclined to hold, is still secreted by the brain; but then Poetry and Religion (and it is really worth knowing) are "a product of the smaller intestines".' Almost a century later T. S. Eliot warns us against the habit of scrutinizing a poet's heart or his soul and ignoring his physiology: 'Those who object to the "artificiality" of Milton or Dryden sometimes tell us to "look into our hearts and write". But that is not looking deep enough; Racine or Donne looked into a good deal more than the heart. One must look into the cerebral cortex, the nervous system, and the digestive tracts.'[3] Dame Edith Sitwell's judgement reinforces Eliot's contentions: 'If we were to ask any of the poets of the past, we should without doubt be told that poetry is just as much a matter of physical aptitude as of spiritual. . . . I believe that a poem begins in the poet's head,

---

[1] Edith Sitwell, 'On My Poetry', *Orpheus*, ii, p. 104.
[2] Cited by Matthiessen, *The Achievement of T. S. Eliot*, 2nd ed., pp. 88–89.
[3] 'The Metaphysical Poets', *Selected Essays*, p. 290.

and then grows in his blood, as a rose grows among its dark leaves.'[1] These attempts to correlate a poet's style with his physique had been anticipated in the middle of the last century by G. H. Lewes. Some of his critical *aperçus* have a curiously modern tone—he advanced the theory that art is a means of resolving what we should now call psychological tensions and, like A. E. Housman, he spoke of the poet's secreting poetry as an oyster secretes a pearl. He believed that the art produced by women was a transposition of the peculiarly feminine forms of suffering, a theory which hints at a close relationship between works of art and the organic make-up of the artist.

Some critics have postulated a direct connexion between the artist's physiology and his achievements. Stendhal was at least half-serious when he wrote: 'There was a splendid portrait of Cardinal Richelieu which I often looked at. Beside it was the coarse, heavy, pompous, silly countenance of Racine. It was because he was so fat that this great poet had felt the sentiments whose memory is indispensable for creating *Andromache* and *Phèdre*.'[2] Stephen Spender reports a conversation in which Aldous Huxley said to him: 'You and I are the wrong height for the work we wish to do. The great creative geniuses are short and robust "pyknic" types with almost no neck to divide the nerves of the body from the centres of the brain. Balzac, Beethoven, Picasso, did not have great stooping bodies to lug around. There was no gulf to divide their minds from the imme- diate communication of their physical senses.'[3] Suspicious as we may be of such biological generalizations, we may yet feel that orthodox literary criticism has, in the past, failed to recognize that such apparently irrelevant factors as a poet's diet, physique, and digestive system may profoundly affect the rhythms, the imagery, and the structure of his poetry. Robert Graves, dis- cussing an encounter of his childhood days with Swinburne, draws attention to the way in which his recollection of the poet's appearance and speech throws light upon his poem 'An Old Saying': 'My picture of him is of a nimble and shrill-voiced gnome dressed in a biscuit-coloured suit with tails and talking

---

[1] *Alexander Pope*, p. 265.
[2] *Memoirs of an Egotist*, p. 129.
[3] *World Within World*, p. 163.

insistently and shrilly at the top of his voice. . . . I can still discern
the insistent shrillness in the assonantal play of "slay . . . faith";
"peace . . . deep"; "sweet sleep"; "nights resign"; "hate . . . waste"
—at which technicians of the Miltonic and Tennysonian schools
would virtuously shudder.'[1] If Graves is correct we must beware
of trying to explain a poet's technique by reference to diction
and to prosody alone, for the origin of a poet's style lies concealed in the roots of his nature. Sir Osbert Sitwell's description
of T. S. Eliot's appearance in 1917 confirms the conjectures of
Robert Graves: '. . . the range and tragic depths of his great
poetry were to be read in the very lines of his face. . . . If it be
or be not true that the technique of a poet is his etheric body, yet,
in this instance, the comparison is particularly apt: for Eliot's
muscular conformation and his carriage and the way he moved
seem to explain the giant muscular control of rhythm he has
acquired.'[2] Dame Edith Sitwell's explanation of why Pope employed the heroic couplet may be contrasted with Christopher
Caudwell's account of the way in which blank verse was suc-
ceeded by the heroic couplet as the common measure of the early
eighteenth century. Caudwell emphasizes the sociological pattern
of an epoch, Dame Edith the lineaments of a solitary man: 'Blanks,
for instance, would have been impossible to a poet of Pope's tiny
and weak body; but the stopped heroic couplet, with its sustain-
ing rhymes, its outward cage (though that cage holds within it
all the waves, and the towers and the gulfs of the world), this was
born to be his measure.'[3] Her theory should not be accepted
unreservedly for, like Caudwell, she has pushed one aspect of
truth to such an extreme that we cannot accept it as valid.
Dryden, Johnson, and Charles Churchill, to name only three
notable exponents of the heroic couplet, were men whose
physique differed markedly from Pope's and from one another's,
yet, like Pope, they found the heroic couplet perfectly adapted
to their needs. We may doubt whether Pope's avoidance of blank
verse and his habitual use of the couplet were determined by his
bodily•peculiarities: the Spenserian stanza would have been an
even more elaborate support for his weak frame, had he felt that

[1] *The Common Asphodel*, p. 314.
[2] *Laughter in the Next Room*, p. 33.
[3] *Alexander Pope*, p. 266.

his physical frailty could be strengthened by encasing it in a metrical corset. Churchill's massive, bruiser-like physique certainly required no prop, yet he constantly had recourse to the heroic couplet. Both Caudwell and Dame Edith deserve our gratitude for reminding us that truth is multifarious and complex, that a nascent capitalism in the body politic, and a sickly deformity in the body of a poet play their part in moulding a poetic style. Nevertheless, before we can hope to understand the origin of Pope's attachment to the couplet we must supplement biological mysticism and sociological analysis by a study of his conscious ambition and of current literary tradition: his worship of Dryden, his avowed intent to attain a perfection hitherto beyond the reach of English poets, and the latent resources of the couplet in 1700.

Physiology alone provides no clue to the source of a poet's rhythms and imagery. We may find that research into a poet's intellectual predispositions and temperamental obsessions helps us to discern the configurations of those forms which lie deep in the subterranean caverns of our being. Imagery and rhythm are the means by which these buried faculties are set free to emerge into the daylight. If a poet is predisposed towards certain themes by the promptings of his nature, we shall not be surprised to discover that some themes appear again and again in his work, as if they held for him an inescapable fascination. This phenomenon is not confined to the art of poetry. Sir Kenneth Clark has pointed out that Leonardo used certain motifs, particularly gestures and poses, throughout his life, irrespective of the subject-matter of the picture, and that Michelangelo was so enchanted by a particular curve that he drew Tityrus rising from a rock on one side of a sheet of paper, traced the design through to the other side and turned it into the figure of Christ rising from the tomb.[1]

We cannot tell why any given line, gesture, or curve should hold an unusual significance for a painter, any more than we can explain the recurrence in a poet's work of a limited range of imagery. Shelley, for example, employs a beautiful image in one of his most luminous evocations of nightfall and of the radiance with which nature clothes a sleeping town:

[1] *The Listener*, 13 Nov. 1941.

Within the surface of the fleeting river
The wrinkled image of the city lay,
Immovably unquiet, and forever
It trembles, but it never fades away.[1]

This symbol of evanescence seems to have troubled Shelley's mind, for it recurs in two other poems, almost as if he were driven to make use of it in obedience to the importunate demands of his nature.[2]

Some such conjecture is necessary if we are to attempt to discover the motives which guide a poet in his choice of images, for even if we maintain that he merely recognizes images already present in the external world—whether they be archetypal or sociological in origin—we still have to explain the principle on which he makes his selection from the great constellation of images which he reviews with meditative gaze. Cecil Day Lewis makes a pertinent comment upon the theory that *The Ancient Mariner* conceals a rebirth archetype and that its pattern of images symbolizes the cycle of frustration, impotence, death, and regeneration which is a fundamental rhythm of existence: 'The theory of archetypes is, of course, highly speculative. But we can at least agree that, if there is anything in the rebirth myth, its promptings would have had a special appeal for Coleridge, since the emotional configuration claimed for it does correspond with the emotional rhythms of the manic-depressive character.'[3]

Granted that a poet's style, rhythms, imagery, and themes may be largely determined by his nature, we must now seek to disentangle the entwining threads of hereditary predispositions and of personal experience which unite, however imperfectly, in the man's total being. Common sense may suggest that poetry is simply a reflection of a man's experience, but a more subtle kind of sense, which is a safer guide through the labyrinth of poetry, warns us against assuming that the relationship between life and art is one of straightforward cause and effect. A few artists, acutely sensitive to the deepest longings and the most powerful subterranean forces of their time, have seemed to possess the clairvoyant power of discerning the future—Keats hinted at the

---

[1] 'Evening: Ponte al Mare, Pisa.'
[2] 'The Witch of Atlas,' l. 513, and 'Ode to Liberty,' l. 76.
[3] *The Poetic Image*, p. 149.

theory of evolution in *Hyperion*; Lawrence foreshadowed the recrudescence of romantic barbarism in Germany; the Futurists heralded the violence and the disintegration of the early twentieth century, just as the Surrealists portrayed, in miniature, the frenzied despair of the middle years of the century. Even so, an artist's work may prefigure the experiences of his life, perhaps because the pattern of his existence and the design of his art flow like twin streams from a common source in the hinterland of his nature. A story by Napoleon, written just before his rise to fame, reads like 'an unconscious and macabre self-prophecy', says Dormer Creston in her biographical study of the Emperor and his son.[1] Herzen's novel *Who Is To Blame?* anticipated, in curious fashion, the domestic tragi-comedy of his wife's adultery, and Verhaeren, whose poems are full of images of railway trains, fell under a train at Rouen station in November 1916.[2]

Graham Hough's study of Rossetti and his friends is particularly relevant to our inquiry.[3] Morris, according to him, was 'haunted by the story of the husband despised for a more brilliant lover',[4] and we may find the clue to this obsession in the obscure regions of his intimate biography. The origins of Rossetti's work are less easy to determine, for the influence upon him of Dante's writings was one of peculiar complexity. Not only was it inbred and hereditary, a kind of natural element from childhood onwards, as Rossetti described it; it also became a more than literary influence.[5] Graham Hough's analysis cannot be bettered:

> The *Vita Nuova* especially is a central part of Rossetti's experience. . . . What Rossetti draws from it is chiefly the idea of a continuing relation to a dead love; and its aptness to his situation after the death of Elizabeth Siddal needs no remark. What is more remarkable is that he seems to have been possessed by this complex of ideas while she was still alive even before he had met her. . . . It is almost as if Elizabeth Siddal had to die in order to fulfil her role in his poetic myth.[6]

It is impossible to lay down any formula which would indicate the precise relationships between the diverse forces that animate a poet's rhythms and liberate the images and the themes upon

---

[1] *In Search of Two Characters*, pp. 16–17.

[2] E. H. Carr, *The Romantic Exiles*, Penguin edition, p. 53, and F. L. Lucas, *Literature and Psychology*, p. 84.

[3] *The Last Romantics.*

[4] Op. cit., p. 131.

[5] Op. cit., pp. 67–68.

[6] Op. cit., pp. 75–76.

which he builds his verse. We cannot, for example, hope to distinguish the exact workings of all the influences that helped to mould the poetry of Swinburne. We may doubt whether Lord Houghton was responsible for corrupting Swinburne's imagination, if only because sadistic reverie and alcohol were the very stimulants for which his nature instinctively craved.[1] Graham Hough has adumbrated the nature of the diverse strands in Swinburne's poetry and, in so doing, has reminded us that literary tradition, sociological conditions, and archetypal images modify and, in their turn, are profoundly modified by, the vagaries of a poet's idiosyncrasies:

> Swinburne's algolagnia would have been the same if no other literature had ever existed; but without Gautier and Baudelaire he would have had considerable difficulty in finding means to express his abnormalities. Any full treatment of the culture of the period would have to explain the lavish and eccentric display of erotic symbolism that made its appearance on both sides of the Channel after the middle of the century—the obsession with various illicit alliances between love, pain and death; the *femme fatale* or the vampire; homosexuality, male and female; hermaphroditism, and all the rest of it. No doubt some of the mythological embodiments of these states of mind, notably the conception of woman as some sort of mysterious fatality, were what Jung would call archetypes, personifications of forces and ideas buried very deep in the human psyche, which social and literary decorum had formerly prevented from finding expression. But others were the result of purely private aberrations of the erotic sensibility.[2]

Similarly, the recurrence in the verse of Poe and of James Thomson of a beautiful young woman doomed to an early death may be explained by reference to archetypal symbols: but it is significant that both men lost their mothers at an early age. Rilke's obsession with roses and with young girls may also derive from some configuration of his innermost nature which haunted him until the very end of his life—he died, symbolically, from blood-poisoning contracted from scratching himself on the thorn of a rose given to him by a young girl.

One of the marks by which we recognize a poet is his ability to stamp the images which he uses—no matter what their source—with the indelible mark of his imagination. They must come fresh

---

[1] James Pope-Hennessy, *Monckton Milnes: The Flight of Youth*, gives an admirable picture of Swinburne's relationship with Lord Houghton.

[2] Op. cit., p. 191.

from the poet's mint before we can accept their authenticity. Think how the age-old symbols of wine and flowers are employed by Herrick to present his beautifully composed vision of the world; how Gérard de Nerval gave personal expression to the plastic images of antiquity which drifted before him in outline; how Edwin Muir incorporates the heraldic images, the labyrinths, and the symbols of incarnation which he finds everywhere in Rome, into his mythological universe. Unless the poet has completely absorbed the images which offer themselves to him, unless they have become part of his flesh and blood, there will be a sense of strain in his use of them. He may attempt to write poetry of universal import by making a great parade of his archetypal images; he may draw attention to his highly original sensibility by racking his brains for ingenious or fantastic metaphors; he may assert his contemporary awareness by flaunting his modernity in the choice of images: but all this will be in vain if the images fail to represent with complete fidelity the private and unique vision which he is trying to delineate.

In our attempt to ascertain the source of a poet's images and rhythms we have, up to now, forgotten or ignored the fact that he need not confine his imagination to the realm of archetypal patterns or to the limited field within which his inherited predispositions seek to imprison him. He has free access to a world of immeasurable richness, of inexhaustible fertility—to the world of experience and of memory, the nature and extent of which we must now proceed to examine. For even if the archetypal patterns are unchanging, the poet's ever-maturing imagination gradually reveals to him the full significance of these primordial images; and although he can never wholly transcend the limitations of his temperament, his poetry is, in part, a record of his conflict and his final reconciliation with the promptings of his nature. Its rhythms and its images will bear the imprint of his experience, and we may discern in a poem what Coleridge remarked in every countenance—a prophecy and a history.

Chapter Seven

OUR understanding of poetry has been enlarged and enriched in the past fifty years by three great contributions to our knowledge of human beings and of society: the Marxist investigation of social change; the Freudian analysis of the human psyche; and the exploration of the part played in our lives by time and by memory. It is probable that the Proustian evocation of things past, although it lacks the intellectual drive and acuteness of Marxism and the metaphysical implications of Freudianism, throws more light than the other two systems upon the workings of the poetic imagination.

Hobbes, it will be remembered, quoted with approval the ancient Greek belief that Memory was the mother of the Muses, and Wordsworth stressed the importance of recollection for the poet. His fondness for dwelling upon

> old unhappy far off things
> And battles long ago

like his attempt, in the early 1790s, to escape to the timeless world of mathematics, was dictated by his desire to contemplate humanity and human emotions when they had been purged by distance: he thanks God that men

> Did first present themselves thus purified
> Removed, and to a distance that was fit.[1]

In the twentieth century we have come to believe that a poet's imagery and rhythms are largely determined by memory and by experience; that the poetic imagination is an exercise of memory, an ability to recall past events, to trace in them a formal pattern of beauty and to impose it upon the flux of being; that an intimate knowledge of ourselves enables us to enter into the hearts and minds of other men and that the poet, with his great memory, is peculiarly well fitted to perform this act of imaginative sympathy.

Proust's delineation of childhood helps us to understand some-

---

[1] Cf. Willey, *The Eighteenth Century Background*, pp. 288–9.

thing of the subtle way in which experience and memory work upon our senses. In his description we may learn how deeply our memories sink into our minds, how tenaciously they cling to the fabric of our being, and how, unknown to us, they lie dormant for years, only to emerge unexpectedly when our senses are stirred by some trivial influence with a strange power to summon up the past.

Psycho-analysis has confirmed Proust's intuitive discovery that our lives may be profoundly and permanently affected by incidents which occurred in our childhood, even if we have no conscious recollection of them. The danger of psycho-analytical literary criticism is that it tends to limit the source of a writer's imagery to one type of experience. William Empson roundly declares that 'Wordsworth frankly had no inspiration other than his use, when a boy, of the mountains as a totem or father-substitute . . .'.[1] In fact, Wordsworth's passion for mountains was not as simple and unequivocal as Empson suggests: it was neither a psychological abnormality nor a visionary longing. He studied mountains with the scientific eagerness of the geologist, studied them as they were, not as the means of gratifying some obscure impulse but with the desire to understand their origin, their structure, and their characteristics. Nor did he derive inspiration solely from them. He has told us that for every hour spent thinking about poetry he spent twelve hours meditating upon public affairs. Finally, to stress the unique importance of mountains in Wordsworth's emotional life is to overlook his love for Dorothy which suffuses so much of his early poetry, and to ignore the claims of Annette Vallon to be the decisive factor in the poet's development, a thesis which Sir Herbert Read has maintained with his customary fervour and ingenuity.

Yet there is no doubt that the configurations of a poet's verse may be insensibly moulded by the impress of his childhood experiences. It has been suggested that Blake's employment of gold as a symbol of warmth, energy, and holiness, and his use of the image of a square as the symbol of an ordered freedom derive from his memories of Golden Square, where he was born.[2] T. S. Eliot's *Four Quartets* remind us that no expatriate can disavow

---

[1] Op. cit., p. 20.
[2] Bernard Blackstone, *English Blake*, p. 4.

his childhood, even if he desires to do so. He has told us that the Mississippi has impressed itself more deeply upon his memory than any landscape in the world, and it may well be that the wonderful potency of the river imagery in *The Dry Salvages* is derived from the poet's childhood memories. The sea imagery also is unusually rich, perhaps because the poet is drawing upon early recollections of that north-east coast of Cape Ann, Massachusetts, where three rocks, Les Trois Sauvages, rise from the sea.

There is no reason to believe that Eliot's ability to draw upon his early recollections is unique. Among prose writers, Gibbon and Newman were, as children, enthralled by Arabian tales, and although their subsequent careers diverged so widely, both were impelled by their childhood impressions to construct a universe in which the pleasurable emotions induced by the marvellous tales might be experienced once again and perpetuated.[1] Ruskin's debt to the Old Testament is glaringly obvious, a debt contracted when, as a child, he was obliged to commit long passages of the Bible to memory; Stevenson's precocious imagination was similarly inflamed by the fierce rhythms of the Calvinist psalms which his nurse read to him. If only we knew more about the nurses of poets, prose-writers, and other artists we might gain a valuable insight into the hidden forces that mould an artistic style. Some artists have recognized that their earliest experiences have been decisive and that our lives may be overshadowed by the almost forgotten figure of a nurse, a gardener, a rag and bone man, or some terrifying object that haunted our childhood dreams. The figure may be cruel and malevolent, like the master at Eton who flogged Swinburne in the pine-woods and who permitted him to dab his face with eau-de-cologne; the object may be a symbol of sadistic reverie, like the flogging-block which was one of the two features of the Etonian landscape that Swinburne desired to see again;[2] or a childhood may for ever be associated with a gentle teacher and a peaceful garden. Samuel Palmer, for example, had a nurse who was deeply read in the Bible and in *Paradise Lost*:

---

[1] J. B. Yeats, op. cit., p. 258, says that Newman, who, as a child, had wished the Arabian tales to be true, held ideas 'not because they were true but because they were agreeable to his artistic nature.' This applies also to Gibbon.

[2] The other was the river.

When less than four years old, as I was standing with her, watching the shadows on the wall from the branches of an elm behind which the moon had risen, she transferred and fixed the fleeting image in my memory by repeating the couplet:

> Vain man, the vision of a moment made,
> Dream of a dream and shadow of a shade.[1]

I never forgot these shadows and am often trying to paint them.

William Empson has an illuminating comment to make about nineteenth-century English poets:

Almost all of them ... exploited a sort of tap-root into the world of their childhood, where they were able to conceive things poetically, and whatever they might be writing about they would suck up from this limited and perverted world an unvarying sap which was their poetical inspiration. Mr. Harold Nicolson has written excellently about Swinburne's fixation on to the excitements of his early reading and experience, and about the unique position in the life of Tennyson occupied by the moaning of a cold wind round a child frightened for its identity upon the fens.[2]

Peter Quennell points to even subtler impressions as the source of a poetic style:

It is impressions such as these—the rumour of a woman's skirts, evocative of a maternal tenderness, a swimming haze of lights that may, perhaps, recall our earliest adventure into the realms of scenic illusion—that interbreed and multiply, and are the prime factors to which any poetic style, even the most complicated and allusive, can ultimately be reduced.[3]

The proportion of images in a poet's work directly traceable to reminiscences of childhood will, of course, vary from writer to writer. The images in Wordsworth's poetry serve almost as signposts pointing to the tracks which lead to his youthful experiences, and in his 'Ode on the Intimations of Immortality' he is paying a lifetime's tribute to the source of his genius and even, it may be, regretfully bidding that genius farewell. It is less easy to relate the images of Keats or of Shelley to their childhood memories, although we may explain Shelley's attachment to snakes by his fondness for an old snake in the garden of Field Place.

[1] Edward Young, *Paraphrase of Job*, xxxviii, ll. 187–8.
[2] Op. cit., p. 20.
[3] *Baudelaire and the Symbolists*, p. 21.

Biographical interpretation of poetry is full of pitfalls, especially for fools.[1] Helen Gardner's story of the Belgian critic who thought that Little Gidding was 'un petit garçon cher à T. S. Eliot' is a warning to us all.[2] We should, therefore, be grateful to any poet who attempts to analyse the sources of his verse. Louis MacNeice, in explaining the recurrence of certain themes in his poems by reference to his childhood, his father's house, and the family servants, has given us valuable information about what he conceives to be the origins of his poetic imagery:

My favourite reading at about the age of eight was the Book of Revelation but, long before that, Biblical imagery had been engrained in me. On top of this I had more than my share of old wives' tales from our Roman Catholic cook and others, of Calvinist alarums from our Presbyterian housekeeper, and of nightmares from various causes. I also had certain early contacts with both mental illness and mental deficiency (these latter may explain the *petrification* images which appear pretty often in my poems, e.g. in *Perseus*). I should add that our house was lit by oil lamps (not enough of them) and so was full of shadows. And in general the daily routine was monotonous, there were few other children to play with and I hardly ever went away to stay. These circumstances between them must have supplied me with many images of fear, anxiety, loneliness or monotony (to be used very often quite out of a personal context). They may also explain—by reaction—what I now think an excessive preoccupation in my earlier work with things dazzling, high-coloured, quick-moving, hedonistic or up-to-date.[3]

His father's church, says MacNeice, inspired him with terror, and he puts this forward as one reason 'why church bells have for me a sinister association, e.g. in my poem *Sunday Morning*', where he compares them with skulls. In another poem, 'Perseus', he writes:

Or look in the looking-glass in the end room—
You will find it full of eyes,
The ancient smiles of men cut out with scissors and kept in mirrors.

[1] Not only for fools. Pierre Legouis has pointed out how sadly Sir Herbert Read went astray in his Freudian exegesis of Wordsworth's emotional history. Sir Herbert found it highly significant that Wordsworth should have admired Le Brun's painting of the Virgin, failing to notice that the subject of the painting was not the Virgin but the Magdalene. Sir Herbert acknowledged his error: 'As for substituting the Virgin for the Magdalene —there M. Legouis has this Freudian nigger by the toe.' Psycho-analytical literary criticism, to be valid, must submit to the discipline of the literary critic and of the historian. Cf. *The Road to Xanadu*, where Livingston Lowes dissects Robert Graves's Freudian analysis of 'Kubla Khan'. The admission made by Sir Herbert Read is to be found in the *T.L.S.*, 18 May 1951.   [2] *The Art of T. S. Eliot*, p. 44, footnote.
[3] Experiences With Images', *Orpheus*, ii, pp.129-30.

The explanation of this dream-like image must be sought in the events of the poet's childhood:

I am describing a mood of terror when everything seems to be unreal, petrified—hence the Gorgon's head which dominates the poem. Such a mood being especially common among children, 'the end room' implies a child's fear of long corridors. In such a mood, both when a child and when grown-up, I remember looking in mirrors and (a) thinking that my own face looked like a strange face, especially in the eyes, and (b) being fascinated and alarmed by the mysterious gleams of light *glancing* off the mirror.[1]

It would, of course, be wrong to assume that a poet's childhood experiences and memories are the sole or even the chief determinant factors in the formation of his poetic style, nor must we fall into the error of supposing that we can reconstruct a poet's intimate biography simply by analysing the images of his verse. Certain events may prove too intractable for transmutation into poetry, and it is therefore probable that the most significant experiences of childhood, partly because of their mysterious, inexplicable quality, will resist the poet's attempt to assimilate them into poetry. Or it may be that the poet himself is inhibited from giving expression to the obscurely felt events and emotions which agitated his childish sensibilities. Thus, Louis MacNeice, in an illuminating footnote, speaks of an image which haunts him but which he has never employed in his verse: 'Almost the most disastrous experience of my childhood is for ever associated in my mind with a doubled-up poplar twig—but I have never yet used this image as a symbol of Evil.'[2] We can, however, legitimately claim that, although subsequent experience will modify the impressions of childhood and the temperamental endowments with which one is born, a study of a poet's formative years will usually reveal the sources of his imagery and of his rhythms.

Here we must pause for a moment to ask ourselves what, in this context, we mean by experience. We can say, without equivocation, that any attempt to distinguish between thought, emotion, action, observation of the visible world, reading, study of the arts, reverie, and dreaming is foredoomed to failure because all these

[1] *Modern Poetry*, pp. 174–5. Cyril Connolly makes a brilliant observation on this theme when he writes: '. . . the one golden recipe for Art is the ferment of an unhappy childhood working through a noble imagination'. *Ideas and Places*, p. 136.

[2] *Orpheus*, ii, p. 130, footnote.

modes of experience are, for the poet, of equal validity. Some poets need the spur of travel, of adventure, or of sex to stimulate their imagination; others can turn into poetry the humdrum routine of daily life; a third type of poet feeds his imagination upon poetry itself, upon works of pictorial art, or upon the ever-varying moods and appearance of the landscape or of Nature. We may lament Hopkins's utter submission to the demands of his religious order, and consider Yeats's dabbling with the occult a mixture of superstitious nonsense and comic vanity, but the point is that such devotion to an apparently erroneous system of belief or mode of behaviour may well have been the mainspring of the poet's imaginative life. Jack Isaacs gives an admirable description of the various sources from which a poet may derive his imagery, and reminds us that poetry is incredibly rich and multifarious: 'Chaucer, Spenser, Marlowe, Donne, Coleridge, Keats and Shelley, all sought their imagery. They dug in fields and in mines of imagery, mythology, philosophy, geometry, military history, geography, chemistry, the Bible, anthropology, psychology and war.'[1] The mark of a poet is the ability to turn into poetry everything that happens to him, to discover in apparently unpropitious events the raw material of his art, and to transfigure what appears to be arid, sterile, and commonplace. We can never pontificate about what ought to be the source of a poet's imagery, but must be content to observe humbly the diversity of sources upon which poets have actually drawn. A remark of Whitehead's will help to remind us that poets may derive their sustenance in unexpected ways: 'What the hills were to the youth of Words-worth, a chemical laboratory was to Shelley.'[2] The nineteenth-century prejudice in favour of what the moralists of that period regarded as natural should not blind us to the truth that the artificial forms created by man are, for a poet, as fit an object of reverence and admiration as the vegetable kingdom beloved of Wordsworthians. Baudelaire, says Peter Quennell, applauds 'la majesté superlative des formes artificielles' and celebrates the strength and the delicacy of ocean-going ships: 'The pedantic beauty of great sailing ships, moored alongside the quay,—each the monstrous edifice of patience and knowledge, every shroud and spar tightly threaded against some known, calculated danger,

---

[1] *The Background of Modern Poetry*, pp. 37–38. [2] Ibid., p. 73.

quiescent, yet, while it rocks its yards across the sun, each apparently meditating an immediate, urgent flight, made frequent and profound inroads on his sensibility.'[1]

Henry James has given us an unrivalled description of the way in which experience is absorbed into the blood and transformed into imaginative energy. After recounting the tale of an English woman novelist who, on glimpsing a pasteur's household seated at a finished meal, created an exact picture of the nature and the way of life characteristic of young French Protestants, James defines experience and its mode of operation:

Experience is never limited, and it is never complete; it is an immense sensibility, a kind of huge spiderweb, of the finest silken threads, suspended in the chamber of consciousness and catching every air-borne particle in its tissue. It is the very atmosphere of the mind, and when the mind is imaginative—much more when it happens to be that of a man of genius— it takes to itself the faintest hints of life, it converts the very pulses of air into revelations. . . . The power to guess the unseen from the seen, to trace the implication of things, to judge the whole piece by the pattern, the condition of feeling life, in general, so completely that you are well on your way to knowing any possible corner of it—this cluster of gifts may almost be said to constitute experience, and they occur in country and in town, and in the most differing stages of education.[2]

Sometimes, long after a war is finished, a mine laid by the navy of one of the combatants will drift into the main ocean trade-routes and blow to pieces an unsuspecting vessel. Even so, an experience which has for years lain submerged beneath the surface of the conscious mind, will suddenly explode and release a flood of memories about old and half-forgotten conflicts. Wordsworth knew that experiences sank deep into his mind, accumulating all the richness of a sea-change, and re-emerging unexpectedly:

> Nor is it I who play the part,
> But a shy spirit in my heart,
> That comes and goes—will sometimes leap
> From hiding-places ten years deep.[3]

Unlike Scott, who noted down the beauties of Nature in a little

---

[1] Op. cit., pp. 19–20.   [2] Cited by Matthiessen, op. cit., pp. 54–55.
[3] 'The Waggoner', part iv.

book, Wordsworth deliberately allowed his experiences to mature in the recesses of his mind, knowing that they would present themselves to him as soon as time had ripened them. We have already seen how certain images and rhythms lie buried in a poet's being from childhood onward, and must now examine the way in which the experiences and memories of adult life reappear in a poet's work.

The genesis of 'Resolution and Independence' has been traced by Professor Smith to an encounter on 26 September 1800 between William and Dorothy Wordsworth and an old man. They met him on the Grasmere road in the late evening as he was begging his way to Carlisle. The poem was begun twenty months later on 3 May 1802 and finished on 4 July, during which period Wordsworth was experiencing a mood of dejection, although at the time of the actual meeting he was in good spirits. In the poem Wordsworth is represented as being alone; the meeting takes place on the moor at sunrise after a night of wind and rain; the old man is no longer a former leech-gatherer turned beggar but a leech-gatherer who has met all his trials with fortitude and who has retained his independence. It is noteworthy that all these changes helped to create the kind of emotional atmosphere which Wordsworth's imagination found so congenial—solitude, the aftermath of a storm, a great, lonely stretch of countryside, a noble countryman untainted by the world's contagion. Whether or not Wordsworth deliberately tampered with the recollected facts is immaterial: just as an efficient ruling-class will intuitively pursue a course of action that will confirm its own privileged position, so a poet will intuitively select and arrange his memories in order that he may the more easily turn them into poetry.

Wordsworth seems to have remembered dreams, hallucinations, and waking reveries as vividly as he recalled experiences of his normal daily life. He tells us that he allowed his waking imagination to play repeatedly upon his dream of the Arab, that mounted Bedouin, that semi-Quixote, which he describes in Book V of *The Prelude* and which forms the starting-point of W. H. Auden's disquisition upon Romantic symbols in *The Enchafèd Flood*. It is probable that this crucial dream belongs to his Cambridge days and that its glory and its freshness persisted through the years. We know that the appalling scenes which he witnessed in revolutionary Paris profoundly impressed themselves upon his memory. In October 1792 he heard a voice cry 'Sleep no more', as if to remind him of the terrors endured by Macbeth, and we know that the nightmares brought on by his having been present at the execution of Gorsas troubled him long afterwards. One final example of Wordsworth's power to transfer his recollections of past events to a different context must suffice. In August 1793, when walking on Salisbury Plain, he had a waking-dream of ghastly Druidical rites. In Book IV of *The Excursion* this vision is seen by a Pastor, not upon Salisbury Plain, but in the Lake District, in the Vale of St. John, where mountain stones form a Druidic circle.

It seems likely that Wordsworth deliberately exploited his recollections in order to achieve his poetic ends, and that he was fully aware of what he was doing. Coleridge, on the other hand, was probably ignorant of the mental processes which transmuted his past actions, dreams, observations, and reading into the flawless patterns of his greatest poetry. Thanks to Professor Lowes, we can retrace, in detail, the road to Xanadu which Coleridge trod, and distinguish the myriad impressions which were sifted and refined by his remarkable sensibility, until they were ready to combine in a poetic harmony. A remarkable example of the subterranean way in which memory insidiously works is to be found in a letter from Horace Walpole to Madame du Deffand, 27 January 1775.[1] One day, upon entering the Great Court at Trinity, he recognized the courtyard of Otranto. After reflecting upon this coincidence, he realized that a previous visit to Trinity must have remained vividly in his memory for the space of a year and combined with his daily observation of Strawberry Hill to form the imaginary castle.

This sudden, involuntary, onrush of memory which assails the poet may provide him with a theme for a poem, or even with a stanza perfectly formed. Stephen Spender describes an experience during the Spanish civil war in the following words: 'Suddenly the front seemed to me like a love relationship between the two sides, locked here in their opposite trenches, committed to one another unto death, unable to separate, and for a visitor to

[1] R. W. Ketton-Cremer, *Horace Walpole*, p. 194.

intervene in their deathly orgasm seemed a terrible frivolity.'[1]
Some weeks later he was standing on a station platform:

In broad daylight the train arrived. I stared out of the carriage window,
in a state of mind when fatigue seems to open a door upon a further awakening, on an involuntary awareness of the darkest movements of thought
within the mind. Lines suddenly ran into my mind, as though gliding with
the movement of the train:

> Clean silence drops at night when a little walk
> Divides the sleeping armies, each
> Huddled in linen woven by remote hands.
> When the machines are stilled, a common suffering
> Whitens the air with breath and makes both one
> As though these enemies slept in each other's arms.[2]

A naïve prejudice still lingers on that a poet who draws upon
his memories of books, or whose verse is filled with echoes of
other men's words, is less original and virile than one who repro-
duces his memories of the external world. The truth is that almost
every poet of merit has drawn upon his reading in order to enrich
his experience of daily life, and to impose a coherent order upon
the whirling images that clamour for admission to the body of his
verse. The facile distinction between life and literature is meaningless in this context, since both are raw material of equal value
to the poet. Shakespeare's omnivorous sensibility absorbed everything and transformed it into poetry—the way in which the
current of the river swirled beneath the bridge at Stratford; the
reactions of the snail to danger; a lecherous petty official flogging
a whore; an old wives' tale; a fragment of a ballad; the latest
medical jargon; a passage from a chronicle. Poets as diverse as
Coleridge, Virgil, and Petronius all believed in vast reading as the
mainspring of inspiration, a view shared by Milton who, although
he dutifully attributed his flow of verse to the visitation of the
Muse, prudently spent his evenings 'reading some choice Poets,
by way of refreshment after the day's toyl, and to store his Fancy
against Morning.'[3]

Some poets designedly incorporate into their verse the
cadences, phrases, and images of their predecessors in order to

[1] *World Within World*, p. 223.
[2] Ibid., p. 228.
[3] John Phillips, *The Life of Mr. John Milton* (*Early Lives of Milton*, ed. Helen
Darbishire p. 33).

produce a carefully calculated effect.[1] Marlowe makes Faustus cry out in wonder at the vision of Helen:

> Was this the face that launch'd a thousand ships

—a reminiscence of Lucan who employs a similar phrase when contemplating Helen's reputed skull. Faustus's agonized demand that time shall stand still is given even greater poignancy by his quotation of a line from Ovid

> O lente lente currite noctis equi

which, in the Latin poet, was the prayer of a lover who desired that the night of love might be prolonged. Marlowe draws upon his memories of earlier poets and gives an ironical twist to what he recalls.

Pope's borrowings from the work of other men are an essential element of his style. A particularly brilliant example is the allusion to the famous lines of Horace:

> non sum qualis eram bonae
> sub regno Cinarae

Pope transmutes these lines into a couplet which extends the range of Horace's meaning by widening the reference from the personal to the communal:

> I am not now, alas! the man
> As in the gentle Reign of my Queen Anne.

Horace is lamenting the decline in his fortunes since the days when he loved Cynara; he is regretting the passing of youth and of passion. Pope is giving expression to a similar emotion, but his reference to 'my Queen Anne' is a regretful, backward glance to the days when the last Stuart was on the throne and the fortunes of his brilliant friends were at their zenith. He is speaking for a circle of men whose disappointed hopes tinged their lives with a restless, bitter melancholy. Finally, by equating the early eighteenth-century world of fashion with the first Augustan epoch, Pope is drawing the attention of his readers to an historical parallel which they delighted to contemplate. Horace's lines thus form a nucleus around which a whole complex of emotions has crystallized.

---

[1] Hopkins objected to this device: 'The echos are a disease of education, literature is full of them; but they remain a disease, an evil.' *Letters*, i, p. 206.

Occasionally, a song or a book, heard or read long before, will suddenly flash once again into the poet's mind without his conscious volition. In extreme cases, there is not even the recognition that he is reproducing another man's work, so thoroughly has the imagery and the rhythm been absorbed into the memory. This is especially true of young poets who fall so utterly beneath the spell of a greatly admired writer that they tend to reproduce the very accents of their chosen master, with no avowed intention of writing pastiche. A passage from a book read long ago, a tune heard in a café, a painting once seen in a great museum, may linger in the mind for many years, gradually sinking into oblivion, until it unexpectedly rises to the surface in a shape that has been modified by the pressure of the experiences undergone in the intervening years.

A striking example of the way in which a half-forgotten passage from a book may give rise to a poem in after years is to be found in Browning's account of how he came to write *The Ring and the Book*. Italy gave him the beauty, the intensity, the voluptuous, melodious, sensuous harmony that his temperament imperatively demanded. After living in the Mediterranean warmth, he was able to draw upon a reservoir of memories that helped to dissolve the foggy gloom of Victorian London and to dispel the inspissated atmosphere of earnest metaphysical speculation into which he was often tempted to plunge. His imagination leaped in response to all that he had heard and seen in Italy, to the street-vendors' cries, to the glowing frescoes, to the monumental statues or to a toccata of Galuppi's, which he had heard whistled or sung on every street corner on his visit to Venice in 1838 and which evoked for him the past glories of the decaying city where Shelley, the idol of his youth, had once glided in the painted gondolas. In 1864 he was in Cambo and the landscape, bathed by the hot August sun, reminded him of the days which he had spent in Italy. Four years previously he had purchased 'for a lira on a stall in Florence on another summer's day' a book which contained an account of a murder committed in Renaissance Italy. Elizabeth Browning did not approve of her husband's fascinated brooding upon evil—of all the great Victorians, Browning was the best qualified, emotionally and intellectually, to apprehend the reality of evil—and the impressions engendered by his reading the 'square old yellow book' had not formulated themselves into any coherent pattern in his conscious mind. Suddenly, as he contemplated the Pas de Roland, he saw, as in a vision, the total plan of the poem that was eventually to become *The Ring and the Book*.[1]

T. S. Eliot's elaborate tesselation of other men's poetry and prose into the body of his work is too well known to call for any detailed commentary upon his technique. The one point on which there may still exist some doubt is the extent to which he is consciously incorporating quotations into his poetry and the extent to which his unconscious mind is fishing up reminiscences of his past reading as the occasion demands. F. O. Matthiessen has pointed out that *Gerontion* almost certainly owes much to passages from A. C. Benson's study of Pater and to *The Education of Henry Adams*.[2] I think it probable that Eliot was not fully aware of his indebtedness to his sources when he wrote this poem, and consider it likely that the echoes of Kipling, Dowson, and Whitman, which various critics have discovered in his work, are less the result of deliberate imitation of these poets than a reappearance of images and of rhythms which had lain in his memory for years, only to re-emerge at a favourable moment after having suffered a sea-change. Professor Hausermann's article in *Life and Letters* lends colour to my belief that T. S. Eliot is not invariably aware of the sources from which his imagery is derived and that, as with all great poets, his nervous sensibility secretes poetry as infallibly and as automatically as an oyster secretes pearls. Professor Hausermann quotes a letter about the imagery of *East Coker* in which Eliot says: 'I think that the imagery of the first section (though taken from the village itself) may have been influenced by recollections of *Gemelhausen*, which I have not read for many years.' *Gemelhausen*, it seems, is the story of a village which, placed under Papal interdict, can neither live nor die but which, once in a hundred years for the space of a single day, resumes its ghostly revelry before sinking again into the earth.[3]

If poets themselves cannot tell us with any certainty whence

---

[1] Betty Miller, *Robert Browning: A Portrait*, p. 263.
[2] Op. cit., pp. 73–74.
[3] Helen Gardner, *The Art of T. S. Eliot*, p. 165, footnote.

they have derived their own images, a critic should beware of making dogmatic judgements on this subject. We may guess as best we can, but only the poet (and not always even he) can confirm the accuracy of our diagnosis. One of W. H. Auden's finest poems, 'Musée des Beaux Arts', is a meditation upon the nature of suffering, inspired by Brueghel's painting of the fall of Icarus. Before we could hope to discover the genesis of this poem we should have to know the circumstances in which Auden saw the painting; how long had elapsed between his seeing the picture and his writing the poem; and whether he had read any critical commentary upon the painting's significance. It is possible, for example, that he had read and partially forgotten the following passage: 'History is made up of juggernauts, revolting to human beings in their blindness, supremely humorous in their stupidity ... in Brueghel's "Fall of Icarus" the true humour of the tragedy is not so much the pair of naked legs sticking out of the water, as the complete unconcern of all the potential onlookers; not even the fisherman who sits on the shore notices what has happened.'[1] Auden's poem is a variation upon this ironical theme:

> About suffering they were never wrong,
> The Old Masters: how well they understood
> The human position. . . .
> They never forgot
> That even the dreadful martyrdom must run its course
> Anyhow in a corner, some untidy spot
> Where the dogs go on with their doggy life and
>   the torturer's horse
> Scratches its innocent behind on a tree.
>
> In Brueghel's Icarus, for instance: how everything turns away
> Quite leisurely from the disaster; the ploughman may
> Have heard the splash, the forsaken cry,
> But for him it was not an important failure; the sun shone
> As it had to on the white legs disappearing into the green
> Water; and the expensive delicate ship that must have seen
> Something amazing, a boy falling out of the sky,
> Had somewhere to get to and sailed calmly on.

A picture seen in Brussels, a passage from an historian, reflection upon human cruelty and stupidity—it is from elements such as

[1] L. B. Namier, *England in the Age of the American Revolution*, p. 149.

these that a poet creates an ordered pattern wherein his sense-perceptions are united in a rhythmical harmony.

I have tried to show in this chapter the way in which different types of experience, retained in the poet's memory, interact upon one another and help to determine the imagery and the rhythms of his verse. I propose to end this chapter by briefly and sketchily examining the poetry of W. B. Yeats in order to demonstrate how a poet imposes unity upon the multitudinous sense-impressions to which he is subjected from youth upwards, and how archetypal patterns, observation of nature, intimate biographical facts, political opinions, mystical beliefs, remembered paintings, and recollected fragments of verse and prose leave their mark upon the body of his work. I choose Yeats as my example, partly because he was the greatest poet of his time and partly because his elaborate, highly complex art readily lends itself to this particular type of exegesis.

Certain recurrent images in Yeats's poetry repay careful study, and help us to understand the way in which his poetic imagination habitually worked. Unlike Shakespeare, who normally subordinated his imagery to the development of his dramatic theme, Yeats allowed his poems to develop from the interplay of his chosen images. This method of composition can succeed only if the images themselves are sufficiently rich and complex to generate a variety of emotional responses, and the extraordinary potency of Yeats's imagery is a distinguishing feature of his verse. The most fruitful single image in his work is the Tower. Milton, Shelley, Villiers de l'Isle Adam, and Donne, all of whom Yeats passionately admired, had used this image as a symbol of the search for wisdom pursued in solitude. Such an image appealed irresistibly to Yeats's temperament, and the fact that kindred spirits had been fascinated by it invested it for him with the glamour of an archetypal symbol. As such, it provided him with the means of access to all that was eternally recurrent and primeval, to a world beyond the reach of the shallow materialism of rationalistic man: 'It is only by ancient symbols . . . that any highly subjective art can escape from the barrenness and shallowness of a too conscious arrangement into the abundance and depth of nature.'[1]

[1] *Essays*, p. 106.

His purchase of the tower at Ballylee provided him with an archetypal symbol visibly rooted in his daily existence. It came to stand for a bewildering variety of ideas, all of which were incorporated into the texture of his verse. It symbolized lonely meditation, security, the ancient ceremony of the Anglo-Irish tradition, aristocracy, action, and war. In its ruined state it took on the nature of the contemporary world:

> Is every modern nation like the tower,
> Half dead at the top?[1]

and during the Troubles, when it was threatened by fire, it fore-shadowed violence and disintegration, like the sixteenth card in the Tarot Pack, the lightning-struck tower. Above all, by remind-ing him of those poets and painters who had nourished his spirit, it served as an image of artistic glory:

> He has found, after the manner of his kind,
> More images, chosen this place to live in
> Because, it may be, of the candle-light
> From the far tower where Milton's Platonist
> Sat late, or Shelley's visionary prince:
> The lonely light that Samuel Palmer engraved,
> An image of mysterious wisdom won by toil.[2]

This bare list of the symbolic meanings which resided in the image of the Tower gives no idea of the subtle richness which Yeats lavished upon it, and I am concerned here only with the variety of the sources upon which Yeats drew when he employed this particular symbol. A great poet makes use of his daily observation, his reading, his metaphysical speculation, and the course of contemporary politics, deriving from all these facets of experience the imagery which lends distinction to his verse and kindles his creative faculties. Again and again, in Yeats, we find that his memories of books and of paintings are fused with his personal biography and his observation of the world to form one magnificent image. The image of Byzantium, for example, is compounded of diverse recollections which are miraculously welded into a perfected whole. Yeats had visited Ravenna in 1907 with Lady Gregory and had journeyed to Sicily with his wife in 1924. As a result of his reading of history which he had under-

---

[1] 'Blood and the Moon.'   [2] 'Phases of the Moon.'

taken to illustrate 'A Vision', he had come to believe that 'in early Byzantium, maybe never before or since in recorded history, religious, aesthetic and practical life were one'.[1] Moreover, Byzantium was to him the symbol of completeness and of ecstasy, not the Christian heaven nor the Buddhist Nirvana, but a condition in which the immortal soul delighted in an intensely joyful sensuality.

The very language of the poem, 'Sailing to Byzantium', bears the traces of the poetry and the painting he had loved so long, and even incorporates certain phrases which he had used many years before in his prose writings. Thus, in stanza II, 'soul clap its hands and sing' is a reminiscence of Blake; the juxtaposition of fire and music in stanza III echoes the phrase in 'Per Amica Silentia Lunae': 'in the condition of fire is all music and all rest'; his prayer that he may be gathered 'into the artifice of eternity' is adumbrated in the passage from *The Tables of the Law* (1895) in which he writes of 'that supreme art which is to win us from life and gather us into eternity like doves into their dovecots'; finally, his reference to the golden bough in the last stanza is probably coloured by his memory of Turner's painting *The Golden Bough*, at which he had stared for hours in his childhood.[2]

In 'Nineteen Hundred and Nineteen' he employs the imagery of weasels fighting in a hole to convey his sense of the political degradation into which Ireland had sunk. During his wanderings in the woods at Coole, he had seen weasels fighting and running across the woodland paths, so that this image may well have been drawn from his observation in the countryside, but Dr. Jeffares suggests that he may also have recollected a passage from Landor's *Imaginary Conversation* between Windham and Sheridan on Church Establishment in Ireland: 'Turn out the weasel against the rat, and at least while they are fighting neither of them can corrode the rafters or infest the larder.'[3]

Memories of early years and recollections of books combined with the turbulent events of his life to renew his stock of imagery. The rough beast of 'The Second Coming' was, indeed, an image

---

[1] 'A Vision', p. 279.
[2] Ellmann, *Yeats: The Man and the Masks*, pp. 258–9.
[3] *W. B. Yeats, Man and Poet*.

out of *Spiritus Mundi*, but it was also a memory summoned from the 1880s when MacGregor Mathers had conjured up the form of a Titan rising from the desert. The beautiful celebration of sensuality in 'Supernatural Songs' owes something to the Steinach glandular operation which Yeats underwent in 1934, but it owes more to Yeats's preoccupation with sex and the dead, the only two topics that 'can be of the slightest interest to a serious and studious mind'.[1] His friend Edwin Ellis, fifty years before, who had been his collaborator in the book on Blake, used to speak only of religion and sex, and Swedenborg, whom Yeats revered, had indulged in curious speculations upon these themes. In a letter to Mrs. Shakespear, 24 July 1934, Yeats spoke of work in progress: 'I have another poem in my head where a monk read his breviary at midnight on the tomb of long dead lovers on the anniversary of their death, for on that night they are united above the tomb, their embrace being not partial but a conflagration of the entire body and so shedding the light he reads by.' In an earlier letter to Mrs. Shakespear, dated 21 February 1933, he had recalled 'the saying of Swedenborg's that the sexual intercourse of angels is a conflagration of the whole being'. Memories of Ellis, of Swedenborg, and of past love, are reanimated by the miraculous spurt of energy which followed his operation: the resulting poem burns with a supernatural flame of joy:

> The miracle that gave them such a death
> Transfigured to pure substance what had once
> Been bone and sinew; when such bodies join
> There is no touching here, nor touching there,
> Nor straining joy, but whole is joined to whole;
> For the intercourse of angels is a light
> Where for the moment both seem lost, consumed.

Yeats's ability to transmute into poetry his memories of books and of pictures, as well as the raw material of daily life, remained unimpaired until the end of his life. The influence of Blake, for example, continually irradiates his verse, suggesting appropriate images, animating the rhythms, and helping him to find a pattern of blessedness in the sensual agony of an existence where blind men batter blind men. Dr. Jeffares cites a remarkable example of Yeats's power to retain a single phrase, to brood upon it, and

[1] Letter to Mrs. Shakespear, 2 Oct. 1927.

finally to transform it into a magnificent line of poetry.[1] Swinburne, in his book on Blake, made a contemptuous reference to Yeats's essay on the poet's work and spoke of Blake as a man who was 'fitfully audacious and fancifully delirious'. Years later, in his poem *September 1913*, Yeats, remembering this scornful judgement upon Blake and an insulting remark about the Celts which accompanied it, proudly adopted one of Swinburne's adjectives and applied it to those who had devoted their lives to Ireland:

> Was it for this the wild geese spread
> The grey wing upon every tide;
> For this that all that blood was shed,
> For this Edward Fitzgerald died,
> And Robert Emmett and Wolfe Tone,
> All that delirium of the brave?
> Romantic Ireland's dead and gone,
> It's with O'Leary in the grave.

Yeats's debt to Blake is visible not only in his constant employment of such words as 'lineaments' and 'copulate' which frequently occur in Blake's writings, but also in the sensual grandeur, prophetic majesty, and abounding zest that distinguish the poems of Yeats's last period, 1933–9. Occasionally, the reminiscences of Blake are miraculously fused with other memories that apparently belong to a totally different order of experiences. F. R. Higgins points out Yeats's remarkable power of juxtaposing two dissimilar moods: 'There were, for him, only two commingling states of verse. One, simple, bucolic, or rabelaisian, the other, intellectual, exotic, or visionary.'[2] These two commingling states are clearly visible in one of his most superb achievements, 'News For The Delphic Oracle', wherein he displays a consummate mastery of rhythm, image, and syntax. T. R. Henn has shown that Yeats's verse is often loaded with reminiscences of paintings which he had admired, and there is little doubt that, in this particular poem, he was haunted by a recollection of 'The Marriage of Peleus and Thetis'.[3] The classical serenity and decorum of Poussin's painting has been overwhelmed by a naked sensuality, a brutality of expression, and a tremendous zestful vitality which rises to a Dionysian frenzy, without becoming either ugly or uncontrolled:

[1] Op. cit., pp. 172–3.
[2] *Scattreing Branches*, p. 152.
[3] *The Lonely Tower*, pp. 225–54.

Slim adolescence that a nymph has stripped,
Peleus on Thetis stares.
Her limbs are delicate as an eyelid,
Love has blinded him with tears;
But Thetis' belly listens.
Down the mountain walls
From where Pan's cavern is
Intolerable music falls.
Foul goat-head, brutal arm appear,
Belly, shoulder, bum,
Flash fish-like; nymphs and satyrs
Copulate in the foam.

These are the very accents of Yeats in his tremendous final period, but they contain a hint of Blake's youthful fire and frolic which exploded in parts of *The Island in the Moon*. Indeed, the nearest parallel that I know to the sensual levity which characterizes some of Yeats's last poems is to be found in Blake's early extravaganza, and in particular in one song which displays a savage, ironic gaiety that Yeats came to adopt as he grew older:

Hail Matrimony, made of Love!
To thy wide gates how great a drove
On purpose to be yoked do come;
Widows and maids and youths also,
That lightly trip on beauty's toe,
Or sit on beauty's bum.

Yeats himself recognized that all poetic imagery ultimately comes from experience and that the search for its origins leads us into strange, dark places of whose existence we are scarcely aware. In a poignant survey of his life's work he reviewed the images which, at various stages of his career, had dominated his poetry. All had now deserted him, and he was left to face the desolation of reality alone:

Those masterful images because complete
Grew in pure mind, but out of what began?
A mound of refuse or the sweepings of a street,
Old kettles, old bottles, and a broken can,
Old iron, old bone, old rags, that raving slut
Who keeps the till. Now that my ladder's gone,
I must lie down where all the ladders start,
In the foul rag-and-bone shop of the heart.[1]

[1] *The Circus Animals' Desertion.*

Our greatest living poet has, in his graver music, restated Yeats's declaration that poetry is born when we brood upon our experience of the past—not merely upon the events of our own life, upon our personal joys and sorrows, but upon our reading, our philosophical speculation about the human situation, our sense of the past. It is no accident that the images in *Four Quartets* are drawn from so wide a field, from the four elements, from childhood memories, from adult experience, from English history, and from Greek and Indian metaphysics. All form part of the pattern of dead and living, the pattern which it is the poet's task and privilege to discern and to embody in the words of his poem:

> As we grow older
> The world becomes stranger, the pattern more complicated
> Of dead and living. Not the intense moment
> Isolated, with no before and after,
> But a lifetime burning in every moment
> And not the lifetime of one man only
> But of old stones that cannot be deciphered.[1]

[1] *East Coker*, v.

Chapter Eight

In the last chapter we saw how memory and experience provided the poet with a flood of images and rhythms, and how a wide variety of memories might often be found inextricably twined together in a single image. We must now inquire into the means by which the poet imposes a formal pattern upon the rhythms and images that surge through his mind, and into his motives for doing so.

It is often assumed that the poet is primarily concerned with communicating a meaning or transmitting a feeling. Investigation into the meaning of meaning and into the nature of communication would require a book in itself, and I am content merely to state my belief that the poet's overmastering impulse is something other than the wish to convey an idea or an emotion to an audience. For, as both I. A. Richards and T. S. Eliot have insisted, meaning and communication, like experience, are ambiguous words, especially in the context of poetry and the poetic process.

W. H. Auden, even in his undergraduate days, insisted that he was, as a poet, less preoccupied with emotional experiences than with the ordered patterns of words in which they were precipitated and embodied.[1] Matthew Arnold had expressed a similar opinion in his strictures upon the common practice of his own day: 'More and more I feel bent against the modern English habit (too much encouraged by Wordsworth) of using poetry as a channel for thinking aloud instead of making anything.'[2] When a poet is absorbed in making a poem, the contours of his philosophical speculations and beliefs may appear more firmly and clearly than if he deliberately parades them before the world. Nothing is of poetic significance until it has been ordered into a poetic pattern, and concentration on this pattern may permit feelings and thoughts to manifest themselves unhampered by the fever and fidget of the poet's conscious mind. Eliot once told

[1] Stephen Spender, *World Within World*, p. 59.
[2] *Unpublished Letters of Matthew Arnold*, ed. Arnold Whitridge, p. 17, cited by G. Tillotson, *Criticism and the Nineteenth Century*, pp. 208–9.

A. L. Rowse that 'he could never write a poem unless he tricked himself into the belief that it was only a technical problem to be solved.'[1] Lawrence Durrell, in his essay on Henry Miller, also minimizes the importance of statement and of dogma in poetry:

> For the creative man the whole world of philosophic or religious ideas is simply a sort of harem from which he chooses now this pretty concubine, now that. . . . The truth is that the artist is at his most immoral when he reaches the domain of ideas. He is concerned, of course, not with the dialectical truth of ideas, but simply with their beauty and appositeness to his own temperamental make-up. He chooses often exactly the *opposite* of what he is, simply in order to provide a counter-balance to his own over-balanced sensibility. Yeats felt an almost sensual attraction for the calm of the Indian sages.[2]

Although we may find it impossible to accept all the implications of this theory, we can welcome the suggestion that poetry is full of complexity, tension, ambiguity, and contradiction, and that there is, in all poetic creation, a reconciliation of the discords that perplex and divide the poet's nature. Some critics believe that all art springs from suffering, and that no poet can wield the bow unless, like Philoctetes, he has first been deeply wounded: 'No one has ever written, painted, sculpted, modelled, constructed, or invented anything, except in order to extricate himself from hell.'[3] The artist is, in Cyril Connolly's phrase, a self-cured neurotic, poetry being, in part, a manifestation of nervous disorder and, in part, a therapeutic process by which the patient heals himself of his affliction. In extreme cases the patient may cling to his disease for fear that the power of writing poetry may cease.[4] Without assigning to suffering and to illness the preeminent place accorded them by such theories, we may acknowledge that poetic composition is a means whereby disharmonies are resolved and conflicting elements reconciled in the formal dance of words. The energy of poetry, to use Blake's terminology, is generated from the dialectical clash of contraries. The

---

[1] A. L. Rowse, *A Cornish Childhood*, p. 218.

[2] *Horizon*, July 1949.

[3] Antoin Artaud, 'Van Gogh, The Suicide Provoked by Society', *Horizon*, Jan. 1948. Artaud endeavoured to escape from his hell by suicide. For a discussion of the relationship of art and neurosis, cf. E. Wilson, *The Wound and the Bow*, Lionel Trilling's essay on this theme in *The Liberal Imagination*, and the section in *The Orators*, entitled 'Letter to a Wound', by W. H. Auden.

[4] Robert Graves, *Goodbye to all that*, p. 381.

absence of any such conflict in most didactic verse is responsible for our comparatively low estimate of this species of poetry, as Robert Graves observed: '. . . In didactic verse, where a sudden doubt arises and the teacher admits himself a blind groper after truth (so Lucretius time and time again) and breaks his main argument in digressions after loveliness and terror, only then does Poetry appear. It flashes out with the surprise and shock of a broken electric circuit.'[1] Browning and Swinburne are examples of poets whose natures were at war with themselves and who, precariously and fleetingly, found in the formal coherence of poetry a compensation and a remedy for the turbulence of their divided personalities. Both, in their later years, having come to terms with society and with themselves, hastened to renounce all that reminded them of their former disequilibrium. 'I never had really much in common with Baudelaire' wrote Swinburne to William Sharp in 1901; Browning likewise disavowed his youthful idolatry of Shelley, choosing to assume a protective cloak of overt normality, much to the perplexity of Henry James who was struck by his 'loud, sound, normal, hearty presence, all so assertive and so whole, all bristling with prompt responses and expected opinions and usual views'.[2] His youthful remorse and uncertainty, engendered by the consciousness of having delivered falsely or imperfectly the message with which he had been entrusted by God, were the mainspring of his poetic imagination. When the passage of time had concealed the deep split in his personality, there was no longer an impelling necessity to resolve the inner conflict in dramatic poems: 'Inspiration extinguished, an excess of energy was released, which expressed itself, jauntily enough, in the garrulous, irascible, highly didactic work of his later years.'[3]

Whether we hold with Yeats that poetry springs from our quarrel with ourselves, or whether we prefer to say with Housman that it exists to harmonize the sadness of the world, we are recognizing the fact that it is a way of restoring order to a fragmentary and disquieting universe, wherein all seems broken and decayed. James Joyce says that the purpose of art is 'to try slowly and humbly and constantly to express, to press out again,

---

[1] *On English Poetry*, p. 99.
[2] Cited by Betty Miller, *Robert Browning*, p. 271.   [3] Ibid., p. 271.

from the gross earth or what it brings forth, from sound and shape and colour which are the prison gates of our soul, an image of the beauty we have come to understand',[1] and Ruskin tells us how, after contemplating a part of the universe, we extricate it from infinity 'as one gathers a violet out of grass; one does not improve either violet or grass in gathering it, but one makes the flower visible; and then the human being has to make its power upon his own heart visible also. . . . And sometimes he may be able to do more than this, and to set it in strange lights, and display it a thousand ways before unknown.'[2] Whitman also exults in the poet's power to create harmony and to cleanse our perceptions:

His thoughts are the hymns of the praise of things . . . he sees eternity in men and women—he does not see men and women as dreams or dots. . . . Now he has passed that way, see after him! there is not left any vestige of despair or misanthropy or cunning or exclusiveness or the ignominy of a nativity or colour, or delusion of hell or the necessity of hell and no man henceforward shall be degraded for ignorance or weakness or sin.[3]

Both Emerson and Whitman compare a poem with a perfect form of nature; both remark that it has an architecture of its own as flawless as 'the flight of the grey gull across the bay, or the mettlesome action of the blood-horse, or the tall leaning of sunflowers on their stalk'.[4] The task of poetry, says Francis Thompson, is 'to see and restore ye divine idea of things, freed from ye disfiguring accidents of their Fall',[5] a belief expressed in almost precisely the same words by John Dennis in his *The Grounds of Criticism in Poetry* (1704).[6]

If such views are correct, it follows that the raw material of poetry will often be ugly, complex, bewildering, and incoherent. Moreover, the poet's constant task will be to impose a unity upon his raw material by fusing together the disparate elements into a perfected whole. The formal perfection of a poem may, indeed, be an indication that the poet is aware of warring, rebellious passions in his divided nature that can be subdued only by the

---

[1] *A Portrait of the Artist.*

[2] Cited by Robin Ironside in an article on Ruskin, *Horizon*, July 1943.

[3] Preface to *Leaves of Grass*.   [4] Ibid.

[5] From an unpublished Notebook of Francis Thompson, cited in Viola Meynell, *Francis Thompson and Wilfrid Meynell*, p. 155.

[6] 'The great design of art is to restore the decay that happened to human nature by the fall, by restoring order.'

redeeming power of his imagination: 'The more he is conscious of an inner disorder, the more value he will place on tidiness in the work as a *defence*.'[1] Swinburne's curious response to pleasure and to pain was one manifestation of a nervous, febrile sensibility that was perpetually threatened by disintegration. In *Poems and Ballads* and in *Atalanta* the promptings of his temperament and his intellectual convictions were beautifully crystallized in the achieved mastery of great verse. Humphrey Hare has shown how this precarious and transient synthesis, attained only by a remarkable exercise of poetic imagination, gradually dissolved, never to be recaptured. He has gone so far as to suggest that the very form of Swinburne's poetry was largely determined by the means that he found of satisfying his erotic needs, and relates the changes in his poetic style to his more and more frequent visits to 'the fair friend who keeps a maison de supplices à la Rodin' in the Euston Road, and who enabled him to assuage the frenetic impulses of his nature. On this theory: '"Mrs. A." was as much responsible for the form of *Songs before Sunrise* as Mazzini himself.'[2]

Part of a poem's vitality springs from the dialectical interplay of opposites, the dramatic tension, and the counterpointing of themes which are found therein. A poet's stature largely depends upon the range and the diversity of ideas and of emotions that he can successfully incorporate into his verse. Shakespeare towers above his fellows because of his incomparable ability to assimilate a bewildering variety of experiences into his consciousness, to retain them there and, finally, to release them, transformed, by imaginative pressure, into poetic wholes. His use of obscenity reveals something of his poetic method: in his work it is almost always dramatically appropriate, an integral part of the total design.[3] Mercutio's playful, glittering, detached obscene speculation is quite different from the cheerful bawdiness of the Nurse or of Mistress Overdone, which, in its turn, is unlike Lear's demoniacal sexual tirades or Hamlet's cruel mockery of Ophelia. Shakespeare embraces obscenity as frankly, and employs it as discerningly, as he welcomes and delineates the exquisite delicacy

---

[1] W. H. Auden, *Tennyson:* an Introduction and a Selection, p. xvii.

[2] Humphrey Hare, *Swinburne*, p. 151.

[3] Chaucer displays a similar mastery of obscenity, e.g. in *The Miller's Tale* he fuses the sacred and obscene, thereby enriching the poem and raising what might be simply a bawdy tale to the level of profound comedy.

of Miranda or of Imogen. Pope, though to a lesser degree than Shakespeare, can fuse a variety of emotions into the flawless amber of his poetry. He scrutinized with calm, melancholy gaze all that was scrubby and smelly in the London of his day, hack poets and translators, the dirty corpses of dogs in the muddy Thames, the greed of the City, and the licentiousness of men whose superficial polish barely concealed their wolfish passions. In his verse, wit, tenderness, sadness, obscenity, and satire are commingled in a liquid harmony.

Assimilation of diverse experiences, followed by a fusion of the disparate elements and their transmutation into poetry—such is the nature of the poetic process. There is a sentence of Wordsworth's which suggests that he fully recognized the necessity of a poet's absorbing into his very being the observations, ideas, and emotions which he turns into poetry: 'The remote discoveries of the chemist, the botanist, or the mineralogist, will be as proper objects as any upon which he is now employed, if the time should ever come when these things shall be manifestly and palpably material to us as enjoying and suffering beings.'[1] Rilke, after stressing the importance for a poet of experiences and memories, warns us that to have such experiences and memories, however varied, is not enough: 'Only when they have turned to blood within us, to glance and gesture, nameless and no longer to be distinguished from ourselves—only then can it happen that in a most rare hour the first word of a poem arises in their midst and goes forth from them.'[2]

As for the necessity of fusion, Coleridge has described how the poet 'brings the whole soul of man into activity', by exercising the Imagination: 'He diffuses a tone and spirit of unity, that blends, and (as it were) *fuses*, each into each, by that synthetic and magical power to which I would exclusively appropriate the name of Imagination. This power ... reveals itself in the balance or reconcilement of opposite or discordant qualities.'[3] T. S. Eliot. in an equally famous passage, singles out as a distinguishing mark of the poet this coadunating power: 'When a poet's mind is perfectly equipped for its work, it is constantly amalgamating

---

[1] George Sampson (editor), *The Lyrical Ballads*, 1798–1805, p. 26 (1944).
[2] *Notebook of Malte Laurids Brigge.*
[3] *Biographia Literaria*, ch. xiv.

disparate experience; the ordinary man's experience is chaotic, irregular, fragmentary. The latter falls in love, or reads Spinoza, and these two experiences have nothing to do with each other, or with the noise of the typewriter or the smell of cooking; in the mind of the poet these experiences are always forming new wholes.'[1] It may be objected that such a description of the poet applies only to those who adopt the metaphysical style, 'a kind of *discordia concors*; a combination of dissimilar images, or discovery of occult resemblances in things apparently unlike', as Dr. Johnson defined it. My belief is that this bringing together of widely divergent material is an essential ingredient in any poetic style that is worth considering. Eliot has drawn attention to this aspect of poetry in *The Use of Poetry*, where he tells us that the poet is one who sees, 'beneath both beauty and ugliness, the boredom, and the horror, and the glory'.[2] In a passage of first-rate importance he reveals his debt to his early masters:

I think that from Baudelaire I learned first, a precedent for the poetical possibilities, never developed by any poet writing in my own language, of the more sordid aspects of the modern metropolis, of the possibility of fusion between the sordidly realistic and the phantasmagoric, the possibility of the juxtaposition of the matter-of-fact and the fantastic. From him, as from Laforgue, I learned that the sort of material that I had, the sort of experience that an adolescent had had, in an industrial city in America, could be the material for poetry; and that the source of new poetry might be found in what had been regarded hitherto as the impossible, the sterile, the intractably unpoetic. That, in fact, the business of the poet was to make poetry out of the unexplored resources of the unpoetical; that the poet, in fact, was committed by his profession to turn the unpoetical into poetry.[3]

A hundred years before, Clough had ironically remarked:

Juxtaposition, in short; and what is juxtaposition?

Croker knew the answer to that question. In an anonymous review of Tennyson's poems in the *Quarterly*, April 1833, he sneered at the poet's attempt to amalgamate divergent modes of experience: 'Observe how all ages become present to the mind of

---

[1] *Selected Essays*, p. 287. Shelley makes a similar observation: 'Poetry subdues to union under its light yoke all irreconcilable things.'

[2] p. 106.

[3] 'Talk on Dante', *The Adelphi*, First Quarter, 1951. The frugal, ironic genius of Cavafy made poetry from such unpromising raw material as uneasy homosexual love. Cf. 'Their Beginning'.

a great poet; and admire how naturally he combines the funeral cypress of antiquity with the crape hatband of the modern undertaker.'[1] Today we have come to realize that such a conjunction is a legitimate aim of poetry and that a poem is a reconciliation of complex emotions rather than a celebration of a single feeling.

The best way of observing this poetic fusion in action is to glance at a few lines of poetry by writers of different styles. Take a single line of Shakespeare's:

> And summer's lease hath all too short a date

and notice how the dry, legal terms are fused with the warm, evocative word 'summer' to produce an effect of delight, mingled with regret at the realization that the beauty of the summer is confined to a brief spell ordained by an implacable law. Donne, in a passionate disquisition upon love, employs an image drawn from governmental finance to clinch his argument, nor are we conscious of any incongruity, so perfectly have the two emotions and concepts been conjoined:

> And though each spring doe adde to love new heate,
> As princes doe in times of action get
> New taxes, and remit them not in peace,
> No winter shall abate the springs encrease.[2]

Pope's subtle variation of tone and texture can be appreciated only if we read him with every sense alert to the blending of shades of meaning and to the emotional implications beneath the surface. After describing the magnificence of Timon's villa, he imagines a time when the pomp of wealth and the achievement of art will be obliterated:

> Another age shall see the golden Ear
> Embrown the Slope and nod on the parterre,
> Deep Harvests bury all his pride has plann'd,
> And laughing Ceres re-assume the land.[3]

These four lines hold the balance perfectly between two contrasting emotions, regret at the mutability of man's work and acceptance of life's rhythm in which all things endlessly flow

---

[1] Cited by Harold Nicolson, *Tennyson*, p. 112.
[2] 'Love's Growth.'
[3] *Moral Essays*, Epistle IV.

like the sea. The precarious, formal beauty of art crumbles and dissolves in time's oceanic flood, yet this flood is no mere sterile destroyer but a great, fertilizing, natural force, that permits new shapes of beauty to flower for a brief span of years. Timon's villa gives way, not to choking weeds but to golden harvests, and these harvests are deep both because they utterly drown the Augustan marble and the landscape-gardening which Pope himself loved, and because they are the symbol of life's abundant, eternal fertility. Ceres laughs when, like a monarch, she reassumes the land (note how the technical term is exquisitely fused with the romantic warmth of the other phrases); partly in mockery at human pretentiousness, and partly out of joy as she scatters her bounty to the race of men. These lines are a triumph of romantic discernment informed by a radiant intelligence, and it is instructive to compare them with eight beautiful lines by Robert Louis Stevenson, which are on a similar theme:

> We travelled in the print of olden wars,
> Yet all the land was green,
> And love we found, and peace,
> Where fire and war had been.

> They pass and smile, the children of the sword—
> No more the sword they wield,
> And O, how deep the corn
> Along the battlefield.

Pope's lines seem to me superior in every way. Stevenson, in harping upon the contrast between life and death, has to employ abstractions such as love, peace, fire, war, in order to gain his effects; Pope unfolds a sequence of images which contains within itself poetic truth and logic and which reconciles two divergent emotions by counterpointing the one against the other. Stevenson proves himself a skilful writer who presents us with a poetic truism and Pope is revealed as a great poet who enlarges our understanding of the human condition.

I select one further example of Pope's ability to fuse divergent feelings, moods, and beliefs into an imaginative whole. In his 'Epilogue to the Satires' he refers with devastating contempt to the poetasters, Grub-Street hacks, place-men, and flatterers who fawned upon the Hanoverian Court and upon the Whig noblemen whom he detested:

Ye tinsel Insects! whom a Court maintains,
That counts your Beauties only by your Stains,
Spin all your Cobwebs o'er the Eye of Day!
The Muse's wing shall brush you all away.

The ambivalence of the words 'tinsel Insects' and 'Stains' enables
Pope to combine and to juxtapose emotions of disgust with the
conviction that all that lives is beautiful. Even tawdry creatures
may glitter with a silvery flash, and although, in one sense, a stain
is a moral deformity or a physical blemish, in another sense it is a
delicate marking such as distinguishes one butterfly from another.
Pope thus combines a loathing for a Court which values men only
for their corruptness, with a tender evocation of filmy creatures
whose lives are over in a day, and even the two final lines are not
wholly untinged with compassion. There is something pathetic
in the efforts of these noisome little courtiers to lay up treasure
for themselves and to achieve nothing but cobwebs which the
implacable Muse shall destroy in her immortal flight.

Such intellectual compression, evocativeness, and intensity is,
admittedly, characteristic of the Metaphysical rather than of the
Romantic style, but it is found in all fine poetry, in slightly
differing forms. Shelley's line:

Bright as that wandering Eden Lucifer[1]

is a beautiful example of extreme compression of meaning and
intense fusion of ideas. Byron, throughout *Don Juan*, combines
a sardonic wit, a sense of nature's overwhelming beauty, and an
acceptance of human depravity and impotence, notably in his
description of the shipwreck. In particular, his explanation of
why the master-mate was not eaten fuses wit, horror, and
obscenity into three unforgettable lines:

And that which chiefly proved his saving clause,
Was a small present made to him at Cadiz,
By general subscription of the ladies.[2]

Keats's poetry, which is compounded of suggestion, inter-related
ideas, and linked images, manages to combine a brooding upon
death with an evocation of warm sensuality. It is, indeed, the
simultaneous presentation of these conflicting themes that suf-

---

[1] *Epipsychidion*, 459.   [2] *Don Juan*, II, lxxii.

fuses his verse with a mellow beauty and an unearthly melodiousness unparalleled in our poetry:

> But when the melancholy fit shall fall
> Sudden from Heaven like a weeping cloud,
> That fosters the droop-headed flowers all,
> And hides the green hill in an April shroud. . . .[1]

The mingling sun and rain weave a mist that covers the burgeoning hill—such is the obvious sense of the line; but the hill is green
because it is the symbol of youth and of fertility, and the mist of
April, which is soft and white, is also the shroud which brings a
reminder of death to those who respond most passionately to the
joys of sensuality. Keats, no less than Pope, amalgamated dissimilar modes of experience into a poetic harmony, and the better
we understand Keats's high intelligence the more readily we shall
perceive Pope's deep emotion. Both poets were gifted with a
devouring sensibility and with a passionate understanding that,
modifying their every thought and experience, enabled them to
fuse together all the phrases, rhythms, images, and sense impressions with which their memories were saturated. An anonymous
writer has analysed in some detail the probable origin of 'La
Belle Dame Sans Merci' and shown how the esemplastic power
of the poet shaped a number of diverse elements into an organic
unity. In this poem can be traced recollections of Reynolds's
parody of 'Peter Bell'; of mysterious letters to Keats's brother
from 'Amena'; of 'The Eve of St. Mark'; of *The Faerie Queene*,
III, vii. A hangover after a claret party seems to have induced
in Keats a drowsy, mellow state, in which his poetic faculty was
free to operate. These various particles of experience, which had
been lying dormant in his mind, were fused by his transmuting
imagination into poetry.[2] Robert Gittings has shown how, in the
last period of his life, Keats was able to transform into rich poetry
every facet of his experience—a visit to a chapel; a friendship
with a beautiful, mature woman; and the books that he read,
notably *The Anatomy of Melancholy*.[3]

T. S. Eliot has specifically named the 'Ode to a Nightingale'
as a poem which bears out his belief that a poet's mind is akin to
the shred of platinum that acts as a catalyst, enabling oxygen and

---

[1] 'Ode on Melancholy.'
[2] *T.L.S.*, 14 March 1952.   [3] *John Keats, The Living Year.*

sulphur dioxide to form sulphurous acid.[1] His own nightingales, in 'Sweeney Among the Nightingales', serve to bring together a number of feelings and to combine them into a new unity. We may pause here to inquire in what ways, and to what extent, contemporary practice differs from the poetic technique of earlier periods, and whether Eliot's conjunction of a sordid brothel murder and the slaying of Agamemnon is in the same category as the combination of the cypress and the crape hatband which Croker derided.

Jack Isaacs, after quoting Poe's remark that the mystic expression of a sentiment has 'the vast force of an accompaniment in music', speaks of 'the secret and invisible welding of the most contradictory elements, combined with that confusion of the senses, or rather fusion of the senses, which is the hall-mark of modern suggestive writing'.[2] I have suggested that the welding of contradictory elements is to be found in all great English poetry of every period, and I have cited Shakespeare, Milton, and Shelley to indicate that fusion of the senses has been understood and practised for centuries. Even the modern reliance upon a musical indefiniteness, a quasi-symphonic development of poetic themes, and the employment of linked images as a substitute for logical argument is not without older parallels:

> Gently dip, but not too deep,
> For fear you make the golden beard to weep.
> Fair maiden, white and red,
> Comb me smooth and stroke my head,
> And thou shalt have some cockell-bread.

> Gently dip, but not too deep,
> For fear thou make the golden beard to weep.
> Fair maid, white and red,
> Comb me smooth and stroke my head,
> And every hair a sheaf shall be,
> And every sheaf a golden tree.

Peele's images are as logically irrelevant and as poetically effective as those which occur in the song from *Measure for Measure*:

> Take O take those lips away
> That so sweetly were forsworn,

---

[1] *Selected Essays*, pp. 17–18. [2] *The Background of Modern Poetry*, p. 26.

And those eyes the break of day,
   Lights that do mislead the morn;
But my kisses bring again,
         bring again,
Seals of love, but seal'd in vain,
         seal'd in vain.

These lines are indeed ravishing poetry but they are not, as A. E. Housman once asserted, nonsensical:[1] they are an example of subtle poetic sense, of unerring poetic logic. Sung as they are by a Boy to Mariana, they are exquisitely calculated to convey the overpowering sweetness of sexual desire and its utter deceitfulness. The audience, moreover, will be reminded that Angelo has debased the seals of love as shamefully as he has misused the seals of office entrusted to him by the Duke. No abstract statement about infidelity could match the alchemy by which these images and these cadences evoke the tragedy of the deserted Mariana. A third example may be quoted of a poem which, in the words of Rilke, 'names a lyrical total instead of enumerating the various steps necessary to reach the result':[2]

The maidens came
When I was in my mother's bower;
I had all that I would.
The bailey beareth the bell away;
The lily, the rose, the rose I lay.

The silver is white, red is the gold;
The robes they lay in fold.
The bailey beareth the bell away;
The lily, the rose, the rose I lay.

And through the glass window shines the sun.
How should I love, and I so young?
The bailey beareth the bell away;
The lily, the rose, the rose I lay.
                             Anon.

This passing from one image to another in rapid succession is found in Shakespeare, particularly in the later plays, and I understand that Pindar accumulates images in a single sentence without

---

[1] *The Name and Nature of Poetry*, p. 41.
[2] Cited by J. Isaacs, *An Assessment of Contemporary Literature*, p. 168.

making logical transitions. What Coleridge designated 'the glare and glitter of a perpetual, yet broken and heterogeneous imagery' is not so recent an invention as one might think.

Nevertheless, when we have admitted that earlier poets anticipated our contemporary devices, we are justified in claiming that poets of the present time differ markedly from their predecessors, for while we can find isolated examples in older poets of musical suggestiveness and of imagery used in place of normal logical development, the systematic employment of these devices is a legacy of Symbolism. Furthermore, although poets have always fused disparate and contradictory emotions, the juxtaposition of recondite states of mind, the dislocation of language, and the tesselation of startlingly dissimilar images have, in the present century, attained a new pitch of intensity. The praiseworthy desire to reject no facet of human experience as alien to poetry tends to become a determination to incorporate the sordid into poetry as a gesture of defiance or as a proof of technical virtuosity. In either of these two attitudes a sense of strain is all too apparent, and W. H. Auden's remark to Stephen Spender that the gasworks were more poetic than anything else in Oxford was merely an inverted form of Poe's determination to exploit the poetical associations of ravens, bereaved lovers, beautiful dead women, and the sonorous music of the word 'Nevermore'. Both are examples of what Hopkins described as 'frigid fancy with no imagination'. The complexity of our civilization, the discoveries of psycho-analysis, the Surrealist delight in so-called free association of ideas, the new techniques perfected by the film and by the radio, our desire for speed, slickness, streamlined elegance, and sophisticated ingenuity have led us to demand from poetry a concentrated passion and a highly elaborate network of images, in which the leisurely development of a theme is impatiently dismissed as padding.

Yet, despite every change in poetic fashion, every innovation in poetic technique, the poet's task remains what it has always been. Now, as in the past, he must order his experience into a formally satisfying unity and develop that metre-making argument which, according to Emerson, makes a poem 'a thought so passionate and alive, that, like the spirit of a plant or an animal, it has an architecture of its own and adorns nature with a new thing'. I have suggested that a poem grows beneath the surface of the poet's conscious mind and that it takes its origin from the promptings of his animal sensibility, from his response to the images and rhythms that present themselves to him and from his ability to transmute all his experiences and memories into poetry. This work of sifting, refining, and condensing the divergent elements that constitute the flux of being is largely unconscious, and the foundations upon which a poem rests lie hidden and submerged beneath the deep waters of the poet's mind. It would, however, be a grave mistake to depreciate the importance of the conscious, deliberate craftsmanship that goes to the making of a poem. It is noteworthy that Robert Graves, who insists that the primary stage of poetic composition takes place during a trance-like suspension of normal habits of thought, should himself devote immense time and labour to the secondary phase of correction.

Some poets, it is true, feel temperamentally disinclined to revise their work, either through laziness, or from a belief that such polishing is cold and insincere, a calculating, contrived tampering with the spontaneous utterance of the heart. Browning's reluctance to chisel at his rough-hewn creations and Edward Thomas's refusal to take Garnett's advice about making some of his poems a shade neater are examples of this unwillingness to correct a poem in the interests of smoothness and regularity. Byron said that, like a tiger, he must succeed with his first spring or not at all, and Shelley seems to have regarded the conscious intervention of the poet as a regrettable necessity, designed to keep the poem going in the dreary intervals between flashes of inspiration 'by the intertexture of conventional expressions'.[1]

A few poets are able to write down a poem which is almost flawless and which requires only minor corrections, either because, having formed itself in their unconscious minds over a long period, it suddenly emerges into the light complete and perfect, or, because they prefer to commit nothing to paper until they have solved all their problems in their head. Racine would not pen a line of a play until the entire work had taken shape in his mind, just as Mozart habitually composed a whole movement without having to make a pause or a correction. Shakespeare's disinclination to blot a line may have sprung from his power to

[1] F. W. Bateson, op. cit., p. 43.

visualize a five-act play as a long dramatic poem in which every image, rhythm, and theme contributed to the total design.

Such a faculty is rare: most poets resemble Beethoven whose notebooks bear witness to the false starts, the gropings after clarity, and the agonized strivings to discover what one desires to say, which are the normal accompaniments to artistic endeavour. This work of correction demands considerable patience and devotion to minute detail, for every phrase must be scrutinized before it is finally admitted into the text of the poem. The poem's syntax must be rigorously examined, in order that monotonous repetition of definite articles, relative clauses, and feeble conjunctions may be avoided. The sonnets of Mallarmé and of Hopkins, like the last poems of W. B. Yeats, achieve some of their most characteristically beautiful effects by the way in which grammatical devices have been employed to attain the utmost concentration of meaning. It is instructive also to compare the grammatical crudity displayed by Whitman, as he reels off a long catalogue of affirmations in 'A Song of Myself', with the subtle modulations of grammatical form to be found in Spenser or in Milton, both of whom exploit all the resources of syntax in order to control the speed and the rhythm of their verse.[1] The syntactical complexity and beauty of poetry, although often neglected or undervalued, are among those elements which no translator can hope to reproduce in another tongue, and only those who have tried to write poetry can fully appreciate the difficulty of making grammar itself contribute to the shape and to the development of the poem.

Granted that the poet has removed all grammatical weaknesses, structural flaws, unintentional ambiguities, and obscurities that spring from clumsiness of expression, he still has to consider the imagery and the texture of his poem. Coleridge demanded that all images be 'modified by a predominant passion; or by associated thoughts or images awakened by that passion'. Cecil Day Lewis has shown that Keats altered a striking image in *Hyperion* in order to achieve that unity, coherence, and congruity of imagery which alone can preserve a poem from disintegration.[2] The eighth and ninth lines of the poem originally read:

[1] Cf. G. Rostrevor Hamilton, *The Tell-Tale Article*.
[2] *The Poetic Image*, pp. 75–77.

> Not so much life as a young vulture's wing
> Would spread upon a field of green-ear'd corn.

After various emendations, the lines were modified to read:

> Not so much life as on a summer's day
> Robs not one light seed from the feather'd grass.

The image in the first draft is more striking than that in the final version, yet Keats was fully justified in his recasting of the lines. The opening passage of *Hyperion* presents us with a scene of impotent decay, of a god utterly overcome by lassitude. In this context, the introduction of a vulture or of green-ear'd corn, with their associations of strength and of fertility, would have minimized the emotional effect produced by the other images, which were chosen to suggest the atmosphere of moribund stillness in which Saturn was confined.

The best definition of texture in verse is that put forward by Robert Graves:

'Texture' covers the interrelations of all vowels and consonants in a poem considered as mere sound. The skilled craftsman varies the vowel sounds as if they were musical notes so as to give an effect of melodic richness; uses liquid consonants, labials and open vowels for smoothness; aspirates and dentals for force; gutturals for strength; sibilants for flavour, as a cook uses salt. His alliteration is not barbarously insistent, as in Anglo-Saxon poems or *Piers Plowman*, but concealed by the gradual interlacement of two or three alliterative sequences. He gauges the memory-length of the reader's inward ear and plants the second pair of an alliterative word at a point where the memory of the first has begun to blur but has not yet faded. He varies his word-endings, keeping a careful eye on *–ing* and *–y*, and takes care not to interrupt the smooth flow of the line, if this can possibly be avoided, by close correspondence between terminal consonants and the initial consonants that follow them—e.g. *break ground*, *maid's sorrow*, *great toe*.[1]

Having indicated some of the means by which a poet may attain euphony, Graves draws a distinction between those poets who, like Virgil, Dante, and Milton, desire to achieve abstract musical grandeur and the Non-Classicists, who sacrifice euphony in order to convey the more exactly emotional states such as despair, boredom, agony of mind, and uncertainty.[2]

---

[1] R. Graves, *The Common Asphodel*, p. 15.
[2] Ibid., pp. 12–13, p. 15.

In order to illustrate his theory, Robert Graves quotes Leigh Hunt's remark about the lines from 'The Eve of St. Agnes' which describe the supper and which end with the words:

> And lucent syrops, tinct with cinnamon;

Keats, according to Hunt, had read the passage 'with great relish and particularity', and Hunt, while admiring it, shrewdly notes and dismisses a possible criticism of its technique: 'Mr. Wordsworth would have said that the vowels were not varied enough; but Keats knew where his vowels were *not* to be varied.'

Another anecdote of Hunt's serves to underline the difference between the Classicist and the Non-Classicist attitude towards euphony:

Wordsworth found fault with the repetition of the concluding sound of the participles in Shakespeare's line about bees:

> The *singing* masons *building* roofs of gold.

This, he said, was a line which Milton would never have written. Keats thought, on the other hand, that the repetition was in harmony with the continued note of the singers, and that Shakespeare's negligence, if negligence it was, had instinctively felt the thing in the best manner.

It would be false to suppose that there is, in practice, a rigid distinction between Classicists and Non-Classicists, or that a Classicist will never violate the canons of euphony in order to obtain any particular emotional effect that he may desire. Tennyson, for example, though he disliked the hissing sound of the letter *s*, used it in Section VIII of *Maud* to convey the feeling of sudden confusion which assailed the young lovers in the village church. It is instructive, indeed, to compare Tennyson's exquisitely musical handling of vowels and consonants in the poem to Catullus to his employment of sounds and rhythms in this passage from *Maud*, and to realize that this great master of abstract musical grandeur could, when he chose, disregard smoothness and melodic sweetness in the interests of emotional and intellectual congruity:

> And once, but once, she lifted her eyes,
> And suddenly, sweetly, strangely blush'd
> To find they were met by my own;
> And suddenly, sweetly, my heart beat stronger
> And thicker, until I heard no longer

The snowy-banded, dilettante,
Delicate-handed priest intone.

Walter de La Mare made a like sacrifice of euphony to exactitude when he left unaltered the assonance *roves* and *rose* in his
poem *All That's Past*, because no synonym for *roves* was strong
enough.[1] It would be temerarious to assert that all good poets
solve their problems in the same way: Swinburne clearly preferred to subordinate the claims of meaning to the insatiable
demands of his verse's melodic flow, a practice which brought
down upon him one of Hopkins's most trenchant judgements.
Swinburne's poems he dismissed as '"mere arrangements in vowel
sounds", as Mallock says, very thinly costuming a strain of conventional passion, kept up by stimulants, and crying always in a
high head voice about flesh and flowers and democracy and
damnation.'[2] Those who want a neat rule of thumb may derive
comfort from the moral which the Duchess impressed upon
Alice: 'Take care of the sense, and the sounds will take care of
themselves.'

We may even suspect that the abstract musical grandeur of
verse is largely a myth, if only because a poet's response to vowel
and consonantal sounds is highly subjective. Tennyson may have
considered the *s* sound hissing, but Pope employed it to convey
the notion of speed, and Bridges, in commenting upon the chorus
in *Samson Agonistes* which begins 'This, this is he, softly a
while', remarked that 'the sibilants are hushing'.[3]

We should not, however, assume that the claims of euphony
and of meaning are necessarily conflicting: often, an alteration
designed to improve the texture will suggest further modifications that clarify the sense; conversely, the word or phrase
employed to give a precise shade of meaning may involve radical
changes for the better in the musical pattern of the verse. We
saw in chapter four the part played by rhyme and rhythm in
the shaping of a poem; another example of the fruitful interplay between sense and sound is illustrated by Robert Graves's
description of how he redrafted six times the opening lines of his
poem 'Cynics and Romantics'.[4] We may learn from his account

---

[1] Robert Graves, *Goodbye to all that*, p. 395.
[2] *Letters*, i, pp. 72–73.   [3] F. W. Bateson, op. cit., p. 26.
[4] *The Common Asphodel*, pp. 10–12.

how the correction of a jerky line may entail an ugly duplication of prepositions or of vowels, which must be replaced by a more harmonious combination of sounds. The verse now runs more smoothly, but there has been a sacrifice of precision and vividness of meaning which outweighs the minor gain in euphony. A further alteration, which clarifies the sense, introduces an unpleasant assonance and an intrusive alliteration. After these blemishes have been removed, two minor emendations are made in order both to vary the vowel sounds and to give a new precision of utterance to the whole passage. In some such counterpointing of music and of meaning the poem gradually takes shape, until the last subtle modification is made, and, contemplating the perfected work, one can scarcely distinguish the demands of meaning from the exigencies of texture, so harmoniously have they been reconciled.

Poetic revision is a gradual discovery by the poet of what he desires to say, a perpetual endeavour to attain a harmony that seems constantly to elude him. The manuscripts of Milton's poems bear witness to the painful nature of this struggle and to the ceaseless vigilance that the poet must bring to his task of discerning the shape of the poem that he wants to write. Pope and Coleridge have said that the wheels of the poet's chariot take fire while driving,[1] and Yeats has spoken of the endless stitching and unstitching without which the appearance of spontaneity cannot be achieved. Rosamund Tuve's description of Yeats's style brings out something of the complexity of a poet's technique and reminds us that he has to reconcile the demands of grammar, the exigencies of rhyme, the associations called up by the pattern of images, and the reverberations of the poetic music, fusing them all into a meaning wherein sound and sense are perfectly integrated: 'One could not find better Elizabethan examples of decorum justly and delicately maintained in the character of images, and governing: absence or presence of tropes; their complexity, logical tautness, or emotional reach; amplifying or diminishing suggestions through epithet or detail; brevity or expansion; amount and character of rhetorical ornament; all adjusted by syntactical or metrical means, to tone.'[2]

---

[1] Cf. G. Tillotson, *Criticism and the Nineteenth Century*, p. 163.

[2] *Elizabethan and Metaphysical Imagery*, p. 235, cited by T. R. Henn, *The Lonely Tower*, pp. 281–2.

If we compare the first draft of the opening lines of 'Byzantium' with the final version, we may gain some insight into the process by which Yeats transformed the tenuous outline of a dimly imagined theme into the full orchestration of his verse. The first stanza of the poem, which has been preserved in an unpublished notebook of the poet, originally ran as follows:

> When the emperor's brawling soldiers are abed
> The last benighted victims dead or fled—
> When silence falls on the cathedral gong
> And the drunken harlot's song
> A cloudy silence, or a silence lit
> Whether by star or moon
> I tread the emperor's tower
> All my intricacies grown clear and sweet.[1]

In the published version of the poem the stanza reads:

> The unpurged images of day recede;
> The Emperor's drunken soldiery are abed;
> Night resonance recedes, night-walkers' song
> After great cathedral gong;
> A starlit or a moonlit dome disdains[2]
> All that man is,
> All mere complexities,
> The fury and the mire of human veins.

The first improvement to be noted occurs at the very beginning of the stanza: instead of the somewhat abrupt, unsatisfactory exordium of the rough draft, we now have a majestic line that immediately evokes the desired atmosphere of religious awe and of the miraculous purification which must be endured in the holy city of Byzantium. In the context, *night-walker* is more appropriate a word than *harlot*, since the emphasis of the poem is upon the night as opposed to the day. The last four lines of the rough draft have been replaced by a truly magnificent image which takes us back to an earlier poem, 'A Dialogue of Self and Soul', with its defiant cry:

> I am content to live it all again
> And yet again, if it be life to pitch
> Into the frog-spawn of a blind man's ditch,
> A blind man battering blind men

[1] Cited in Richard Ellmann, *Yeats: The Man and the Masks*, p. 274, footnote.
[2] An alternative reading is *distains*.

and which prepares us for the third verse of 'Byzantium' itself:

> Miracle, bird or golden handiwork,
> More miracle than bird or handiwork,
> Planted on the star-lit golden bough,
> Can like the cocks of Hades crow,
> Or, by the moon embittered, scorn aloud
> In glory of changeless metal
> Common bird or petal
> And all complexities of mire or blood.

Not only is the intellectual and the emotional content of the stanza's final version much richer than that of the draft recorded in the notebook; the music of the verse is more profound, the rhyming scheme more intricate and satisfying, the rhythm more incisive. All that is superfluous, tentative, or wavering has been swept away in the passionate sensual music which Yeats alone of the poets of our time has been able to command. We can all recognize the difference in poetic quality between the two versions of the stanza; it is more difficult to guess at the exact way in which the poet wrestled with the recalcitrant words, trying to hammer the lines into a refulgent splendour. For the ardours and endurances inseparable from the task of writing poetry are only partly communicable, and most poets have not wished to reveal the secrets of their art or sullen craft.[1]

Poets in all ages have contemplated the medium of their art with an ambivalent set of emotions. They love it, because only in words can their poems attain palpable form, yet they hate it, because they see in language an intractable Protean element which they must ceaselessly strive to redeem and to transfigure.

There have even been poets who have been haunted by a lingering fear that the effort to write poetry is foredoomed to failure, because they can never express in words that Truth which it is the object of poetry to reveal. Roy Fuller has told us of these gnawing doubts:

> Perhaps the object of art
> Is this: the communication
> Of that which cannot be told.
> Worse: the rich explanation

---

[1] This phrase is taken from Dylan Thomas's poem which begins 'In my art or sullen craft'.

> That there is nothing to tell;
> Only the artificial
> Plot and ambiguous word,
> The forged but sacred missal.[1]

His doubts have been echoed by David Gascoyne who, in his verse and prose alike, has called upon us to accept the fact of Death in its enigmatic significance, and to reject the reassuring consolations offered to us by the philosophical systems which our logical faculties take pleasure in erecting.[2] For language tends to degenerate into verbiage and even poetry, which is language at its most alert and fresh, may obscure the absolute Truth that only the revelation of despair can bring home to us. The accents of profound disquiet, even of deep anguish, that resonate so plangently through his verse have been forced from him by the discovery that poetry can neither lead us to the heart of reality nor solve the riddle of the human situation:

> Before I fall
> Down silent finally, I want to make
> One last attempt at utterance, and tell
> How my absurd desire was to compose
> A single poem with my mental eyes
> Wide open, and without even one lapse
> From that most scrupulous Truth which I pursue
> When not pursuing Poetry.--Perhaps
> Only the poem I can never write is *true*.[3]

If we are inclined to blame poets for yielding to such pessimistic reflections, we should remember that, in this present age of anxiety and introspection, all human activities are subjected to a minute and subtle scrutiny by minds whose knowledge of psycho-analysis leads them to question all established values. It is only to be expected that poets will be tainted by the prevailing malady and that they will become increasingly self-conscious and self-critical. Indeed, we may suspect that a poet who has never been assailed by these doubts is either too stupid to understand the agony that torments the finest spirits among his contemporaries, or too cowardly to contemplate a truth that may wreck his fondest illusions.

---

[1] 'The Emotion of Fiction.'

[2] See his article on Leon Chestov, in *Horizon*, Oct. 1949, and his sequence of poems, 'Miserere'. Cf. Robert Graves's poem 'The Cool Web'. [3] 'Apologia.'

The greatest of our living poets has told us, in his *Four Quartets*, which are, among other things, meditations upon the making of a poem, how exhausting and dispiriting a task it is to bring a poem into the light, and how the struggle often appears to be in vain. Words, he reminds us, are obdurate, tough, hostile, and perverse or, at the best, imprecise, blunted tools. Such reflections, coming as they do from a poet who has achieved a consummate mastery of his art, are salutary as a corrective to glib rhetoric about the golden music and the immortal harmony of verse. They recall to our mind the imperfection of the human condition, and help us to remember that even the finest works of our hands are fragmentary and transitory. A reminder of this nature may be deemed superfluous in the second half of a century which has seen the crumbling of so many certainties and the mockery of so many deluding hopes. The danger is, rather, that we shall abandon an extravagant, shallow optimism for an abysmal, but equally extravagant, despair in which an excessive concentration upon pain, evil, irrationality, and hatred will lead us to deny the value of every human activity. It is, therefore, important to remember that even those poets whose verse is, at times, resonant with despondency and frustration have acknowledged that their task is not wholly beyond their strength. T. S. Eliot, despite his forebodings, can envisage a poem

> where every word is at home,
> Taking its place to support the others,
> The word neither diffident nor ostentatious,
> An easy commerce of the old and new,
> The common word exact without vulgarity,
> The formal word precise but not pedantic,
> The complete consort dancing together.[1]

David Gascoyne himself has borne witness to the ultimate value of poetry, and we can accept his testimony the more readily because he has faced the possibility of finding nothing but emptiness in his search for poetic truth. His words may serve to remind us that the growth of a poem, which we have endeavoured to trace in these pages, must always defy analysis and remain both a mystery and a source of wonder:

[1] *Little Gidding*, v.

THE FIRE AND THE FOUNTAIN

... Words are marks
That flicker through men's minds like quick black dust;
That falling, finally obliterate the faint
Glow their speech emanates. Too soon all sparks
Of vivid meaning are extinguished by
The saturated wadding of Man's tongue ...
And yet, I lie, I lie:
Can even Omega discount
The startling miracle of human song?[1]

[1] 'Lines'.

Select Bibliography

THE list of books which follows is not intended to be an exhaustive guide to the best critical writings on English poetry. It is simply a list of the modern prose works to which I am indebted, in greater or lesser degree, for certain facts and ideas contained in my essay. The main primary sources upon which I have drawn are the poetical works of the writers discussed in this essay, together with those prose writings of Sidney, Ben Jonson, Dryden, Samuel Johnson, Coleridge, Wordsworth, Shelley, and Keats which throw light upon my chosen theme.

The date given after each book is that of the first edition, and when a later edition has been used the date is given of that edition also.

AUDEN, W. H. *Tennyson: An Introduction and a Selection.* Phœnix House, 1946.
—— *The Enchafèd Flood.* Faber, 1951.
BATESON, F. W. *English Poetry: A Critical Introduction.* Longmans, 1950.
BELGION, M. *The Human Parrot.* O.U.P., 1931.
BLACKSTONE, B. *English Blake.* C.U.P., 1949.
BODKIN, M. *Archetypal Patterns in Poetry.* O.U.P., 1934.
BOWRA, C. M. *The Heritage of Symbolism.* Macmillan, 1943.
—— *The Creative Experiment.* Macmillan, 1948.
CAPETANAKIS, D. *A Greek Poet in England.* John Lehmann, 1947.
CAUDWELL, C. *Illusion and Reality.* Macmillan, 1937.
CLARK, G. N. *Science and Social Welfare in the Age of Newton.* O.U.P., 1937.
COWL, R. P. *The Theory of Poetry in England.* Macmillan, 1914.
DARBISHIRE, H. *The Early Lives of Milton.* Constable, 1932.
ELIOT, T. S. *Selected Essays.* Faber, 1932.
—— *The Use of Poetry and the Use of Criticism.* Faber, 1933.
—— *The Music of Poetry.* Glasgow University Publications, 1942.
ELLMANN, R. *Yeats: The Man and the Masks.* Macmillan, 1949.
EMPSON, W. *Seven Types of Ambiguity.* Chatto & Windus, 1930, 2nd ed., 1947.
GARDNER, W. H. *Gerard Manley Hopkins.* Martin Secker & Warburg, 1944.
GITTINGS, R. *John Keats: The Living Year.* Heinemann, 1954.
GRAVES, R. *On English Poetry.* Heinemann, 1922.
—— *The Common Asphodel.* Hamish Hamilton, 1949.
HALLIDAY, F. E. *Shakespeare and his Critics.* Duckworth, 1949.
HARDING, R. E. *An Anatomy of Inspiration.* Heffer, 1942.
HARE, H. *Swinburne.* H. F. & G. Witherby, 1949.
HENN, T. E. *The Lonely Tower: Studies in the Poetry of W. B. Yeats* Methuen, 1950.

HONE, J. M. *W. B. Yeats, 1865–1939.* Macmillan, 1942.

HOPKINS, G. M. *Letters to Robert Bridges.* ed. C. C. Abbott. O.U.P., 1935.

—— *The Correspondence of Gerard Manley Hopkins and Richard Watson Dixon.* ed. C. C. Abbott. O.U.P., 1935.

—— *Further Letters of Gerard Manley Hopkins.* ed. C. C. Abbott. O.U.P., 1938.

—— *The Notebooks and Papers of Gerard Manley Hopkins.* ed. H. House. O.U.P., 1937.

HOUGH, G. *The Last Romantics.* Duckworth, 1949.

HUXLEY, A. *Texts and Pretexts.* Chatto & Windus, 1932.

—— *Vulgarity in Literature.* Chatto & Windus, 1940.

INGE, W. R. *Christian Mysticism.* Methuen, 1899. 7th ed. 1933.

ISAACS, J. *An Assessment of Twentieth Century Literature.* Martin Secker & Warburg, 1951.

—— *The Background of Modern Poetry.* Bell, 1951.

JEFFARES, N. *W. B. Yeats: Man and Poet.* Routledge & Kegan Paul, 1949.

LAWRENCE, D. H. *The Letters of D. H. Lawrence.* ed. Aldous Huxley. Heinemann, 1932.

LEAVIS, F. R. *New Bearings in English Poetry.* Chatto & Windus, 1932.

LEWIS, C. DAY. *Poetry For You.* Blackwell, 1944.

—— *The Poetic Image.* Cape, 1947.

LEWIS, C. S. *Rehabilitations.* O.U.P., 1939.

LOWES, J. L. *The Road to Xanadu.* Constable, rev. ed. 1931.

MACNEICE, L. *Modern Poetry: A Personal Essay.* O.U.P., 1938.

MATTHIESSEN, F. O. *The Achievement of T. S. Eliot.* O.U.P., 1935.

MILLER, B. *Robert Browning: A Portrait.* John Murray, 1952.

MORTIMER, R. *Channel Packet.* The Hogarth Press, 1943.

MURPHY, G. *The Modern Poet.* Sidgwick & Jackson, 1938.

NAMIER, L. B. *England in the Age of the American Revolution.* Macmillan, 1930.

NICOLSON, H. *Tennyson.* Constable, 1922. 2nd ed. 1951.

POPE-HENNESSY, JAMES. *Monckton Milnes: The Flight of Youth.* Constable, 1951.

POUND, E. *Literary Essays of Ezra Pound.* ed. T. S. Eliot. Faber, 1954.

QUENNELL, P. *Baudelaire and the Symbolists.* Chatto & Windus, 1929.

READ, H. *Wordsworth.* Cape, 1930.

—— *Collected Essays in Literary Criticism.* Faber, 1938.

—— *The True Voice of Feeling.* Faber, 1953.

RICHARDS, I. A. *Practical Criticism.* Routledge & Kegan Paul, 1929.

ROBERTS, M. *Critique of Poetry.* Cape, 1934.

SITWELL, E. *Alexander Pope.* Faber, 1930.

SITWELL, O. *Laughter in the Next Room.* Macmillan, 1949.

SMITH, J. C. *A Study of Wordsworth.* Oliver & Boyd, 1944.

SPARROW, J. *Sense and Poetry.* Constable, 1934.

SPENDER, S. *World Within World.* Hamish Hamilton, 1951.

TENNYSON, C. *Alfred Tennyson.* Macmillan, 1949.

TILLOTSON, G. *On The Poetry of Pope.* O.U.P., 1938.

TILLOTSON, G. *Essays in Criticism and Research.* C.U.P., 1942.
—— *Criticism and the Nineteenth Century.* (Athlone Press) Constable, 1951.
TRILLING, L. *The Liberal Imagination.* Martin Secker & Warburg, 1951.
WILLEY, B. *The Seventeenth Century Background.* Chatto & Windus, 1934.
—— *The Eighteenth Century Background.* Chatto & Windus, 1940.
WILSON, E. *The Wound and the Bow.* W. H. Allen, 1941.
YEATS, J. B. *Letters to his Son W. B. Yeats and Others.* Faber, 1944.
YEATS, W. B. *Essays.* Macmillan, 1924.
—— *The Bounty of Sweden.* Cuala Press, 1925. Macmillan, 1936.
—— *A Vision.* T. Werner Laurie, 1925. Macmillan, 1937.
—— *Letters on Poetry to Dorothy Wellesley.* ed. Dorothy Wellesley. O.U.P., 1940.
YOUNG, G. M. *Daylight and Champaign.* Cape, 1937.
ZIMMERN, A. *The Greek Commonwealth.* O.U.P., 1915. 5th ed. 1932.

Supplement to the Bibliography (1965)

The following works, some of which were published after the compilation of the Bibliography, throw light upon the matters discussed in this book.

ABRAMS, M. H. *The Minor and the Lamp.* O.U.P., New York, 1953.
ALLEN, W. *Writers and Writing.* Phoenix House, 1954.
BARTLETT, P. *Poems in Process.* O.U.P., 1954.
BERRY, F. *Poetry and the Physical Voice.* Routledge & Kegan Paul, 1962.
GHISELIN, B. *The Creative Process.* University of California Press, 1952.
HOUSMAN, A. E. *The Name and Nature of Poetry.* C.U.P., 1933.
KERMODE, F. *Romantic Image.* Routledge & Kegan Paul, 1957.
MELCHIORI, G. *The Tightrope Walkers.* Routledge & Kegan Paul, 1956.
SKELTON, R. *The Poetic Pattern.* Routledge & Kegan Paul, 1956.
SPENDER, S. *The Making of a Poem.* Hamish Hamilton, 1955.
STALLWORTHY, J. *Between the Lines.* Clarendon Press, 1963.
WHALLEY, G. *Poetic Process.* Routledge & Kegan Paul, 1953.

Index

246

60

DATE DUE